Latest titles in the McGraw-Hill Training Series

Details of these and other titles in the series are available from:
The Product Manager, Professional Books, McGraw-Hill Book Company Europe,
Shoppenhangers Road, Maidenhead, Berkshire SL6 2QL, United Kingdom
Tel: 01628 23432 Fax: 01628 770224

Learning to change

A resource for trainers, managers and learners based on Self-Organised Learning

Sheila Harri-Augstein
Ian M. Webb

McGRAW-HILL BOOK COMPANY

London · New York · St Louis · San Francisco · Auckland
Bogotá · Caracas · Lisbon · Madrid · Mexico · Milan
Montreal · New Delhi · Panama · Paris · San Juan · São Paulo
Singapore · Sydney · Tokyo · Toronto

Published by
McGRAW-HILL Book Company Europe
Shoppenhangers Road, Maidenhead, Berkshire, SL6 2QL, England
Telephone: 01628 23432
Fax: 01628 770224

British Library Cataloguing in Publication Data
Harri-Augstein, Sheila
 Learning to Change: Resource for Trainers,
 Managers and Learners Based on
 Self-Organised Learning. – (McGraw-Hill
 Training Series)
 I. Title II. Webb, Ian III. Series
 153.15

 ISBN 0-07-707896-9

Library of Congress Cataloging-in-Publication Data
Harri-Augstein, E. Sheila.
 Learning to change: a resource for trainers, managers and learners
 based on self organised learning / Sheila Harri-Augstein and Ian M.
 Cameron-Webb.
  p. cm.
 Includes bibliographical references and index.
 ISBN 0-07-707896-9
 1. Employees–Training of. 2. Self-culture. 3. Learning,
 Psychology of. I. Cameron-Webb, Ian M. II. Title.
 HF5549.5.T7H315 1995   95-791
 658.3'124–dc20   CIP

12345 CUP 98765

Typeset by BookEns Limited, Royston, Herts.
and printed and bound in Great Britain at the University Press, Cambridge

Printed on permanent paper in compliance with ISO Standard 9706

Contents

This book is dedicated to:

Ray, Geoff, Pete, John, Sid, Maurie, Eddie, John Paul, Willie, and all those 'SOL Coaches' with whom we have worked on the job.

Series preface

Training and development are now firmly centre stage in most organisations, if not all. Nothing unusual in that—for some organisations. They have always seen training and development as part of the heart of their businesses—but more and more must see it that same way.

The demographic trends through the 1990s will inject into the marketplace severe competition for good people who will need good training. Young people without conventional qualifications, skilled workers in redundant crafts, people out of work, women wishing to return to work—all will require excellent training to fit them to meet the job demands of the 1990s and beyond.

But excellent training does not spring from what we have done well in the past. T&D specialists are in a new ball game. 'Maintenance' training—training to keep up skill levels to do what we have always done—will be less in demand. Rather, organisation, work and market change training are now much more important and will remain so for some time. Changing organisations and people is no easy task, requiring special skills and expertise which, sadly, many T&D specialists do not possess.

To work as a 'change' specialist requires us to get to centre stage—to the heart of the company's business. This means we have to ask about future goals and strategies, and even be involved in their development, at least as far as T&D policies are concerned.

This demands excellent communication skills, political expertise, negotiating ability, diagnostic skills—indeed, all the skills a good internal consultant requires.

The implications for T&D specialists are considerable. It is not enough merely to be skilled in the basics of training, we must also begin to act like business people and to think in business terms and talk the language of business. We must be able to resource training not just from within but by using the vast array of external resources. We must be able to manage our activities as well as any other manager. We must share in the creation and communication of the company's vision. We must never let the goals of the company out of our sight.

In short, we may have to grow and change with the business. It will be hard. We shall not only have to demonstrate relevance but also value for money and achievement of results. We shall be our own boss, as accountable for results as any other line manager, and we shall have to deal with fewer internal resources.

The challenge is on, as many T&D specialists have demonstrated to me over the past few years. We need to be capable of meeting that challenge. This is why McGraw-Hill Book Company Europe have planned and launched this major new training series—to help us meet that challenge.

The series covers all aspects of T&D and provides the knowledge base from which we can develop plans to meet the challenge. They are practical books for the professional person. They are a starting point for planning our journey into the twenty-first century.

Use them well. Don't just read them. Highlight key ideas, thoughts, action pointers or whatever, and have a go at doing something with them. Through experimentation we evolve; through stagnation we die.

I know that all the authors in the McGraw-Hill Training Series would want me to wish you good luck. Have a great journey into the twenty-first century.

ROGER BENNETT
Series Editor

About the series editor

Roger Bennett has over 20 years' experience in training, management education, research and consulting. He has long been involved with trainer training and trainer effectiveness. He has carried out research into trainer effectiveness, and conducted workshops, seminars, and conferences on the subject around the world. He has written extensively on the subject including the book *Improving Trainer Effectiveness*, Gower. His work has taken him all over the world and has involved directors of companies as well as managers and trainers.

Dr Bennett has worked in engineering, several business schools (including the International Management Centre, where he launched the UK's first masters degree in T&D), and has been a board director of two companies. He is the editor of the *Journal of European Industrial Training* and was series editor of the ITD's *Get In There* workbook and video package for the managers of training departments. He now runs his own business called The Management Development Consultancy.

Acknowledgements

The authors are especially indebted to Professor Laurie Thomas for his support. The imaginative developments of the reflective tools and techniques as well as the conversational paradigm of Self-Organised Learning were originated by him. We are grateful to him for access to the CSHL Integrated Repertory Grid Software, and in particular the FOCUS and CHANGE grid programs to analyse the data in Chapters 3, 5 and 6.

We also appreciate the support given by the series editor, Roger Bennett, who as external examiner for Ian's PhD, saw the value of the 'Personal Learning Contract' as a tool for reflective learning on the job. He also recognised the contribution that SOL, backed by the methodology of the 'Learning Conversation', can make within the world of training and development.

We are especially grateful to the editorial and production teams at McGraw-Hill—Julia Riddlesdell, Anthea Coombs, Kate Allen, Vicky Baker, Ros Comer and Elaine Gaymer—for the professional support and personal attention they gave us. Working with them was a salutary experience.

Figure acknowledgements The authors and publishers are grateful to Routledge for permission to reproduce Figures 3.6, 4.1, 4.2, 7.1 and 8.1. These figures previously appeared as Figures 5, 12, 20, 26, 30 in Harri-Augstein, E.S., and Thomas, L.F., (1991) *Learning Conversations*, Routledge, London.

Foreword

This book explains simply and clearly how people may increase their capacity to learn. The authors, Sheila and Ian, show how trainers, managers and learners can achieve this. They focus on the diverse habitats of work, at all levels of the social hierarchy within commercial, industrial and government enterprises. However, their message has significant implications for all types of enterprise engaged in change. To be enabled to develop personal learning potential, and hence one's capacity to learn, is a rare achievement. When it happens, a quantum leap in learning competence takes place. It results in each subsequent skill, task or topic being learnt significantly better and in more cost-effective ways. This is no wild claim. It is the most repeatedly validated outcome from many years of action research carried out at the Centre for the Study of Human Learning (CSHL) in Brunel University, UK.

This academic learning community was founded by Sheila and me as a postgraduate school and as a research and consulting institute. The term 'academic' is used here to indicate an informed and systematic search for valid knowledge and innovative techniques. Members of the CSHL also belong to other institutions including banks, marriage guidance clinics, industrial companies, the Metropolitan Police, commercial organisations, drug addiction centres, large management consultancy companies, the London Fire Service, the Cabinet Office of the Civil Service, the Social Services, The Zen Foundation, hospitals, The Royal Mail Businesses, teacher training colleges, psychotherapy units, Olympic sports squads, a strategic planning unit, a teaching therapy organisation offering the Alexander Technique and a commercial language teaching college (to name but a few). The CSHL functions as a global learning community using Internet and other hi-tech communication channels to coordinate members living and working in Europe and other parts of the world, including Australia, Iran, Canada, Mexico, the USA and India.

Ian was one of our recruits. He was awarded his PhD in Human Learning in 1990 and after a stint of management teaching formed his own independent training consultancy. As an associate of the CSHL and as an honorary senior lecturer he retains close working links. For his PhD, supervised by Sheila, Ian carried out a series of sensitive and innovative studies on a one-to-one and small-group basis with learners in a variety of educational and training contexts. He applied various CSHL techniques and methods, especially the Personal Learning Contract (PLC), to produce some very interesting and, indeed, rather outstanding results.

Early in her career, Sheila was a prime mover in introducing learning-to-learn to advanced 'A' and 'S' level and undergraduate science teaching. She extended this work within higher education during her PhD studies with me at CSHL in the early 1970s. During this time she conceived the notion of a 'Learning Conversation', which evolved into a unique approach for addressing processes of learning. Together, we developed this into an explicit methodology and invented a whole series of new techniques for recording learning activities and helping individuals reflect upon their experiences. Later, during her years as senior lecturer in the psychology of education at Loughborough University, she introduced the theory and practice of Learning Conversations into the teacher training curriculum. She also introduced self-assessment and peer-evaluation into trainee teachers' assignments and examinations. At this time she also worked as tutor, monitor, examiner and member of a course design team for the Open University. At the next stage in her career Sheila re-joined the CSHL as my deputy to launch a series of action research projects in government, commercial and industrial contexts.

We have installed Self-Organised Learning (SOL) in the Ministry of Defence, in a number of industrial and commercial companies and in the Royal Mail letters and parcels businesses. Working with Sheila, conducting Learning Conversations on the job has always been inspiring. I experienced new insights as I observed her:

- explaining SOL to a captain in the Gurkha Rifles by encouraging him to make a series of origami paper penguins, and then use this experience to reflect on how he organised his learning;
- standing on Reading railway station at midnight helping a firstline Post Office supervisor to reflect upon why the over-run of mail to Paddington was 55 per cent (and her delight three weeks later when Paddington confirmed that he had reduced it to 3 per cent in the previous week);
- using the repertory grid conversationally to help the senior managers in Kelloggs UK reflect upon, and then systematically re-define, the quality of one of their brands of breakfast cereal;
- helping two Royal Naval officers—one of whom was on Air Intercept Control duty in HMS *Sheffield* when it was sunk by a missile in the Falklands—relive the experience on a computer-driven simulator; they were having one deep 'ah-ha' learning experience after another;
- conversing with a Zen Master about SOL and Zen as alternative paths to self-fulfilment;
- explaining to a well-known captain of industry that psychologists from the CSHL do not shrink people's heads, they expand them; and then going on to use the opportunity to get him to reflect rather

rigorously, in a head-expanding way, on how he did his job.
- eliciting Personal Learning Contracts as she conducted tutorials with post-graduate students, so enabling them to appreciate the power of the PLC and reflective tool.

In formulating the theory of Self-Organised Learning and by inventing and developing the methods of the Learning Conversation, the CSHL has made a major contribution to the theory and practice of education and training over the past 25 years. The current vogue for 'independent learning', 'open learning', 'empowerment', 'learning organisations', 'distance learning', 'learning companies' and even 'innovative learning' reflects many of the ideas that we pioneered in the 1960s and 1970s. At that time such progressive ideas were often greeted with alarm and hostility. The current preoccupation with such conceptions of learning carries the seeds of its own destruction. As with many other 'flavours of the month' in education, training and management, what starts out as a powerful set of ideas is easily misunderstood. It is then misrepresented, and exploited by the politically and professionally ambitious. Thus the original ideas become so distorted that they lose their quality, their utility and finally their credibility. This cannot happen to SOL and Learning Conversations because the approach is robustly embedded in practice and in the real experience of people.

Despite the apparent simplicity of the concept, 'learning' is often misunderstood because it is all too easily equated with training or it is treated as a 'product'. As the reader will discover, SOL is always concerned with the quality and the specific content of what is being learned; but it is the process of learning that is, here, always centrally addressed. For the Self-Organised Learner, 'learning' is not just successfully submitting to being taught, trained or instructed. Nor is it what happens incidentally to the lucky learner as he or she acquires more experience. It is personal to each learner, and needs to be consciously understood and organised by each learner, in his or her own terms.

For Self-Organised Learners, each and every event becomes an opportunity for experimenting and developing personal skills, competences and creativity. Once initiated, this process cannot be stopped by the insightful or even the politically bigoted; what happens is that when self-organisation is thwarted in one area, it blossoms in another. Self-organised learners seek new challenges; they question and expect valid feedback and discriminating appraisal. This spark should be cherished and nourished by an organised system of support.

The theory of SOL and its enabling methodology of the Learning Conversation are rooted in Personal Construct Psychology (PCP), cybernetics, knowledge engineering and transformational management theory. SOL is contributing to the evolving new psychology which is emerging in various forms in different parts of the world.

Enabling SOL is fundamental to modern-day management. Any

enterprise will remain viable if its members are regularly encouraged to review what they should know, the skills they should have and what they should expect to achieve. It will become successful if its members are enabled to acquire the knowledge and skills they have identified, use them well and continue to revise their understanding and their performance in the light of their experience.

The enterprise will really begin to take off when its trainers and its managers:

- enable each member of staff to investigate exactly what it is they need to know and be able to do, to get the job done with quality, cost-effectively and reasonably fast;
- encourage them to acquire these skills and knowledge, continually testing them out, refining them and updating them from experience on the job;
- enable all staff and all teams to take responsibility for their own learning; then develop their capacity to learn so that they become capable of life-long learning.

This book invites every manager to become a Learning Manager. Each manager will continually be learning on the job; and managers will be supporting the learning of each of those for whom they are responsible. Part of the trainer's role becomes that of supporting the manager to develop the skills for carrying out these activities with competence and flair. Sheila and Ian directly address trainers and suggest how they might transform their views of their job, becoming more skilled and competent in enabling effective learning to take place on the job.

The organisational application of Learning Conversations to enable individuals and teams to become more self-organised in their learning entails a personal paradigm shift by all concerned. This requires a significant change in one's whole pattern of understanding of what learning is all about. Sheila and Ian have done a magnificent job in offering the readers an opportunity to make this shift by experimenting with their own learning as they converse with this book.

LAURIE F. THOMAS
Professor of Human Learning, Brunel University, UK
Carl Rogers Memorial Professor, Clayton University, USA

Notes for readers from a SOL Coach

For most of my lifelong career in the Post Office I had to learn the hard way. By the time I was a senior planning manager with special responsibility for training, I was given the opportunity to develop more skills and I became a SOL Coach. In many ways this transformed my life and how I did my job. I experienced many 'Learning Conversations' and over a period of two years I kept a diary of my thoughts and feelings as I practised SOL on the job. Extracts from this diary are reproduced below for the benefit of trainers and managers who read this book.

I have initiated several 'Learning Projects' as a SOL Coach. These have included:

- Learning Conversations to create an awareness of the effects of 'orderliness and tidyness' on office performance.
- Developing, running and evaluating SOL workshops for newly appointed supervisors to help them research their jobs by hands-on experience.
- Developing and testing my 'personal problem solving algorithm' as a planner
- Working with the Christmas team to develop 'personal work plans' to ensure the smooth despatch of mail during this busy period.
- Working with my full-time SOL Coach to support the smooth transition from the old mail letter sorting office to the new system.

Part of my Personal Learning Biography which records some of these activities is presented in Figure 7.4. Each project was judged to be successful when evaluated against SOL criteria and the 'objective measures' within my office.

My introduction to Self-Organised Learning (SOL)

In 1985 representatives from CSHL at Brunel University visited our post office to study the work performed by postal supervisors. Their objective was to consider new methods to be used either as an alternative or as additions to the current methods being used to improve the standards of supervision.

I was one of the supervisors interviewed and I remember that I was more than a little sceptical and I questioned the purpose of the interviews. It had been one of my duties to organise training sessions and I thought that the existing sessions were quite adequate and did not involve expensive outside training. However, during the interviews with the CSHL people I began to realise that there was more to it and I became more inquisitive and interested. In 1986 I attended a SOL course and became a part-time SOL Coach.

Self-Organised Learning has helped me quite considerably. In the course of my work in planning, I have to think about the work or problem and analyse it critically. It was always normal practice to perform this work by traditional methods that had been used for years and never questioned. Since attending the SOL course I now ask myself 'Is there a better way or perhaps a quicker one?' Of course, it does not necessarily follow that there is, but at least I think about it and do not just accept matters.

I have found SOL to be a very personal thing and if accepted it can help in many different ways, both at home and at work. It is a personality builder as it makes you more confident, you see things differently and more clearly. SOL should not be considered 'an overnight success story', but once the seeds are sown they will grow, although they grow more quickly in some people and more slowly in others because we are all individuals with our own individual pace.

I have become more aware of how I do my job, I certainly give matters more thought and I examine myself for my strengths, faults or weaknesses. I think the most noticeable change is that I find myself looking at problems on a much broader horizon. For example, I realised that our post office, along with others countrywide, was going through various inspections and fault-finding missions, all of which should improve our business. I felt, however, that insufficient thought was being given to staff motivation. My thoughts evolved into proposals which have been given to management for consideration. I credit Self-Organised Learning for my interest and insight in this matter.

Reflections: the humorous side of SOL

After returning home from the SOL course, I began to review the course and wondered if something was missing from the curriculum of 'Learning to Learn', namely 'Learning to Think'. I was not sure exactly what I had learned and this seemed to be the general feeling among the other course participants. All of us were saying, albeit in different ways, that we were unsure of exactly how to put SOL into practice. We had learned a great deal on the course but because the method was completely new to us and perhaps a little strange, it was difficult to grasp.

Preparation of a Learning Programme

I began thinking about a possible Learning Programme and tried to work out a pattern we could follow. First, I thought that a meeting between SOL Coaches and their assistants should be set up to discuss how all the Coaches could work on the same wavelength, not necessarily in the same way, but as a team. I felt that this could make for better informed and more efficient and confident supervisors who are able to go on learning and support the learning of others on the job.

It was while I was thinking about preparing a Learning Programme and working on a flowchart that the word 'FEAR' came into my head. I recalled that this word had been mentioned on the SOL course—the fear of failure, of not being as good as the next person, not really knowing the answers, when a nod of the head suggests confirmation but is really the disguise for not wanting to speak out.

I then realised that I was talking to myself—a sign of madness it is said! I found that almost for the first time in my life I was digging deep into myself, questioning, reflecting, exploring and playing with my mind. For days and weeks I experienced a mixture of apprehension, fear and excitement. Was I going mad? Or was this the seed of the inner Learning Conversation that we had been introduced to on the course?

I have come to realise that it is possible to become a more balanced person if you can learn to think inwardly as part of the Learning to Learn techniques. There is close similarity between learning and thinking, and with the Learning Conversation method I have been made to think, by means of discussion and by asking myself questions and answering them myself.

The enemy of SOL

It is hard to believe that Self-Organised Learning, which can only benefit people, can have an enemy, but it does. How many times, I wonder, does the SOL Coach hear the words 'It's just a gimmick' or 'It's just one big con—somebody trying to tell us how to do our job', and so on.

It is common knowledge that many people are adverse to change, particularly when it affects them personally. In the Post Office we are all aware of the drastic changes taking place and how things are going to differ in the future, particularly in the supervisory grades. I have found that new staff are more responsive to SOL simply because they are keen to receive as much help as they can to be successful in their jobs.

I have noticed that established supervisors with many years of experience seem to shy away from anything different from the norm, they prefer to carry on as they always have—'robotishly'. If the set pattern looks like altering, you will hear a barrage of reasons as to why the new methods will not work even before anything new has been introduced! The established supervisors, set in their ways, find it hard to change. SOL becomes something they do not understand, they resent anyone who tells them it will help them improve, that it will encourage them to question themselves about how they do their job. The supervisors will always reply that 'There is only one way to learn this job, and that is with long experience—the hard way!' They are really afraid that they might reveal certain weaknesses by taking part in SOL. 'It is a brain-washing technique,' I have heard someone say, and 'We do not need SOL, with our experience we know it all,' was another comment. It is not an easy task to convince established supervisors that SOL can only be of benefit to them. Sometimes a supervisor may already be practising SOL to some extent and not be aware of it. The enemy of Self-Organised Learning is fear in the individual.

Speaking personally, I shall continue to endeavour to transform 'training' and to become an enabler of change on the job.

R.W.

General introduction

Agenda board

- Training and learning

- Self-Organised Learning as a radical approach

- How the book is organised

- How the book may be used

- Suggested activity: action plan: designing an SOL workshop

This book is intended for the training practitioner. The term 'training practitioner' tends to suggest someone with training in their job title; however, the book will be of practical value to *all enablers of learning* and this will include trainers, managers and supervisors as well as consultants, counsellors, tutors and human resource providers generally.

There is a growing movement away from 'content-based' training towards 'process' management. Self-Organised Learning (SOL) is firmly based in processes of learning and learning to learn and is 'content' free. This means that any topic, task or skill can be approached through the SOL methodology; topics from law, accountancy, economics, management theory, statistics, science and engineering to more practical tasks such as operating a lathe, a computer or a check-out machine, to people-oriented activities such as dealing with customers, getting the best out of employees and encouraging team leadership. These represent a small selection of topics, tasks and skills which may be learnt effectively through the practice of processes related to SOL.

With the aid of this book, *training practitioners will be in a position to enable their clients to become better learners.* This will be achieved through greater awareness and self-management of personal learning processes, which will contribute greatly towards improved and lasting results in organisational effectiveness.

Some of the examples and procedures used in the book are based on the doctoral research of Ian Webb, one of the co-authors. The original techniques and the methodology of 'Learning Conversations' and SOL have been developed over 20 years of action research in industry, education and government by Dr Sheila Harri-Augstein and Professor Laurie Thomas, founder directors of the Centre for the Study of Human Learning and the Postgraduate Division of Human Learning based at Brunel University.

Training and learning

Technology, organisations, communities and life in general is changing at an ever-increasing pace, and individuals as well as all forms of working and social groups have to be able to develop *strategies for change*. In order to cope with the pressures that often arise, we have to learn new ways of mentally tackling situations, which frequently involve changes in procedures, the manner in which we relate to others and the ways in which we physically perform tasks. Escalating change is not confined to Europe but is a worldwide phenomenon that is gaining momentum. Sudden change as opposed to gradual change, referred to by Charles Handy as discontinuous change, can bring about high levels of stress in many people. Often they find themselves deeply threatened by a future in which they have no strategy to cope let alone to survive and grow.

The answer that frequently emerges is to encourage all those involved in change to undergo 'training' or 'retraining'. There are many problems associated with this approach, not least of which are the *personal myths* held by the majority of individuals and by trainers themselves. One such myth commonly held by learners relates to the belief that the older we become the less we are able to learn! Here are some sayings reflecting personally held myths about 'age and learning' that we have probably all heard:

- *'If I lose my job, I shall be on the shelf for life—it's too late for me to change now.'* (A 40-year-old executive.)
- *'You can't teach an old dog new tricks.'* (A 50-year-old post office supervisor.)
- *'My memory is going; I am definitely getting older.'* (A 30-year-old schoolteacher.)
- *'I have heard that brain cells die off and are not replaced after the age of 21; goodness knows how much of a brain I have got left now that I am reaching 40.'* (A researcher in the pharmaceutical industry.)
- *'Older people have used up most of the brain's capacity, so they have a problem when learning anything new. If my learning is to be successful some part of my memory has to be destroyed to make way for new knowledge.'* (A 35-year-old mature student.)

One classic *trainer held myth* relates to the 'control of learning'. All too often trainers assume that if training is carried out effectively, with a well-organised programme using carefully controlled training materials, and assessed rigorously using objective criteria, then learning will automatically take place! Trainers caught up in this myth fail to appreciate that *trainers' purposes and learners' purposes are seldom identical* and that real learning can only take place when each individual's learning needs and personal background is seriously taken into account. Figure I1.1 shows how the trainer's 'purposes' and 'expected outcomes' are often not the same as the learner's 'purposes' and 'expected outcomes'. These represent two *different perspectives* on learning. The Learning Conversation allows the trainer and learners to *negotiate shared purposes*, and to *agree standards for evaluating the quality of the outcomes*.

With inappropriate myths like these, and many more predominating in the training/learning culture, it is not surprising that when we have to adapt to change through a process of learning—often forced upon us by outside influences—stress arises which, in turn, can lead to poor performance, an inability to cope and all too often illness and absenteeism.

It is a sad fact that in the UK, for a variety of reasons, many organisations large and small pay scant regard to training. Those few proactive and insightful organisations that provide training for their staff often find that, when changes in work practice and technologies are introduced, and people are 'trained' to meet these new demands, the staff fail to adapt to further unforeseen changes. This involves trainers in more work, carrying out further training in the form of courses, workshops or traditional coaching. In the long run this is neither cost-effective for the

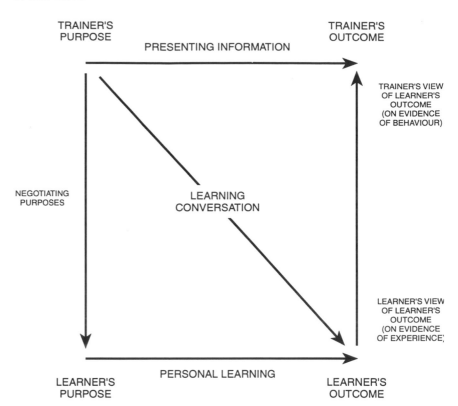

Figure I1.1   *Perspectives on training and learning*

company nor significantly productive of trainer time and effort. Training is essentially designed to be *expert-organised*, leaving the learner little room for manoeuvre and may well be concerned with reducing the number of 'short cuts' taken by staff who feel they have found 'better' but not approved ways of carrying out their work. Again, individual learners are often designated to attend training sessions without prior consultation and with little or no involvement in the design of their course.

When asking people to express what they wish to get from a course, the following comments are commonplace:

- *'To be frank I don't know why I'm here, I was just told to come along.'*
- *'My boss sent me.'*
- *'I received this memo about joining only last Friday, and when I tried to get out of this course because it isn't really relevant for me, I was told I had no option but to attend. I am hopping mad!'*
- *'What a waste of time! I have got loads of real work to do at the office, I really resent this.'*
- *'I thought this course dealt with learning about total quality but it's largely about the skills of accountancy.'*

This is hardly an ideal situation to help develop real and on-going learning!

Any serious book that aims to address learning directly must concern itself with the accelerating pace of change, the ever-spiralling demands for new skills and competences, and the relevance of learning in a person's job and in life. This book aims to do just that, and much more. It aims to familiarise individuals and groups who may need to learn together, with a compendium of techniques and procedures by which they can develop and conduct 'Learning Conversations' for enhancing their *capacity to learn*. Self-Organised Learners have the capacity to continue to develop their *learning* on the job and in life. For them the learning curve is characterised by an infinite growth potential.

The book aims to open up the mind to the exciting possibilities offered by SOL in enabling individuals and teams to develop their own abilities to manage change constructively by making the most of all learning opportunities and experiences and by loosening their dependence on other organised behaviours and standards. The book is designed to introduce the natural yet radical concept of SOL. It offers a very practical approach, encouraging the reader to use the techniques and procedures to *learn by experimentation* and by *reflection in action* on the job.

Many books have been written on the subject of self-development and learning to learn with a wide variety of stand-alone tools to help the learner to progress. Such books are, in the main, highly prescriptive despite the claim to be process-based. They do not invite 'freedom to learn'; nor do they promote self responsibility and continuous learning. They perpetuate what we would call *other-organised learning*. We aim to do something very different.

The content-independent *reflective learning tools* to be introduced are systematically designed to open up the process of SOL. Each is selected for use according to the needs of the individual at any given situation, time or place. Our experience shows that as learners increase their competence in learning they are gradually able to discard these tools instead of using them as a crutch to be relied upon for ever. The tools will have served their purpose to *enhance awareness of personal perception* as well as *personal performance*, promoting an enduring change within the person. Such learners will be able to conduct effective on-going 'Learning Conversations' with themselves, which can endure through life.

The SOL journey should not be viewed as a solitary activity: on the contrary it takes place within a *social environment* which encompasses the world of work, study and life as a whole. We invite readers to consider ways in which *learning partners* may be recruited to help in the quest towards SOL. Suggestions are given on how to develop *conversational networks of learners* operating in project teams or in small groups, or as a 'learning section' and a 'learning department'. Towards the end of the book, we indicate how an entire organisation can also recruit SOL for promoting learning throughout the company.

Trainers and managers are encouraged to reflect on their role of enabling others to develop competence in learning and how to make the best use of the opportunities that present themselves inside and outside the workplace for promoting personal development and team learning. Once this has been achieved various tools and strategies are offered for the management of SOL within the organisation.

The book is written in such a way as to encourage readers to *experiment* and *converse with themselves* about the ways in which they are learning as they progress through each chapter.

Self-Organised Learning as a radical approach

Learning is increasingly becoming the focus of attention in the workplace, with many approaches to helping people become better learners. Action learning, active learning, accelerated learning, learning sets, autonomous learning, independent learning, experiential learning, self-directed learning, neurolinguistic programming (NLP), open learning and learning style inventories have each, at some point, been 'flavour of the month' and there are no shortages of source material from which to examine the subject of learning. The key issue with these approaches, in our view, is that despite the apparent focus on learning, they are often primarily aimed at helping the trainer to use a preplanned and pre-organised 'learning package' as distinct from providing tools and techniques for enabling the learner to develop a continuous capacity to learn. A deep-rooted myth prevails: as a 'professional', the trainer should be in a position to know exactly what learning is necessary in others and how to structure and organise the learning activities to meet predictable needs.

Self-Organised Learning is totally different in that it genuinely focuses on the learner, who is enabled to develop responsibility for diagnosing personal needs and for developing personal standards of quality as well as for managing his or her own learning. The approach involves identifying appropriate resources, which will include people who may be in a position to offer their experiences and expertise. Learners are guided to explore the work situation and the often unexpected yet rich resources within themselves as well as in their whole environment. Part of the resources that may legitimately be offered include formal courses and workshops, but learners will have identified their needs and enrolled themselves. Such learners find it uncomfortable to submit themselves passively to being directed and instructed in what, for them, may be a purposeless manner. They would rather actively engage in the learning process in ways that meets their unique needs.

Many trainers who are accustomed to running courses and workshops in a predefined and highly structured manner are likely to find self-organised learners initially difficult to cope with, but once a shift in attitude is made they readily learn to accept new challenges, to move towards identifying individual needs and to meet the developing purposes of each of their clients. Trainers can then begin to see themselves as enabling learners to go forward to learn on the job, by systematically engaging them in Learning Conversations, thus supporting the process all the way.

How the book is organised

Each chapter begins with an *Agenda board* outlining the framework of the contents, and ends with a section featuring *Suggested activities* for developing the skills involved. Towards the end of each chapter we develop the *definition of Self-Organised Learning* and in the last chapter invite you to define the term for yourself.

In this general introduction we have explored how Self-Organised Learning relates to training and have introduced the concept as a radical approach.

In Chapter 1 we offer a basic definition of Self-Organised Learning, which is elaborated on as the reader progresses through the book. This chapter explains Self-Organised Learning and covers some of the benefits to individuals, teams and organisations.

Chapter 2 is concerned with getting started by challenging personal and professional myths about learning. There are suggested activities that will help to increase understanding of how personal myths can affect learning. We introduce and guide the reader through the process of setting up learning experiments, and making sense of learning.

In Chapter 3 we show the reader how to model the experience of learning using the repertory grid as a tool. Procedures are offered for analysing the results of the grid and the reader is shown how to support the learner to stand back and reflect on these results. Some mini exercises are offered throughout the chapter so that a step-by-step mastering of the method is achieved. The Self-Organised Learner is here seen as a 'personal scientist' researching learning.

Chapter 4 addresses itself to the need for developing a language with which to converse about learning and how this can help to develop skills and competences and the learner's capacity to learn. It describes exactly what we mean by a 'Learning Conversation' and introduces the role of the 'Learning Coach'. The different dialogues and the three levels of the Learning Conversation are explained.

In Chapter 5 we introduce the reader to the Personal Learning Contract as a major learning tool. We explain what we mean by the 'personal' learning contract and differentiate our meaning from the commonly held view of what a learning contract is. We take the reader through the procedure step by step and build up the process from a simple tool towards a more complex 'real life' instrument.

In Chapter 6 we illustrate Personal Learning Contracts by presenting examples of 'real life' applications from a wide variety of backgrounds to show the reader how the process works in action. This chapter is also intended to give the reader some ideas for using this tool as a training practitioner.

Chapter 7 is devoted to methods for measuring progress in learning. There is a suggested framework for measuring progress in SOL called the Personal Learning Biography. As well as measuring the effects of improved learning on task-based activities, this biography can be used as an evaluation tool.

Chapter 8 focuses on the practical organisational application of the SOL approach and elaborates on the development of a learning system involving a Learning Manager and Learning Coaches, and the setting up of learning networks among staff. We indicate how SOL may be introduced into an organisation, and how it may be encouraged to develop and become part of the learning culture.

How the book may be used

We suggest that while readers work their way through the book they perform the recommended activities and so experience SOL for themselves. We do not advocate that the entire text should be read before experimenting with learning. An overview of the approach can usefully be gained from the flow chart of the book, the table of contents and the agenda board at the beginning of each chapter. The previous section presented a brief summary of the ideas, techniques and processes relating to each chapter.

Some of the *learning tools* referred to can be used in isolation to the overall methodology and the benefits can be experienced almost immediately. However, the real science of SOL and the full pay-offs that the whole methodology brings can only develop when individuals accept responsibility for their own learning, thus creating a *personal project*. Such a project involves experimenting with all the tools and procedures in a variety of learning tasks and situations. This requires competence in carrying out all three *levels* of the 'Learning Conversation' as well as practice in the three *dialogues* of learning.

So! We suggest that you experiment with your learning *right away*, and then you can begin to consider how to support others to develop their SOL skills. Some readers may wish to use the methodology for helping others to develop competence in learning without experimenting too much themselves. This is, to some, extent possible but it would be difficult to envisage helping others develop the skills of learning conversations when one has no personal experience of the process! An advanced driving instructor needs not only to be an experienced driver before tutoring pupils for the advanced test, but must also be experienced in the tutoring process. Simply reading a book on advanced driving techniques and tutoring techniques, without personal experimentation, is unlikely to be helpful to either the trainer or the learner!

Quite simply, the SOL methodology is not just a package that can be passed on. It demands insight, understanding and specific skills which need to be mastered. On the other hand, given some support for learning, we have been very impressed by the speed with which some learners can become self-organised. In the book we describe how the training practitioner can offer this kind of work-based support for developing Self-Organised Learners.

Suggested activity

Action plan: designing an SOL workshop

Imagine that you have been given an opportunity to design a '3-day event' focusing directly on individual *processes of learning*. This may involve up to 30 participants, and should empower individuals, teams and an organisation as a whole to effectively change.

We invite you to produce specifications and a design brief for this event, giving emphasis to SOL.

Part of each day should be organised to enable individuals to *research the nature of their own jobs* and to *exchange experiences* on what they did (or intend to do) to learn the skills involved. Part of the day should be structured to *generate opportunities for feedback-for-learning*.

Consider carefully the resources to be offered, the nature of the exercises to be introduced, and your own responsibilities while running the course. Try to *identify your own various roles*

1 Construct a comprehensive yet flexible *process-based* plan for each activity.
2 Develop at least two *alternative plans* for the whole event.
3 Design a scheme for using *feedback generated by the learner* to *evaluate the effectiveness* of each plan.

We invite you to use this book to build on this activity, making revisions to your plans, and trying these out in different situations for clients of varying backgrounds and needs. Try to develop a fresh approach—*as an enabler of learning.*

1 What is Self-Organised Learning?

Agenda board

- The basic principles and background of Self-Organised Learning
- Tools for change
- The characteristics of a Self-Organised Learner
- Some benefits of Self-Organised Learning
- Suggested activity: designing a SOL workshop: revisions and elaborations

Basic principles and background of Self-Organised Learning

Self-Organised Learning (SOL) is a process which has to be personally experienced in order to be properly understood. Here we shall start with a basic definition which will become more personally meaningful as readers work through the book. By using the book as a resource for their practice, readers can develop an appreciation of how SOL can empower the person, on the job and in life.

SOL is defined as:

The personal construction of **meaning**—*a system of 'personal knowing'*

and

Meaning is the basis for all our **actions**.

Let us elaborate a little on this basic definition.

Each and every experience allows us to construct personal meanings, made up of thoughts and feelings, which underlie all our anticipations and our actions. This process is basic to human life; indeed, we would go as far as to say that it is basic to all organisms with brains. Our actions include everyday tasks such as cleaning one's teeth, deciding what to wear on a particular day, ordering work priorities for the day, working through the first meeting of the day, organising a report, or attending to a problem with the car. Actions may be more complex or of a less frequent occurrence—for example, working on a programme of self-development, chairing a critical meeting, handling a tricky disciplinary offence, sorting out a 'sticky' personal relationship, completing a water-skiing slalom course at great speed, or even building one's own home. Actions may involve major life events—for example, constructing a new life after redundancy, or divorce, or even living positively through the stages of a terminal illness.

Towards the end of each chapter we shall return to this definition and elaborate on it further. At the end of the book we invite you to define Self-Organised Learning in your own terms!

The methodology intrinsic to the SOL approach involves *Learning Conversations* for challenging robotic patterns of thoughts, feelings and actions, and for exploring new degrees of personal freedom. It is based on the fundamental notion that no one can 'cause' learning in someone else. Attempting to control learning from the outside can only result in producing dependent, inflexible, non-adaptive individuals who perform like robots. We call such learners *other organised*, not self-organised. They are neither creative nor able to engage constructively with change.

By getting to grips with the ideas and experimenting with the Learning Conversation techniques, readers will gain practical experience and will be in a position to give a critical appreciation of what SOL is and what it can achieve. Here, we aim to explain its background and to introduce some of the basic principles.

Self-Organised Learning has emerged from the humanistic, cognitive and behaviourist movements within psychology, and forms part of the rapidly growing 'New Psychology'. This focuses on a science of the 'whole person' in which both experience and behaviour are integrated into a 'psychological whole'. SOL explores how people's thoughts and feelings, perceptions and cognitions influence their actions, the ways in which people interact with their environment—their *personal worlds*. SOL offers a 'total quality' approach and focuses on developing an individual's *capacity to learn*, through experience on the job and in life. Readers may be familiar with the ideas of Carl Rogers and George Kelly, two leading figures within humanistic psychology. For Rogers, 'freedom to learn' was a key concept and Kelly saw 'behaviour as an experiment initiated by the whole person'. Rogers drew attention to the importance of the 'psychological conditions' necessary for personal growth, i. e. for becoming, in his words, a 'fully-functioning person'. He saw the role of a facilitator as removing the obstacles to growth thus allowing the person to 'flower'. He developed *'congruence'*, i. e. becoming at one with the learner while remaining true to oneself; *'empathy'*, i. e. entering into the world of a learner; and *'unconditional positive regard'*, i. e. truly accepting this world, as psychological procedures for promoting personal growth. The facilitator can thus converse with the learners in ways that *mirror their processes*, heightening awareness and facilitating growth.

The 'support' functions of the Learning Conversation within SOL recruits a Rogerian approach to facilitate personal reflection. Given such support, individuals are able to live more fully in and with each and all of their feelings and thoughts; make increasing use of their senses, and to use this information in awareness. The 'personal science' unique to Rogers allows the individual to gain deep recognition that 'the whole self is more than just conscious awareness'. Participants learn to *trust their own processes* and remain open to the consequences of their actions and of change. While Rogers focuses on the *conditions* for personal growth, Kelly was more concerned with *systematically representing personal experience* in the form of 'personal constructs'. No two people see their world in the same way and *their construct systems act as unique sets of spectacles* through which they perceive and make sense of their world. It is important, therefore, to elicit individuals' construct systems and help them to reflect on their own functioning. Kelly helps us to appreciate why a group of managers attending the same meeting will interpret the agenda differently and prepare different solutions to apparently the same problem. Likewise, each reader of this book will comprehend it differently and will react differently to it.

A person's construct system develops through the course of his or her particular life history and may change through the passage of time. *SOL makes a science of this change process*. It builds on Kelly's metaphor of 'the person as scientist', i. e. making sense of the world by building a personal theory of it. Such personal theories form the basis of subsequent anticipations and actions. 'Good scientists' go on to revise and occasionally transform their theories in the light of their on-going experiments. But people, i. e. learners, are often not very skilled as scientists and their models of their world are often implicitly held in almost total non-awareness. Such models become impossible to revise and individuals become very impoverished as a result. This inhibits their growth.

SOL builds on the 'biographical account' and repertory grid technique originally developed by Kelly and transforms these as reflective tools for learners. The 'Learning Conversation' methodology and the three stages of SOL awareness (to be described later) are rooted in the psychology of Rogers and Kelly, and evolve this further towards a conversational science.

SOL, feedback and purposiveness

A growing awareness of personal functioning depends on an ability to *model* each and every aspect of the human process. How does a person's meaning system influence his or her anticipations and actions? How do the results of actions feed back to revise understanding?

To answer these questions SOL leans heavily on ideas within *Cybernetics*—the science of communication and control. This is based on the *study of the flow of information through a system* and the way this is used by the system to control itself, i. e. to *self-organise*.

Imagine the system to be a person. Self-control involves generating personal criteria of competence, and this depends on the aims and intentions of the system. This is central to SOL. To appreciate how purposes help to control the functioning of a system, one needs to understand the principle of feedback. *Negative feedback*, as, for example, in the control of a central-heating system, is based on an *error-correcting mechanism*, which is important for reinforcing a stable system, i. e. for maintaining an equilibrium. Take, for example, a room in which the temperature has been set at, say, 65°C. The thermostat switches the boiler on and off as the room temperature exceeds or goes below this preset value. Trial-and-error type learning can be explained with this principle, but there is more to learning than this. Negative feedback operates within a *closed system* and does not allow for change and growth. *Positive feedback* allows for greater diversity and change to be introduced. It allows for an elaboration of a person's meanings by introducing variety and a wider range of purposes. A simple mechanical example would be when sound is fed back in an oscillator, so that it becomes amplified, theoretically to an infinite degree of loudness. So a *new response is reinforced*. New *patterns* of sound can be similarly reinforced.

Feedback is thus a fundamental concept in learning. Negative feedback based on an error-correcting mechanism, as, for example, in expert debriefing, top-down job appraisal, and exam assessments, does not support SOL. Positive feedback, internally generated by Self-Organised Learners as they engage in on-the-job activities and life experiences, allows them to construct and reconstruct their personal meanings. These are the building blocks from which they model their world and act on it.

Such personal meanings become the *emergent structures* which enable self-organisation and lead to deep and relevant change. Meanings are constantly being revised through a dense web of open, positive feedback and self-regulation according to the degree of fitness and viability in the environment.

Through SOL a person is enabled to explore an increasing variety of purposes for learning, and to try out and develop an increasing range of successful strategies for achieving these purposes by making use of positive feedback. This more open type of feedback leads to a richer system of personal knowledge and greater personal competence.

Learning on the job offers a rich environment for generating diversity and change, but only when *SOL awareness with open feedback is practised*. Without such awareness and self-control an individual rapidly stabilises into 'robotic patterns' of thoughts, feelings and actions. SOL is therefore important for greater *adaptiveness* within a rapidly changing environment enabling survival and growth.

SOL, relativity, chaos theory and complexity

Learning is a messy and rather untidy business, and necessarily so! You cannot fully know what you are going to learn until you have learnt it! As you progress, you might even change your mind about what you are going to learn and how you intend to learn it. In a sense, learning is open-ended and unpredictable. Now we must dip into the realms of recent trends in modern science to begin to understand this fascinating phenomenon. Bear with our digression into science a little longer, since this is important for a fuller appreciation of SOL.

Heisenberg's 'uncertainty principle' has shown us that even scientific 'truths' are relative. Put very simply, 'light' exists as particles of matter and as waves of energy. It has two basic properties, related to its mass and its energy. In order to measure the speed of light accurately scientific observation has shown that its mass becomes less predictable and vice versa. The two perspectives from which light is measured have to be taken into account so that the 'truth' about light is essentially *relative*.

To understand the 'truth' about a fully functioning person it is also essential to enter the realms of relativity. One must study the whole person from at least *two psychological perspectives, personal experience and behaviour*. When observing personal experience it is impossible to predict exactly how this influences behaviour. When observing behaviour, i. e. action, it is impossible to predict how this relates to personal experience. But what individuals can do is *converse with themselves in awareness* and explore the possible relationships between experience and action. This depends on developing a frame of reference: how personal meanings, needs and purposes lead to anticipations and actions and how the results of actions feed back and lead to revised (new) meanings. Individuals can learn to develop these conversational skills for themselves. The 'uncertainty principle' and 'relativity' are thus central to SOL.

In our experience, the process of change nearly always involves *disintegration*. We have all experienced getting worse at something before getting better! Think of trying to improve your tennis service, golf stroke, computer programming skills, or even your skills in chairing a meeting! Now, *very small changes* in thoughts, feelings, perceptions, and actions can bring about rapid disintegration, creating personal *disorder*, until new patterns of skill begin to emerge. This is chaos theory in action! SOL not only allows individuals to explore this process of disintegration, and to learn from it, but also to go on testing out and rebuilding new patterns until greater skill and competence are achieved. The whole process becomes a joyful, exciting voyage of discovery rather than a pain to be endured until some semblance of competence is somehow arrived at. We invite readers to experience the SOL process and discover for themselves!

Learning operates on the *edge of chaos*, somewhere between a stable system of order and an unstable system of disorder! It is here that personal meaning, a person's system of personal knowing (see definition of SOL on page 2) gets constructed. At the two extremes of the behaviour of all systems, ORDER and CHAOS pervades. Between these two extremes, at the edge of chaos one finds COMPLEXITY! This is a class of behaviours in which the components of the system are neither stable nor in a state of randomness. Complexity is now recognised as the state that allows information to organise and reorganise itself to increasing degrees of sophistication. This is the state *that allows the person to construct new and more complex meanings*. The LIFE process itself in all its diversity and complexity thrives on the edge of chaos, only rarely stabilising into fixed patterns. Such extremes rapidly result in the extinction of a species, as Charles Darwin has shown in his theory of natural selection.

SOL encourages learners to thrive on the edge of chaos, a state easily recognised in today's competitive, fast-changing world. Frozen meanings and fixed attitudes need to be opened up and revised and a whole new repertoire of constructs need to be explored. Each of us has constantly to forge new metaphors for working and for living.

Crises, uncertainties, changes imposed from the outside shadow of everyday life and personal stress becomes symptomatic of ever-increasing chaos. Personal experimentation, on the other hand, introduces diversity, flexibility, innovation and growth. The edge of chaos is vast with possibilities beyond the boundaries of our current imagination.

It allows for *perpetual novelty* and, as some eastern philosophies suggest, for a state of being 'continuously reborn'.

A case has been made for SOL as a *progressive state of 'being'* in which personal growth and change generated from within are constantly negotiated. Immense possibilities open up for communities and for organisations which consciously set out to support this process. Learning becomes transformed as a process of total quality and this is an in-depth approach steeped in the new science, and involving the whole person. In one sense learning can be likened to surfing on the crest of a powerful wave, depending on mental skill, agility and immense awareness from moment to moment. The thrill of ultimate success gives it meaning and learning becomes the joyful experience it should be. In Chapter 3 we shall remind you of learning as a process on the edge of chaos, as we explain about the 'drop in the learning curve' during change and about the need to challenge our robots.

SOL and awareness Research has revealed that there are three essential stages in becoming aware of the personal process of learning, and these stages are illustrated in Figure 1. 1.

First is the robotic non-reflective stage where the learner tackles a task and is almost completely unaware of how the task was actually done. Second is the stage when the learner concentrates in detail on the *doing aspects* of the task itself, observes this process and develops a greater awareness of the thoughts and feelings related to it, so enabling the learner to *experiment with change* in the ways in which the task is performed. The third stage involves observation of the processes of *how learning takes place* so that the person develops an awareness of his or her own learning skills. The evidences accruing from stage 2 become the source for reflecting on *how* we learn and how we *think* and *feel* about it. Learners then learn to build on this new experience, and learn to describe this process for themselves. Increasing awareness can lead to a quantum leap increase in levels of personal skills and competence. It often leads to higher levels of personal motivation and a desire to look constructively at change. Self-organised learners look curiously at the way things work rather than robotically and non-consciously carrying out tasks in the same way each time without questioning whether or not they can be improved. The methodology for developing stage 2 and stage 3 awareness depends initially on some outside support. The SOL coach provides this by engaging learners in a series of Learning Conversations. Learners will also need to seek others, including specialists and experts, as a resource for their learning and this may involve attending courses at appropriate times as they identify their specific needs, but these will form part of a *strategy they will have developed for themselves*, in conjunction initially with their SOL coach. Instead of being passive receivers of training they will actively engage in a Learning Conversation with their chosen resources, people, media and

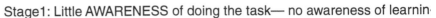

Stage1: Little AWARENESS of doing the task— no awareness of learnin

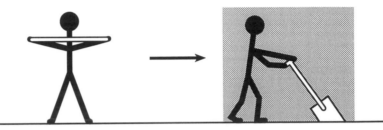

Stage 2: AWARENESS of doing the task

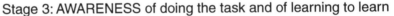

Stage 3: AWARENESS of doing the task and of learning to learn

Figure 1.1   *The three stages of SOL*

technology, in order to make sense of them, i. e. to construct their personal meanings and so achieve their unique learning needs.

Readers should not conclude that the transition from one stage to another is simple and straightforward. In reality the process can take some time and will involve much personal experimentation. In fact, many learners have commented that SOL is highly enjoyable and rewarding, but that it is a lifetime commitment and indeed becomes a *way of life*. Awareness of our own unique processes of learning is an ever-evolving phenomenon. Despite this, much can be achieved in the short term. As soon as a start is made, SOL leads to significant effects. Readers, therefore, should not conclude that the path towards SOL is necessarily long and that, in the tough arena of work, it simply may not be a feasible option. Our action research has shown that this is definitely not the case.

Once the learner starts to engage in SOL, improvements in skills and competence, in attitude, and in motivation develop very rapidly. The individuals drive the process with support from the SOL coach and the Learning Manager. The SOL coach may be either an operational junior or a middle manager experienced in SOL, or a training practitioner temporarily seconded to support learning on the job. The learning manager may be a volunteer senior manager who agrees to devote a small proportion of work time to coordinating and monitoring the SOL process in his or her work domain.

We find that Self-Organised Learners become driven by the constant need to question the way in which they do things on the job, and this is underpinned by the knowledge and ability to structure and manage their own strategies for coping with and initiating change.

Tools for change

The book takes the reader chapter by chapter through some of the core *learning tools* for enabling self-organised change. Let us briefly put these tools into some psychological context.

Greater awareness of personal behaviour depends on some *record of action*. A human observer or a machine can record the learner's performance and use this record for 'talkback'. During talkback special techniques are used so that the learner is encouraged to *reflect on how these details of behaviour relate to personal experience*. Videos, computer logs and learning partners (shadowing) can be used to enable talkback. Part of the task of the Learning Coach is to help the learners engage in their own talkback. This is a very different process to the use of videos for micro teaching where an expert observes the learner's actions, debriefs the learner and issues instructions for improvements. Many training situations follow the same pattern. The tools are specifically designed to help learners make better sense of their actions and to improve the quality of their performance.

While some form of external observation can record behaviour, *only the learner has direct access to his or her own experience*. The repertory grid and other 'meaning-eliciting' tools, to be introduced in Chapters 2 and 3, are used to elicit and heighten awareness of 'personal meanings' systematically and to show how these are constructed and recruited to influence actions.

The Personal Learning Contract (PLC) procedure described in Chapters 5 and 6 is another core-learning tool and develops this further. It allows the learners to explore the *relationship* between personal experience and action systematically so that they can model this for themselves. Initial 'plans for change' derived from personal histories become transformed through experimentation, action, reflection and review. The learners' *capabilities for learning* are thus enhanced.

These awareness-raising learning tools allow the learners, often for the first time, to *become observers of their own processes*. This is a very powerful experience which can lead to significant change. The tools allow the learners to *stand outside themselves and so to see themselves from a new perspective*.

We are at a moment of profound change in our personal, work-related and social lives. These tools, used within a Learning Conversation and initially supported by the SOL coach, enable individuals to get deeper insights into processes of change, and to become proactively involved in shaping their immediate and longer term futures.

SOL is a supreme expression of individual freedom. It can lead to a self-transformation of personal skills and competences. When Self-Organised Learners live and work together, very powerful forces of growth are put into action. These tools for SOL allow individuals and teams to go beyond the apparent limits of their intellectual and practical selves towards greater skill, competence and creativity.

To better appreciate the radical nature of SOL, we have elaborated on its background, its basic principles and some of the tools and techniques involved. Readers are asked to tolerate the oversimplifications and digressions into psychology and modern science, but our aim has been to show how *SOL is a powerful new approach for the training practitioner*. It can never be degraded to the 'flavour of the month' since its effects are long term and can endure for life. SOL is becoming increasingly recognised as part of a new and rapidly growing science. Its methodology has psychological structure and is process based. This distinguishes it from other apparently learner-centred approaches which can be manipulative and prescriptive, lack deep structure and are more concerned with superficial short-term change. SOL delivers an enduring transformation of personal learning skills, competences and capabilities. It enhances our capacity to learn. It empowers the individual.

The characteristics of a Self-Organised Learner

There are a number of essential characteristics for a self-organised learner, and some of these are summarised below:

1 Individuals must *accept responsibility* for their own learning rather than being dependent on the initiatives and directives of others.
2 There must be an achievement of an *awareness of how one learns*, and this involves:
   (a) recognising individual needs, and developing these into clearly expressed purposes;
   (b) initiating flexible learning strategies and recruiting appropriate

resources for achieving the expressed purposes;
(c) self-evaluation of the quality of the achieved outcomes;
(d) critically reviewing this cycle of activity;
(e) planning and implementing more effective cycles of learning activity to meet future needs.

3 There must be an appreciation of the *dynamic nature* of the learning process and a continuous striving for greater self-organisation.

4 The Self-Organised Learners need to recognise and *challenge* existing partially developed skills, including learning to learn so that such skills are transformed to achieve greater competence.

5 The Self-Organised Learners need to digest, challenge and redefine SOL in *their own terms*. This creative aspect of SOL expertise generates new dimensions of personal innovation and experimentation.

6 There must be a continuous effort towards achieving a 'quantum leap' improvement in the individual's *capacity for learning*.

7 The individual learner must believe in the value of SOL and *practise it as a way of life* in his or her job and in all social contexts. Such individuals who act as Self-Organised Learners are in many ways acting as Kelly's 'personal scientist'. They are actively involved in developing their own theories or hypotheses about given events, testing these out in practice, generating feedback of the consequences of their actions, and revising their 'theory' on the basis of such on-going experiments involving themselves. The quality of their actions depends on the richness of this whole activity. The three levels of awareness, the Learning Conversations and the tools, driven by the MA(R)4S reflective process (explained fully in Chapters 4 and 5), are designed to empower individuals with ways for achieving a better management of this proactive process called Self-Organised Learning.

Thus, Self-Organised Learners act as *complex adaptive systems* in a constant state of revision. They are constantly anticipating events, based on their experience and how they model the world. These models are revised in the light of feedback from actions on the world. Thus, for example, in situation *xyz*, bearing in mind experience *abc*, action *lmn* is likely to be best. But if situation *xyz* changes to *xrs* or *ejh* then action *pyu* may be more appropriate. The Self-Organised Learners will test this, generate feedback from the results of actions, and revise the model. They will also remain watchful of processes of change and adapt accordingly.

The Self-Organised Learner is continually exploring new niches to be exploited as *new opportunities for learning* and for living. A Self-Organised Learner's appetite for diversity is continually growing. He or she is never in a state of equilibrium, but is constantly juggling between stability and chaos. If a person operates mainly in equilibrium, seeking a status quo in most situations, he or she is psychologically dead.

A Self-Organised Learner is *part of a rich web of interactions* with the social, technological and physical world. Awareness, reflectivity and a growing sense of consciousness enables the learner to emerge from a genetically and culturally encoded past to become more of a free agent, with a capacity to develop and grow. It is our human capacity for adaptiveness, for SOL, that allows us to evolve our consciousness and our models of the world. We are thus empowered to change our world constructively: our world of work, home and leisure. By healthy competition, cooperation and purpose we can creatively evolve alternative futures. Thus, we can escape from the incessant process of decay and chaos dictated by the second law of the universe. Learning as a process of *self-organisation is the vehicle for living and working on the edge of chaos.*

Some benefits of Self-Organised Learning

There are many advantages to adopting SOL, and some of the more generally reported are listed below.

Individuals

- Improved personal job satisfaction.
- Improved contributions to the job.
- Improved relationships with other members of a team.
- Effective adaptation to changes in work practice and demands for new skills.
- Better use of training and personal development opportunities.
- Rapid advancement on the ladder of promotion, where appropriate.
- Learning on the job is viewed as an on-going way of life which is challenging, exciting and personally constructive.

Teams

- More cohesive teams, working with improved understanding.
- Team work is seen as personally relevant to individual members.
- The team is seen by individuals as a positive learning environment.
- Reduces problems frequently encountered by individuals who see themselves as 'outside' the team.
- The team is supportive of individuals, and individuals are supportive of the team.

Organisations

- Realistic policies, strategies and tactics may be readily related into positive courses of action once the commitment of learners has been gained.
- Efficiency and total quality develop as learners and teams proactively seek to improve their performance.
- Change is managed more effectively instead of expending undue energy on crisis management. Instead crises if and when they occur will be used as 'opportunities for learning'.
- Realistically achievable personal improvement plans are developed as a part of the performance review and planning process.

- Improved morale throughout the workforce as SOL expands its horizons.
- Improved team building and problem-solving activities.

Summary

In this chapter we have explained how SOL draws on humanistic psychology, cognitive science and cybernetics and integrates these sciences into a conversational science of learning. We have indicated how feedback, relativity and uncertainty, as well as chaos and complexity, are part of the process of learning. We have outlined the characteristic features of an SOL system and described some of the benefits of the approach. We have emphasised that SOL is based on learning from experience and is essentially a natural and practical process.

In Chapter 2 we shall explore how personal and professional myths about learning can be both constructive and destructive. We aim to encourage the reader to identify these myths and we show how they may be challenged when appropriate and reshaped into more viable beliefs and values which empower processes of Self-Organised Learning.

Suggested activity

Designing a SOL workshop: revisions and elaborations

At the end of the General Introduction we introduced a basic activity— designing an SOL workshop— and we suggested that readers should return to this at any time. This may be an appropriate opportunity for further reflection and analysis.

1 Consider the ideas put forward in this chapter.
2 Summarise these as you understand them and then try to organise them into some meaningful pattern.
3 Can this pattern of personal meaning created by you be used as a resource for the design brief of the 3-day workshop?
4 How might you create a supportive learning environment for the workshop?
5 Try to evaluate how some of these ideas might be useful for the modern-day training practitioner.

2 Challenging personal and professional myths about learning: the first steps towards SOL

Agenda board

- Beliefs, values and personal learning myths
- Disabling and enabling myths
- Awareness and the Learning Conversation for challenging personal myths
- Learner myths about learning and trainer myths about learning
- Exploring the range of learner myths
- Mini activity: identify personal learning myths
- A category system for personal learning myths
- Trainer myths explained
- Definitions of learning and Self-Organised Learning
- Suggested activity: identifying trainer myths

Introduction

Most people are at least partially 'disabled as learners'. Expectations about learning are low. Learning, like breathing, remains a ubiquitous process that happens to us rather than a consciously controlled process that can be improved. The high flyer who quickly develops some remarkable expertise is considered to be exceptional or 'gifted'! Yet, in our experience, the high flier is someone who, having given time to learn *how* to learn, has learnt how to fly! No topic, task or skill appears to be too difficult to tackle; each is approached as an interesting and challenging exercise. Given an opportunity to observe such an individual, our expectations about learning can be completely transformed. Most of us, regardless of age, background, experience or so-called IQ, can really take off and fly if we so choose. The skills of learning can be learnt: primarily this depends on adopting a challenging and positive stance and getting to grips with one's own learning processes.

Try to think of someone you know at work, in your family circle or, more generally, whose passage through life has significantly changed and who has developed skills and competences which neither of you believed possible. Then try and consider how such a development could have occurred. Our point is that our beliefs, values and prejudices actually condition the ways we approach our own learning. If someone believes they are 'dumb', 'stupid', 'unmusical', 'poor at solving problems or making decisions', not 'gifted at public speaking', 'not talented in maths or essay writing', 'physically inept at tennis, cricket, or water-skiing', it is very easy to confirm one's belief. It is more difficult to transcend one's apparent handicap! Yet time and time again budding Self-Organised Learners have shown that it can be done!

Personal learning myths

Each of us has deeply held robot-like myths about almost everything within our range of experience. This is demonstrably true about our own learning. Such myths have been acquired through mishaps in life, or simply because significant people in our lives have made assumptions about our learning so that creating myths have been perpetuated. At any age personal myths can become ultra-stable and apparently unchangeable! This leads to a person's performance taking on a robot-like function. Body and mind have taken on the role of automaton. In times of enormous change and when crises loom such a person finds it difficult to cope and readily succumbs to the effects of stress. Individuals who so suffer are victims of their own personal myths about themselves and about their learning capabilities.

We cannot make an immediate change in our personal myths about learning, but it is in our power to bring these myths purposefully and self-critically into greater awareness and recognise them for what they are: temporary accounts we make about ourselves from which we can begin to experiment and change.

The *Learning Conversation* is a vehicle for exploring the relativity of our personal myths, as imperfect or partial reflections of our processes at any particular moment in time. Within a Learning Conversation learners can create opportunities to challenge the underlying values of their myths and experience the excitement of deconstructing and rebuilding new patterns of beliefs and values. Learners can then discover those myths that are seriously disabling, and develop a strategy to convert them into more productive myths that can work for personal growth.

After only four years of climbing practice Rebecca Stevens revealed that all she needed to learn to get to the top of the world was a 'head for heights'! This she was able to develop quickly, enabling her constructively to believe that she could make it. The term 'myth' is thus meant to carry all its positive and allegorical as well as negative implications. As we live and work we are constantly developing a vast and complex range of personal myths about 'topics', 'tasks', 'people', 'machines' or any physical events. These myths work with different qualities of effectiveness for the range of situations, purposes and events within which we function. While acknowledging that many are disabling, some, like Rebecca's, can be very enabling!

The ideas, techniques and activities we offer throughout this book are designed to enable learners to experiment-in-action both on the job and in life generally in full awareness of the processes that these myths trigger from within. Once this level of awareness has been achieved a person can develop effective myths built from raw experience.

Let us now begin to explore personal myths about learning from at least *two basic perspectives*: myths that learners have about their own learning capabilities, and myths that trainers have about the learning of others. In the latter case such myths may well constrain rather than transform their clients learning. In the former case, learner myths can powerfully disable or more powerfully enable the development of new competences. When training practitioners adopt a Learning Conversation stance, they and their client learners can work together for personal growth. Such experiences can result in a transformation of their values and related personal myths. This is very different to the more usual 'content driven' training events which can alienate learners and serve to reinforce disabling myths. We shall now proceed to introduce you to some simple conversational exercises designed to enable you to appreciate the range of personal myths about learning that exist in most social settings. We also offer a category system within which such myths can be described and identified. The chapter ends by returning to the definition of Self-Organised Learning (SOL) summarised in the General Introduction. It will then become apparent that SOL—no more than a myth—has been constructed from action research and can be harnessed to richly enhance your capacity to learn.

Identifying personal learning myths

Spend an hour each day observing someone at work or leisure. Look out for what appears to be ritualistic patterns of behaviour and see if you can identify conversational exchanges which may reveal a system of beliefs constraining personal growth.

Now do the same on yourself! Being a spectator of yourself-in-action is not easy, but is a skill that can be learnt! Initially, you will find that you forget to watch yourself but you can invent various strategies to remind yourself! This is a first step towards greater awareness and is a prerequisite on the way to becoming a Self-Organised Learner. In each case try to identify personal myths which clearly signify either negative attitudes towards change or powerfully positive beliefs conducive to growth. Soon you will detect such personal myths in almost *any sample of conversation* within wide-ranging situations and circumstances.

The attitudes and assumptions that any individuals bring to each learning situation, and therefore their capacity to learn from it, are influenced by the cumulative impact of their past history. An obvious example is a group of trainees in a classical training situation obediently taking their seats for a lecture. Often they become passive recipients of information, rather than questioning learners. Trainee helicopter pilots, naval officers and even senior managers in industry and government on some refresher course readily and intuitively adopt a submissive role in this school-type setting.

The most easily identified myths are usually about the physical or social conditions of learning. Others are more concerned with the processes and skills of learning. These are only partially recognised by the learners, who appear to be locked in a 'language void', unable to describe and identify the myths that condition their learning. Deep implicit myths are often held about personal innate capacities for learning. Management trainees trying to master accountancy and computer skills have often stated a belief in their lack of talent for maths. Similarly, other trainees and apprentices firmly believe they have a lack of talent for 'writing', 'athletics', 'chess', 'house repairs', 'juggling' or 'chairing a meeting'.

Another dimension of personal learning myths relates to the set patterns of behaviour we exhibit when we try to remember or imagine any particular learning event. Some remember their learning in visual terms, others sub-vocalise or have auditory memories, or 'feel' themselves doing things. Each believes that his or her own brand of imagery is the universal way to learn. This deeply hidden source of personal myths about learning takes time to explore and identify. The increased learning potential that lies in experimenting with more consciously controlled multiple imageries is itself sufficient justification for giving time to the encouragement of greater awareness of one's own processes. What is true for the blind, deaf and dumb in the external world is also true for the internally disabled in their world of reconstruction and imagination. SOL is partly a matter of developing the skills for exercising, choice over the mode of thinking/feeling and remembering learning.

More insidiously, some negatively held personal myths come clothed as positive personal attributes! Many individuals stifle their personal learning by implicitly formulating a supposedly positive characteristic:

- I'm a toughie.
- I operate through common sense.
- I believe in academic purity.
- I am hard headed and logical.
- I have shrewd business nous.
- I am keenly practical in my method.

These traits can be used for avoidance of suppression of certain other characteristics in learners which might enrich their experience and enhance their learning powers. What is true for individuals applies also to team learning, and even to institution learning. Trainees in the police force, from the most junior to the most senior on the promotional ladder, almost exclusively adopt a macho approach to learning. A tight and logical approach prevails in the world of law, and a highly empathetic stance filters through therapeutic training. Each profession might enrich its competences were it to adopt a more open and flexible multi-trait approach to suit learning needs.

Other very rigidly held personal myths become constructed to excuse poor performance:

- I've not got that kind of intelligence.
- My personality does not allow me to.
- It's against my nature.
- I have to take account of my health.
- I am much too creative a person to get into that type of work.

These myths are expressed as 'objective facts' which explain away many operational incompetences in the factory, in the boardroom, in the surgery, on the sports field, on the battleship and in the prison. It is implied that such 'facts' are inborn and innate and, therefore, not much can be done to change them. Interestingly such assumptions are often only dimly recognised by the individuals possessing them and are fiercely defended within a Learning Conversation. Much support and hard evidence is required to open up the minds and entice such hostile learners to experiment with change.

Mini-activity **Identifying personal learning myths**

We suggest that you perform these activities personally before en-couraging learners to undertake them so that you are aware of the potential benefits to individual competence.

1 Identify one task, topic or skill which is currently important to you.
2 Make a note of this.
3 Consider all the conditions, physical and social, within which you are continuing to learn the specified task, topic or skill.
4 Note these and, on a five-point scale, rate each separately in terms of:
   (a) Very good for me to learn in.
   (b) Fairly good for me to learn in.
   (c) Average for me to learn in.
   (d) Difficult for me to learn in.
   (e) Impossible for me to learn in.
5 List all the 'learning skills' relevant to your learning. Make a separate list of those learning skills **not relevant to your learning**.
6 Consider your own 'talents' and 'personality traits' in terms of attributes for learning. Note each and, on a five-point scale, note each separately in terms of:
   (a) Makes it very easy for me to learn.
   (b) Makes it easy for me to learn.
   (c) Makes it average for me to learn.
   (d) Makes it difficult for me to learn.
   (e) Makes it very difficult for me to learn.
7 Explore your personal learning myths in other topics, tasks and skills that are important to you and keep a log of your experimental findings!

As you accumulate evidence about your own learning myths, begin to review your potential for change. What have you learnt about your self-organising capacities? Can you revise your personal development plans in the light of accumulating evidence? If possible, exchange these experiences with peers and again review your plans for change.

In Table 2.1 we introduce you to a category system of personal myths about learning which has been developed as a result of 20 years' action research.

Table 2.1: *A simple category system for personal learning myths*

A   **Myths about 'conditions' of learning**

Physical
Time of day: Just after sunrise; just after midnight. *Place*: Small and intimate; airy and well lit. *Span of time*: Short; long. *Body position*: Sitting still; walking; lotus position. *Noise levels*: Peace and quiet; radio as background.

Social
Solitude: Alone; with others; in a team; in a family setting; with a chosen friend; in a unisex context.

B   **Myths about opportunities for learning**

Situation
Within a problem-solving environment ● In a crisis ● When everything is running smoothly ● In a lecture ● Using business games ● In a laboratory doing project work ● 'In anger' on ship ● In an intensive experiential workshop ● With a simulator which logs my action for replay ● In a discussion with a consultant/adviser ● Quality circles ● Using computers ● Using videos/books ● On the job.

Type of event
A week's intensive course ● An outdoor leadership course ● A competitive event ● A final year project ● Preparing for an exam ● Attending a relate session ● A well-structured lecture.

Nature of resources
Spreadsheets ● A counsellor ● Observing an experienced worker ● Videos with rich examples ● Research journals and specialist books ● Work placement ● Feasibility exercises.

C   **Myths about processes of learning**
Learning by: Doing ● Listening ● Questioning ● Feeling ● Making patterns ● Repetition and drill ● Selecting principles ● Making a mental map ● Visualising ● Affirmation.

D   **Myths about capacities for learning**
A memorising capacity ● A mind for figures and relations ● Linguistic skills ● Brainstorming abilities ● A colour sense ● A spatial awareness ● Manipulative skills ● Risk taking ● Long concentration ● Sustained commitment.

E   **Attitudinal myths: personal characteristics, traits and talents**
Practical bent ● Sharp eye ● Feminine touch ● Musical ability ● Persistence and doggedness ● Mathematical talent ● Macho nature.

Only through a gradual but deepening reflection on personal learning experiences can learners distance themselves from their own thoughts and feelings, beliefs and values, to develop an ability to *observe their own learning myths* and experience the *effects they have on personal learning*. The myths that limit their horizons can then be open to change. The Learning Conversation with its various techniques and procedures supports this process.

Trainer myths about learning

Sometimes training practitioners and human resource specialists have one set of myths for their clients and another for themselves as learners! Their beliefs about learning in others have been developed through their professional training and what they have experienced as recipients of traditional training. One has only to attend a training course or conference to witness the dogmatic values that dictate the ways in which learning is approached; vast sums are 'channelised' into 'objective' highly structured and pre-programmed packages, courses and audio-visual support. In such packages self-assessment schemes are based on trainer
criteria specified in advance and assigned to each learner. On occasions learners are invited to negotiate their personal objectives for learning but they are often directed within a framework imposed by the trainer. These objectives and assessments convey a highly behavioural, performance-based stance without allowing for the unique mechanisms of understanding that condition each learner's personal approach.

Again the expert system approach demands a submissive and receptive learner stance, in which degrees of freedom are limited to pre-set pathways towards the right answer. Complete skills must be acquired in logical order according to some highly prescribed task analysis procedure.

Resources are highly organised according to a limited number of fixed learning styles from serialist to holist with a belief that learners learn best when matched to their own learning style. A highly structured learning style inventory based almost exclusively on behavioural categories derived by 'experts' is used to classify learning styles.

On scrutinising packages from these points of view, a welter of training myths is so revealed, covering materials, objectives, course curricula and methods for the evaluation of learning.

Together, then, such 'trainer myths' and 'learner myths' create an almost hidden *conversational frame*, which defines the quality of subsequent learning. The interaction of these myths, often without recognition, determines the ebb and flow of a course, workshop or local training session. If they remain unrecognised (that is, without awareness) the conversational frame remains unnegotiable, and therefore not open to change.

When reflected on fully as part of the developing course, such myths enter into the arena of debate or discussion, and the conversational frame expands and changes its shape and direction. The ingredients of a disastrous course are embedded in the former stance, while a successful yet challenging course emerges from the latter. In our experience it is the hidden or revealed assumptions of both clients/learners and trainers about how learning takes place, which directly influences the course of a training/learning event. The quality of learning should be assessed by considering how learning opportunities are exploited or, alternatively, missed.

Suggested activity

Identifying trainer myths

The terms training, instructing, demonstrating, lecturing, packaging, coaching and counselling define some of the professional activities of training practitioners. How do you carry out any of these or other training activities? Now go through the following steps:

1 Think of the tasks in which you have been personally involved in the last 12 months.
2 List the topics and events on separate cards. For example, a slide presentation on team effectiveness; a group discussion on problem-solving techniques; a briefing on strategic planning, etc. Try to identify 15 to 20 topics/events. As you continue with the activity others may emerge. Add these to your list of cards.
3 Look at each card in turn, and begin to reflect on the 'image of learning' evoked in you by each topic/event. *This process of reflecting on the personal experience is the nub of the activity here advocated.* Now record your thoughts and feelings as items of personal experience in note form on the reverse of each card in turn. Do not censor your reflections. It is important to free associate and allow your thoughts and feelings to flow. Some examples may help:

> Slick and according to plan.
> Structured and tight.
> Smooth and easy.
> Participative and enjoyable.
> Too challenging and too permissive.
> Routine execution without much thought.
> Disciplined freedom.
> Egg on my face—never again.
> External manipulation.

As you continue to reflect new topics/events you will identify an ever-widening range of thoughts and feelings. Try to generate 30–40–60 cards with descriptions of your thoughts and feelings in relation to each topic/event. Generally this is a fairly easy and motivating activity. However, we shall at this point introduce what we term *elicitation cues* for triggering your generation processes. Consider:

- If you were to do it again—how might it be different as an image of learning?
- If you could have been in complete control, what would have been your ideal image?
- What is the worst possible scenario, and what kind of image of learning might this create?
- What if you are asked to switch your training role:
    - a behavioural modification approach?
    - a Rogerian approach?
    - a sitting by 'Nellie' approach?
    - a counselling approach?
    - an 'expert' approach?
    - an open and permissive approach?
    - a directive approach?
    - an explanatory approach?
  Place yourself in each role and see what image of learning is conjured up.
- Finally go through your own client list. If you were to prepare individual learning events for each, what might these be and what images of learning do these elicit?

When you feel you have exhausted your repertoire of 'images of learning' or 'items of experience' you should proceed to the next step.

4 *Sorting and patterns of meaning*: This step involves sorting items which you feel are in any way related into piles, which we shall call *clusters*.

5 Having grouped your items into clusters, place the clusters on a large table (or even the floor). A useful tip at this point is not to place the clusters randomly, but to position them in a manner that appears 'logical' to you.

6 Try to describe each cluster. What is the nature of the commonality shared? Try to draw connecting arrows between various clusters, and label the nature of the relationship on each arrow. (You might usefully use coloured arrows to signify differences.)

7 *Review your myths*: Explore the pattern of relationships made explicit.

- What does the representation of your images of learning reveal about your personal myths?
- Use the representation to review the basic nature of your training activities. Try to challenge them. Stay with the possibility that your ways of thinking/feeling about training may be prejudicial to enabling learning in others.
- Try to identify personal myths that may prevent you from expanding your horizons and developing new enabling skills.

- How would you develop a programme for personal development as a training practitioner?
- What would you see as appropriate topics/events and resources for optimising processes of learning?

Answers to these questions lead to tentative first steps in the direction of using your own experience to manage a personal programme of change. Figure 2.1 illustrates diagrammatically a structure of meaning. PLEASE KEEP THE PAPERWORK AND RESULTS OF THIS ACTIVITY AS YOU MAY WISH TO DO FURTHER WORK ON IT IN CHAPTER 8.

Later, in Chapters 3, 4 and 5, we introduce you to systematic methods based on Personal Learning Contracts (PLCs) for managing a programme of growth. Reflective activities such as the structure of meaning activity and the Personal Learning Contract heighten awareness of learning processes, and promote a more focused and penetrating movement towards Self-Organised Learning.

Definitions of learning and Self-Organised Learning

Many training practitioners define learning as:

The acquisition of *appropriate* knowledge, skills, and attitudes to be assessed according to publicly or expertly acknowledged standards.

Or as

The achievement of *valued* changes in behaviour to be assessed according to predefined norms.

BUT: Who is to decide what is appropriate? Who is to value the changes?

In SOL, the learner's own criteria of judgement and values have priority. Hence, the very personal nature of SOL.

Let us now return to our definition of Self-Organised Learning in Chapter 1:

We see learning as the personal construction of meaning—a system of *personal knowing*. The patterns of meaning we construct are the basis for all our actions in our world.

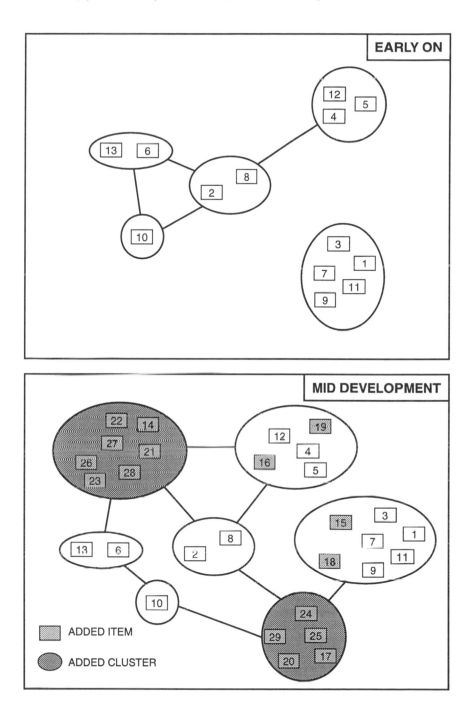

Figure 2.1 *A developing structure of meaning*

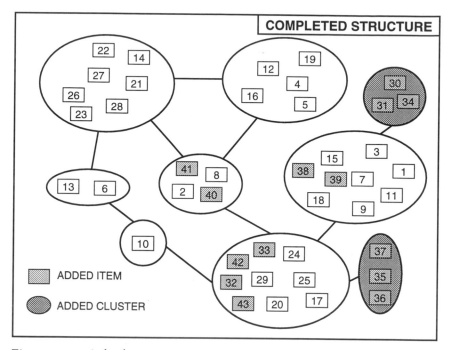

Figure 2.1   *A developing structure of meaning (continued)*

Summary   In this chapter we have tried to explain how our *personal meanings* can usefully be recognised as *personal myths*. These form part of our system of beliefs and values and powerfully influence the ways we learn. Awareness of our personal myths is the first step to enable us to:

- detach ourselves from them and see them for what they are;
- transcend the limits they impose to enrich our personal meanings and so our experiences of the world.

The next chapter takes us one step further into this process.

3 Learning Conversations with the repertory grid: modelling the experiences of learning

Agenda board

- Perceptions, thoughts and feelings as a construing system
- The seven stages of a grid-Learning Conversation
- Talkback with a focused grid: some examples
- Expanding the grid conversation: the CHANGE grid
- Expanding the grid conversation: the EXCHANGE grid
- The Self-Organised Learner as a personal scientist
- Suggested activity: eliciting a personal model of managing people: construing the experience of managing people

Perceptions, thoughts and feelings as a construing system

The thoughts and feelings we experience as we work, play, live and learn can more fully enter into our awareness, by means of conversational encounters with the repertory grid. This technique was originally developed by George Kelly (see Chapter 1) for systematically making personal meaning explicit. *The two-dimensional matrix of the grid represents elements or events within our range of personal experience, and bipolar constructs or dimensions along which these events are differentiated.* Constructs are not a haphazard collection of thoughts and feelings, but form a repertoire of meanings relating to specific domains in our experience. Examples of such domains would be 'people I know well', 'books I have read', 'events when I feel I have really learnt something'. Later in the chapter we list many more examples. Elements and constructs form, as it were, the 'text and subtext of our psyche' influencing the ways in which we perceive, interpret and act in our world. Kelly saw our construing system as a 'unique set of internal spectacles' through which we see and make sense of our world. These spectacles may magnify, clarify and distort. They put some things out of focus as they bring other things into focus.

Kelly would argue that the position, responsibilities and experiences of individuals *have led them to develop a unique set of constructs*. The repertoire of constructs which an individual brings to bear on a particular situation, leads to that situation being viewed by that individual in a way that is unique. Certain aspects may be selected while others are ignored. No two individuals reading the same book will attribute exactly the same meaning to it. Likewise, two individuals attending the same lecture do not necessarily hear the same thing. Even members of a closely knit management group working on a practical task will, in all probability, draw different conclusions. One may see it as 'a statistical exercise', another as 'an opportunity to explore part of the organisation I do not normally have access to', while others may see it as 'rather a chore', 'something which has to be suffered' or 'just another scientific exercise'.

Learning conversations with repertory grids allow us to become more aware of our constructs and also to enrich them, so that we can act more effectively. *Even in the most dire of circumstances, when the going may seem very tough, we are always free to reconstrue the situation, and act differently.* This can be an enormously empowering process. It is the way to greater openness, flexibility, new freedoms, new responsibilities and personal growth. It is the way to enhance our skills, competences and creativity. It is at the heart of an awareness of the construction of personal meaning, which leads to Self-Organised Learning (SOL).

A myriad of conversational exercises with the repertory grid have been invented by Thomas and Harri-Augstein in 20 years of action research. These challenge our ways of looking at the world and invite people to experiment with change. In this chapter we aim to introduce some of these basic exercises that have proved to be very effective in enabling learning on the job, and in empowering individuals and teams to higher standards of excellence.

Every topic, task or skill can be explored in terms of the ways each person construes them. *We can begin to identify 'where I am' and to make plans for 'where I would like to be'.* The Learning Conversation also takes us beyond the grid to explore alternative futures. The examples and suggested activities in this chapter gives some of the flavour of this process. Chapters 4, 5 and 6 expand on this further.

The seven stages of a grid-learning conversation

The grid conversation is initiated by the elicitation of elements and constructs. The process of grid analysis continues this further. The pattern of meanings so revealed can then be reflected upon, so that the conversation becomes an on-going process. A series of grids elicited over time, either in the same topic or in a different domain, take the conversation still further. Again, individuals can exchange grids and so share their understanding of some common experience and continue the conversation by learning together.

Let us describe the seven stages in a grid conversation. As you read through each stage, try to imagine what it would be like to work with a client/learner in this way. Additionally, try to perform the mini-exercises we suggest at certain points. You will then be ready to undertake the complete grid conversation activity that we recommend at the end of this chapter.

Stage 1: Identifying needs and purposes for learning

Applying our approach to the 'grid conversation', the first step is to negotiate an appropriate purpose.

Who sets the purpose? We would suggest that the training practitioner guides the process by which needs and purposes are identified, but it is very important that the client/learner identifies and defines the purposes personally. Creative Learning Conversations begin when practitioner and learner mutually recognise the different contributions each can make at this stage.

Stage 2: Exploring a topic

This must be central to the interests of the client/learner. It could involve some 'problem area' or 'growth point' or some series of events under dispute. Needs and purposes become further clarified as the topic is fully explored. *Stages 1 and 2 develop together as an iterative process.*

Mini-exercise

To experience directly the flavour of negotiating needs and purposes in relation to a topic it is suggested that the reader work with a friend or colleague to explore an appropriate topic area and discuss needs and purposes for 'doing a grid' in this area. Try to tape-record the exercise and listen to it carefully to identify your strategies for guiding the conversation.

Stage 3: Selecting items of experience as elements

Start by selecting 'naturally occurring' events which emerge from a person's experience in a topic area and which are congruent with the emerging purposes for learning. Be sure to encourage events that are close to the original raw experience. By this we mean that the descriptions of the events are steeped in real concrete examples. One of our clients who chose 'Events in my working life from which I really learnt something', as the topic area of her grid, recorded the following elements:

- The day I was told I was in charge of the delivery team for a week.
- Trying to make sense of the paperwork for recording mail throughput.
- The first time I had to discipline a man in public on the sorting office floor.
- When my suggestions for solving a despatch crisis were 'ruled out of court' by my boss.
- A row with my boss over how I tackled the crisis at work when a postman walked out on me.
- A chat about a personal problem I was experiencing at work with a colleague whose opinions I really valued.
- An argument I had with a colleague about timing the tea break.
- Watching my boss as he turned round the tide of opinion during an office dispute.
- When asked to debrief myself on how I performed the task of appraising a member of my team, by my Learning Coach.
- Crashing my car in the fog on the M1 on my way to a business meeting.

Abstract descriptions as opposed to concrete descriptions are ambiguous and lead to difficulties later when the elements (example above) are rated on the constructs in the grid. This is why we emphasise the importance of concrete elements drawn from experience at this stage. The practitioner needs to check the final definition of each element adequately, which reflects the richness of the experience.

It is useful to elicit at least 9 and up to 18 elements and record each on a separate card as fully as possible.

Stage 4: Eliciting constructs

Part of the strength of a grid conversation lies in the highly structured, yet content-independent technique which forces into awareness how items of raw experience get construed. First, the bipolar nature of a construct must be appreciated. This means that any one element acquires meaning when seen in relationship of similarity and difference to at least two other items. Similarity and contrast together assign one dimension of meaning.

The minimum number of elements required to perceive such a relationship is three, and triads (three elements in turn) are used at least at the beginning to elicit a construct. First, place each element elicited in the previous stage on a separate card, then shuffle the cards so that each element is now in a random order. Number each card, on the reverse side, from 1 to however many elements there are. The client/learner is then asked to take the first three cards, requested to think or feel that he or she is back in the events, and asked to state the two that are most alike and the one that is different.

For the sake of illustration, ignoring in this instance what the elements actually are, the personal constructs emerging from similarities and differences of just three elements may emerge as follows:

Similar pair	*Different (singleton)*
(Left-hand pole)	(Right-hand pole)
Pleasant (E1 and E2)	Traumatic (E3)
People-centred (E1 and E3)	Technical (E2)
Difficult (E2 and E3)	Easy to do (E1)

Mini-exercise

Now, to experience this process directly, we suggest you try the following exercise:

Take, for example, 12 job-related tasks and write each task heading on a separate card. Shuffle the cards, so that the order in which the tasks appear is different from the order in which you generated them. We suggest that you attempt to elicit up to 12 personal constructs, and in order to do this 12 sets of three cards (triads) need to be separately considered. A list for selecting the triads is illustrated in Table 3.1, in which no pair of elements should recur until all pairs have been used once.

After considering the first triad (E1, E2, E3) you will have a bipolar construct; that is, from the two elements that you considered to be similar, you will have one construct pole, and from the element that is different you will have the other construct pole. Continue with each of the triads listed in Table 3.1 until construct descriptions begin to repeat themselves, and the learner feels that the repertoire of constructs has been exhausted.

Table 3.1   *The triad table*

E1, E2, E3	E1, E4, E7	E4, E7, E10
E4, E5, E6	E1, E5, E9	E4, E8, E12
E7, E8, E9	E2, E5, E8	E7, E11, E3
E10, E11, E12	E3, E6, E9	E9, E10, E2

When helping the learner through this process, it is very important that both the element and construct descriptions are expressed in the words generated by the learner and that the Learning Coach does not 'put words into the learner's mouth'. It is very easy to fall into the trap of helping the learner, and this must be avoided at all costs, otherwise the verbal labels become those of the practitioner. This can adversely affect the awareness-raising conversation. The skilled construct elicitation process is structured, yet flexible. If the construct provided appears too general or diffuse, the learner must be guided to be more specific. Questions such as 'What do you mean by...?' or such statements as 'Give me an example' can be used to ladder downwards to relate more appropriately to the defined grid purpose.

The success of the grid conversation depends on the quality of the construct elicitation. Time must be given to allow learners to explore and describe their construing of the topic given in their stated purposes for learning.

This stage of the grid conversation is now complete.

Stage 5: Generating the raw grid

The next stage is to map the elements and constructs on to what is known as a raw grid. To do this, place each construct pole description that was generated from 'the pair' of elements on the left-hand side of the grid and the corresponding pole generated from 'the singleton' on the right-hand side of the pole, as shown in Table 3.2.

You will see that the left-hand pole has a '√' and the right-hand pole a '×'. The learner is asked to consider each element in turn, to record whether the element is more closely related to the left- or the right-hand pole of each construct, and to record his or her impression with either a '√' (left-hand pole) or a '×' (right-hand pole). If we assume that E1 represented a task such as interviewing for recruitment and selection, and the left-hand pole of the first construct was 'pleasant' and the right-hand pole was 'traumatic', then if the learner felt that interviewing was more traumatic than pleasant, this would receive a '×'. Encourage the learner to jot down separately why, for later discussion, the event was considered to be more traumatic than pleasant.

Table 3.2 *Generating the grid*

Left pole	E1	E2	E3	E4	E5	E6	E7	E8	E9	E10	E11	E12	Right pole
√													×
C1													C1
C2													C2
C3													C3
C4													C4
C5													C5
C6													C6
C7													C7
C8													C8
C9													C9
C10													C10
C11													C11
C12													C12

The entire grid is then worked on in this manner until it is complete, as shown in Table 3.3.

Table 3.3 *The complete grid*

Left pole	E1	E2	E3	E4	E5	E6	E7	E8	E9	E10	E11	E12	Right pole
√													×
C1	×	√	√	√	×	×	×	×	×	√	√	√	C1
C2	×	√	×	×	√	√	√	×	×	×	√	√	C2
C3	×	×	√	√	√	√	√	√	√	√	√	×	C3
C4	×	√	√	√	√	√	√	√	√	√	√	√	C4
C5	×	×	×	×	×	×	×	×	×	×	×	×	C5
C6	×	√	√	√	√	√	√	√	√	√	√	√	C6
C7	×	√	√	×	×	×	√	√	√	×	×	√	C7
C8	×	√	√	√	√	√	√	√	√	√	√	√	C8
C9	×	√	√	×	√	×	×	×	√	×	√	√	C9
C10	×	√	√	√	√	×	×	×	√	√	√	√	C10
C11	×	√	√	√	√	√	√	√	√	√	√	√	C11
C12	×	√	√	×	×	×	×	×	×	×	×	√	C12

Stage 6: Analysing and identifying the meaning in the raw grid

The grid is now ready to be analysed in preparation for a conversation to help the learner reflect more deeply on the meaning of its contents. We term this analysis 'FOCUSing' and this may be carried out by computer using the special software we have produced or simply by hand. The procedure is illustrated in Figure 3.7 and described later. You will note that space may be made between elements in order to highlight similarities and differences between elements. Although it takes some time in-itially, *learners should be encouraged to analyse their own grid*. This is, in itself, an awareness-raising procedure; the learner is able to understand the process involved and owns the results. The analysis feels like a piece of detective work, as the patterns of meaning begin to emerge. Later, as the practitioner and learner become more experienced and ambitious, instead of a '$\sqrt{}$' or a '×' a five-point scale may be used—1 and 2 for the left-hand pole; 4 and 5 for the right-hand pole; with 3 denoting the half-way stage or that the construct does not apply to the element.

Analysing the grid: general principles

Let us start by describing the basic principles involved. In the completed raw grid the elements have been numbered at random and the constructs numbered in the order in which they were elicited. *The analysis involves re-ordering the elements and then the constructs according to the similarities in rating*. For example, in our raw grid illustrated in Table 3.3, E2 and E12 are rated identically, so during analysis E12 would be moved next to E3 and so on. Similarly with the constructs C4 and C11 both have been rated identically and so would be moved next to each other. This process highlights the meaning in the grid for the learner.

Step-by-step guide to the analysis

Step 1   Look at the *element columns* and search for similarities between the elements. Start by looking for mostly $\sqrt{}$ or mostly × and then for similar distributions of $\sqrt{}$ and × .

Step 2   Make a copy of the raw grid and *cut it up into column strips* to help with the re-ordering process. When this is completed, place the element strips in clusters of similarly rated elements.

Step 3   Paste the strips onto an empty grid form.

Step 4   The *construct rows* are then inspected as with the elements in step 1, but this time look for the similarities in distribution of $\sqrt{}$ and × in rows.

Step 5   Make a copy of the pasted grid and cut the construct rows into strips in a similar fashion to the elements in step 2, place the strips in clusters of similarly rated constructs.

Step 6   Now paste the constructs into an empty grid form. Having re-ordered the element columns and construct rows the analysed hand-FOCUSed grid will reveal the pattern of meaning in it more readily to the learner.

Step 7   Now look at the pattern of meaning and read off the element and construct descriptions in their new order. Usually the grid analysis has quite a profound impact when the learner stands back and reflects on the results.

Figure 3.7 at the end of the chapter offers a detailed guide for hand-FOCUSing your grid.

That is all there is to it. There is no magic; nor do you need a 'head for figures'.

This awareness-raising process of analysing the grid continues the conversation process and many learners have experienced new insights into their own process at this stage. The conversation can now evolve naturally to the next phase, which uses the FOCUSed grid as a 'mirror of the psyche' for a deep reflection.

Stage 7: Talkback conversation with the FOCUSed grid

Let us trace out the steps for reflection on the meaning in the FOCUSed grid.

Step 1 Read the element descriptions and try to relive the experience each embodies.

Step 2 Read the bipolar construct descriptions and try to relive how these emerged.

Step 3 Notice the overall pattern of responses in the grid. Do these simply form a dichotomous patchwork, or a more elaborate form of patchwork?

Step 4 Look at each cluster of elements in turn and assess whether all the elements in one cluster can be subsumed by a more comprehensive verbal label. You are now 'laddering' upwards in the hierarchy of your meaning system.

Step 5 Repeat this process for the construct clusters.

Step 6 Work through the grid repeating steps 4 and 5, looking first at the tight clusters of similar elements and similar constructs, and then at looser clusters.

Step 7 Take a critical look at the pattern as a whole. What does it tell you about your construing of that domain, given your purpose for learning?

Talkback with a FOCUSed grid: some examples

It may be helpful at this point to illustrate a TALKBACK conversation. First, we have chosen a fairly small grid, to give you some flavour of the process. One of our clients who had recently been promoted to senior executive in a large commercial company chose to reflect upon his 'bosses'. These were the directors of one of the divisions of the company. After years of success he was experiencing serious problems at work, and wanted to explore deeply whether this had anything to do with how he related to the directors. Figure 3.1 shows this client's completed raw grid and Figure 3.2 shows the same grid space-FOCUSed.

PROJECT – GRIDS XXX

CONSTRUCT POLE RATED – 1		A	B	C	D	E	F	G	H	I	J		CONSTRUCT POLE RATED – 5
		E1	E2	E3	E4	E5	E6	E7	E8	E9	E10		
EXTROVERT	C1	1	1	5	3	4	3	5	4	2	4	C1	PRIVATE PERSON
OVER-ENTHUSIASTIC	C2	3	2	4	1	5	3	3	4	3	3	C2	CAUTIOUS
DIRECTIVE	C3	1	2	5	2	3	4	3	3	3	4	C3	CONSULTATIVE
DISHONEST	C4	5	1	4	3	4	5	3	4	4	5	C4	HONEST
THINKER	C5	2	3	1	2	5	3	3	3	3	3	C5	PLODDER
DISORGANISED	C6	4	2	1	3	4	5	3	5	5	5	C6	ORGANISED
CLEAR	C7	2	3	1	4	3	2	3	1	1	1	C7	CONFUSED
UNHELPFUL	C8	3	1	5	2	4	5	3	3	4	5	C8	HELPFUL
DEMANDING	C9	1	2	5	3	3	4	3	1	1	2	C9	EASY GOING
NON-DESIRABLE	C10	5	1	4	3	4	4	3	3	3	5	C10	DESIRABLE

Element names (vertical):
VINCENT THOMAS · TONY HOMAN · REGINALD THOMAS · MAXWELL SLADE · JAMES WELLS · HORACE JORMACCEK · FRED HEDWARICK · EDWARD CRUDDS · CHARLES EDWARTHUR · J

Figure 3.1 *Raw grid on company directors*

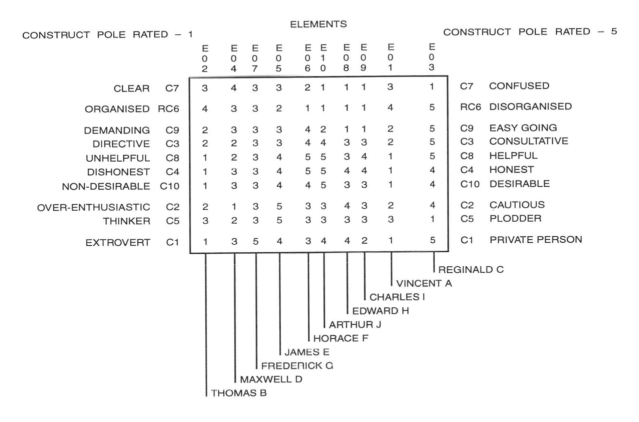

		ELEMENTS										
CONSTRUCT POLE RATED – 1		E02	E04	E07	E05	E06	E10	E08	E09	E01	E03	CONSTRUCT POLE RATED – 5
CLEAR	C7	3	4	3	3	2	1	1	1	3	1	C7 CONFUSED
ORGANISED	RC6	4	3	3	2	1	1	1	1	4	5	RC6 DISORGANISED
DEMANDING	C9	2	3	3	3	4	2	1	1	2	5	C9 EASY GOING
DIRECTIVE	C3	2	2	3	3	4	4	3	3	2	5	C3 CONSULTATIVE
UNHELPFUL	C8	1	2	3	4	5	5	3	4	1	5	C8 HELPFUL
DISHONEST	C4	1	3	3	4	5	5	4	4	1	4	C4 HONEST
NON-DESIRABLE	C10	1	3	3	4	4	5	3	3	1	4	C10 DESIRABLE
OVER-ENTHUSIASTIC	C2	2	1	3	5	3	3	4	3	2	4	C2 CAUTIOUS
THINKER	C5	3	2	3	5	3	3	3	3	3	1	C5 PLODDER
EXTROVERT	C1	1	3	5	4	3	4	4	2	1	5	C1 PRIVATE PERSON

REGINALD C
VINCENT A
CHARLES I
EDWARD H
ARTHUR J
HORACE F
JAMES E
FREDERICK G
MAXWELL D
THOMAS B

Figure 3.2 *Space-FOCUSed grid on company directors*

A five-point scale instead of √ and ✕ was used to rate the elements on the constructs. First he looked at the broad element cluster representing Charles, Edward, Arthur and Horace and began to reflect upon what they had in common. On the whole he saw these four bosses as 'people he felt quite positive about'. This superordinate description of the cluster of elements unifies these four bosses as one construct.

Laddering up the grid conversation gave the client more insight since he had not thought of these four bosses in this way before. He then looked at another element cluster of Maxwell, Frederick and James. He felt less sure of these people as one construct, though generally he was 'rather neutral' towards all three. He felt 'really uncomfortable' about Thomas who did not cluster with any of the other bosses. At this stage of reflection he was not sure about Vincent or Reginald. He then looked at the broad construct cluster comprising C9, C3, C8, C4 and C10. He read the left- and right-hand pole descriptions of each very carefully and began to ask himself why 'non-desirable', 'dishonest', 'unhelpful', 'directive' and 'demanding' were clustered together, and why 'easy going', 'consultative', 'helpful', 'honest' and 'desirable' were clustered together. He really saw these five constructs as one major super-ordinate construct. He had a real 'ah ha' experience when he recognised, and was able to put words to, this over-riding dimension of his thoughts and feelings about his bosses. It was a 'positive glowing feeling' versus a 'negative anxious feeling'.

Now Thomas was, on the whole, seen as described on the negative end of this dimension; while Arthur, Edward, Horace, Charles and even Vincent were seen towards the positive end. But he felt anxious about Vincent's 'bouncy and extrovert' approach. Reginald was the boss he could really identify with, and he especially valued his 'analytical and creative mind'—'as a thinker'.

The four 'positive' bosses—Charles, Edward, Arthur and Horace—were 'clear' and 'organised', but Horace was very demanding. He would have preferred if, as a group, they had a less cautious approach. He decided to make more effort to meet the standards set by all four, and to try to talk to them more often about his progress, asking for more feedback of how he performed the various tasks requested by each of them. He felt he should use Reginald as a role model, and that he should concentrate his energies towards developing a good relationship with him. He would ask Reginald in due course if he would act as his personal mentor and coach. But since Reginald was rather a 'private person' this might prove difficult. On the other hand, he knew the directors were using consultants to help them improve their total quality approach, so he might be lucky. Though Reginald was 'disorganised', perhaps this was why he was also a 'creative thinker'. On the other hand, Thomas, who was also 'disorganised', was not seen as a creative thinker and therefore these two constructs did not necessarily have to correlate. The client decided he would have to be more wary of the 'over-enthusiasm' of Maxwell and Thomas, and not get too involved in tasks they insisted he should do, since by the following month they would probably have moved on to some other hobby horse.

Another client's small space-FOCUSed grid is concerned with a very different topic, as can be seen in Figure 3.3. At 55 she was thinking of taking up an offer of early retirement from academic life, in order to change the course of her career. She had felt for some time that her skills were wasted on academia, and had a yen for working at 'the leading edge' of some commercial enterprise. She thought she would like to seek an opportunity to lead a small but expanding 'green' business. The topic for the first grid featured subjects 'I have enjoyed learning, researching and teaching' to see how her construing might identify other 'subjects' she would need to learn if she were to realise her ambition.

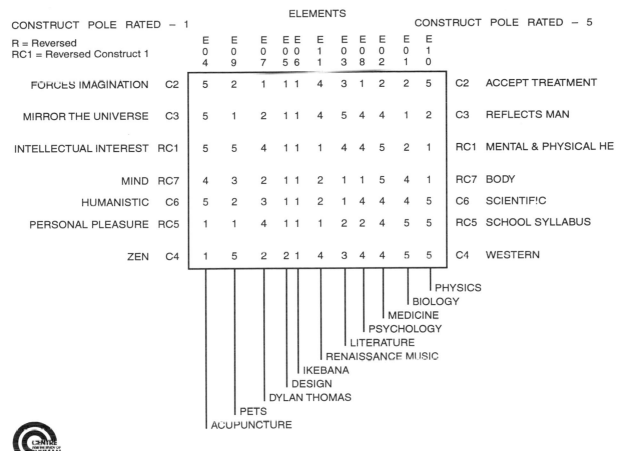

ELEMENTS

CONSTRUCT POLE RATED – 1		E04	E09	E07	E05	E06	E11	E13	E08	E02	E01	E10		CONSTRUCT POLE RATED – 5
FORCES IMAGINATION	C2	5	2	1	1	1	4	3	1	2	2	5	C2	ACCEPT TREATMENT
MIRROR THE UNIVERSE	C3	5	1	2	1	1	4	5	4	4	1	2	C3	REFLECTS MAN
INTELLECTUAL INTEREST	RC1	5	5	4	1	1	1	4	4	5	2	1	RC1	MENTAL & PHYSICAL HE
MIND	RC7	4	3	2	1	1	2	1	1	5	4	1	RC7	BODY
HUMANISTIC	C6	5	2	3	1	1	2	1	4	4	4	5	C6	SCIENTIF!C
PERSONAL PLEASURE	RC5	1	1	4	1	1	1	2	2	4	5	5	RC5	SCHOOL SYLLABUS
ZEN	C4	1	5	2	2	1	4	3	4	4	5	5	C4	WESTERN

R = Reversed
RC1 = Reversed Construct 1

Elements (bottom labels):
PHYSICS
BIOLOGY
MEDICINE
PSYCHOLOGY
LITERATURE
RENAISSANCE MUSIC
IKEBANA
DESIGN
DYLAN THOMAS
PETS
ACUPUNCTURE

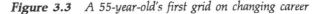

© The Centre for the Study of Human Learning

Figure 3.3   *A 55-year-old's first grid on changing career*

Look at her grid (Figure 3.3) and, bearing the talkback procedure in mind, try to infer what her reflections might have been and what 'new subjects' she might have chosen to familiarise herself with in order to transform herself into a 'businesswoman'. Some of her 'new subjects' are:

- The yin and yang of accountancy.
- The whole person at work.
- Transcendental meditation for anti-stress.
- The art of assertiveness.
- Subjective judgement in quality control.
- Self-responsibility for all learning teams.
- The psychophysics of the work environment.

Now, how do you judge her chances of success?

Our third example is more complicated. This was space-FOCUSed using the CSHL computer package shown in Figure 3.4.

ELEMENTS

CONSTRUCT POLE RATED – 1   CONSTRUCT POLE RATED – 5

Pole (rated 1)	Code	E01	E157	E11-1	E109	E01-8	E1-14	E1046-7	E0053	E0113	E008	E002	E06-1	Code	Pole (rated 5)
REAL	RC3	5	4 4 5	5	5	5	5	4 3 3	4	1	1	2	5 2 1	RC3	IDEALISED NOT REAL
LEAST ATTRACTIVE	RC5	5	3 5 5	5	5	5	5	4 4 2	2	1	1	2	1 2 1	RC5	MOST ATTRACTIVE
LEAST WORTH WHILE	RC12	5	4 5 5	5	5	5	5	4 3 2	1	2	1	2	1 2 1	RC12	MOST WORTH WHILE
WILL LEAST ENJOY	RC11	5	2 5 5	5	5	5	5	5 3 1	1	2	1	3	1 3 1	RC11	WILL MOST ENJOY
WOULD NOT APPLY IF	RC25	5	3 5 5	5	5	5	5	4 4 1	1	2	2	3	2 3 2	RC25	WOULD APPLY IF
SAME OUTLOOK ON LIFE	RC8	5	5 5 5	5	5	5	5	4 4 2	1	2	1	3	1 3 3	RC8	FRESH OUTLOOK
STUCK IN RUT	RC23	5	5 5 5	5	5	5	4	4 4 3	3	3	1	3	3 3 3	RC23	NEW AND CHALLENGING
CONFINED ENVIRONMENT	RC22	5	5 5 5	3	3	4	4	3 3 3	3	3	2	3	2 3 2	RC22	OWN BOSS
WORKING TO OTHERS' RULES	C21	5	5 5 5	4	4	3	4	3 3 3	4	3	2	3	2 3 1	C21	FREEDOM OF OPERATION
CONFINED ENVIRONMENT	RC24	5	4 3 3	4	4	5	4	4 3 2	2	2	2	3	2 2 1	RC24	PUBLIC RELATIONS
LOW FINANCIAL REWARDS	RC26	5	2 1 1	2	4	4	4	4 3 3	3	4	2	3	3 2 2	RC26	HIGH FINANCIAL REWARDS
REQUIRES COURAGE	C4	5	1 2 1	4	3	4	4	3 2 3	4	3	1	3	2 3 5	C4	DOES NOT REQUIRE COURAGE
LOW IN SECURITY	C1	5	1 3 2	5	3	4	4	4 2 3	2	3	1	2	2 2 5	C1	HIGH IN SECURITY
HIGH RISK	C7	5	1 1 1	4	4	4	4	4 2 2	2	2	1	2	2 2 4	C7	LOW RISK
MOST INVOLVED WITH OTHER PEOPLE	C13	5	2 3 3	2	3	1	2	2 1 1	1	1	1	2	2 2 4	C13	LESS INVOLVED WITH PEOPLE
HIGH ORGANISATIONAL INPUT	C15	5	3 3 4	1	3	1	2	3 1 1	1	1	2	4	4 4 5	C15	LOW ORGANISATIONAL INPUT
MOST CREATIVITY	C16	5	3 3 3	4	3	1	3	3 2 1	1	1	3	4	4 4 4	C16	LEAST CREATIVITY

Grid on job choices: senior director.

Left pole	C	Paris Research Job	Join Consultancy Group	Head of Chemistry	Project Management	Patents	Retire with Security	R & D Brussels	My Ideal Job	Head of Research Group	Product Affairs	Warden Nature Reserve	Bookshop	Research Director	Marketing Job	Research Trust	Australian Representative	Run Top-Class Hotel	Restaurant	Right pole	C
SEARCHING FOR NOVELTY	C18	5	3	3	2	2	4	2	2	2	3	2	2	1	2	1	3	4	5	NON-INNOVATIVE	C18
HIGH JOB CONTENT	C9	5	3	3	2	1	4	1	2	2	2	1	2	2	3	2	3	5	3	LOW JOB CONTENT	C9
VARIABILITY	RC20	1	3	2	2	1	3	2	2	2	3	1	2	2	3	3	3	5	5	ROUTINE	RC20
INTELLECTUAL CHALLENGE	C10	1	4	2	2	1	3	1	2	2	2	2	1	1	4	2	3	2	2	NOT INTELLECTUALLY CHALLENGING	C10
DEALING WITH OTHERS	C19	5	5	3	2	2	2	3	3	2	2	1	1	1	2	1	4	2	5	INDEPENDENT	C19
REQUIRES COMPLIANCE	C2	5	5	4	3	4	3	3	3	2	2	1	1	2	2	2	2	2	5	OFFERS FREEDOM OF WORKING	C2
MUST RELATE WELL TO BOSS	C6	5	5	5	2	3	2	3	3	1	1	2	1	2	1	2	3	3	5	NOT IMPORTANT TO RELATE	C6
MORE WITH ACADEMICS	C17	5	5	5	3	3	2	1	2	2	1	1	3	3	2	1	3	5	5	LESS WITH ACADEMICS	C17
DEALING WITH OTHERS	C14	5	4	5	5	2	3	3	4	4	2	2	2	1	3	3	3	5	5	SELF	C14

Figure 3.4 Grid on job choices: senior director.

© The Centre for the Study of Human Learning

41

A senior director in a large company chose 'jobs he had done', 'was currently doing' and 'might like to do in the future' as elements in his first grid conversation. His purpose was to see if the pattern of meaning revealed by his constructs might help him decide what pathway his career might take in the last three years before retirement. After an indepth talkback on his completed grid, and subsequent consultations with colleagues, he finally decided on the option of 'directing project management' within the company. On first glance this may appear surprising since he could have continued to direct the whole research effort as 'Head of Research', which clustered closely with his 'ideal job'. Inspect the grid shown in Figure 3.4 with the talkback procedure in mind. Can you detect why he made the decision? The client admitted that without the 'grid conversation experience' he would have drifted on in his current job, which would probably be better done by someone young and fresh.

Expanding the grid conversation: the CHANGE grid

An individual's capacity for change is partly a function of his or her ability to imagine 'alternative futures'. *It also depends on that person's ability to contract to change in specific directions*, and a commitment to a programme of self-development. These abilities include Self-Organised Learning. The CHANGE grid is essentially a FOCUSed grid of events construed by a person at a certain point in time, superimposed by the same person's later construings of the same topic. *New elements and constructs* are introduced at this later stage and the whole grid is re-rated without reference to how the elements were rated on the constructs in the original grid. The later grid is then FOCUSed again. There are, therefore, *three measures* which reveal *changes* in the scope of the topic.

1 How the new elements cluster in relation to the original elements.
2 How the new constructs cluster in relation to the original constructs.
3 Any significant changes in the ratings of the original elements on the original constructs.

The CHANGE grid computer program does the complete analysis, although by using the hand-FOCUSed method (Figure 3.7) it is possible, though laborious, to analyse the grid without relying on the software. Given the intention and commitment, this manual sorting method is actually a very awareness-raising process offering the client an opportunity to detect his or her own change process. It is also a very private process, which is important to some clients.

Change grids are useful in tracking how a series of Learning Conversations, conducted in the interval between the initial and later stage of the grid, have benefited the client. Has the learner a deepened understanding of the topic? Has the learner's competence in performing particular tasks been advanced?

Here all one can do is refer to this extended conversation of the grid to offer some vision of one direction in which the conversation can grow. Given practice with the basic exercises we have introduced so far, it is quite possible for enterprising training practitioners to 'have a go'. They can refer to 'Self-Organised-Learning. Foundations of a Conversational Science for Psychology' (Harri-Augstein and Thomas (1985)). An example of a CHANGE grid is shown in Figure 3.5.

Expanding the grid conversation: the EXCHANGE grid

How can the sharing of meaning between two or more individuals be made more explicit? Many attempts at *exchanging understanding* can lead to disaster! We have all experienced this frustrating process. At best it leads to some minimal agreement or compromise; at worst it leads to total disagreement and alienation. The problem is universal. We hardly ever see the world as another sees it. How can we then offer our view of the world to another, or enter into theirs? To operate effectively, organisations depend on teams who can transcend the status quo, and who can improve the quality of their shared understanding.

By introducing the EXCHANGE grid procedure, the training practitioner can enable a team to achieve insights into each member's patterns of meaning, and through such insights to better negotiate a mutually productive understanding. Action research with quality control teams, management appraisal teams, job selection teams, production teams, as well as with training consultants working together on specific projects, have shown the effectiveness of EXCHANGE grid conversations. The EXCHANGE grid procedure is essentially very simple, although many innovations are possible. For ease of explanation let us take three individuals working as a team, although it is quite possible to work with groups of five to seven people using the procedure.

Each of the three members of the team completes a repertory grid on some agreed topic and for some agreed purpose. Each elicits his or her own elements and constructs, and each rates his or her own grids. So far we have three completed raw grids on one topic. The three members, A, B, and C, can first simply inspect each others' element and construct cards and try to seek explanations for those elements and constructs they do not understand. This process in itself can be very revealing! The members then copy their elements and constructs onto an empty grid form (i.e. without any ratings). They then go through the following conversational merry-go-round. A gives the empty raw grid form to B and C and asks them to complete it (i.e. the ratings of elements on constructs) as they would imagine A would have done. A's original grid, as well as B's and C's are then FOCUSed and the pattern of meaning in each is inspected for any similarities and differences. B and C are encouraged to try to understand the elements and constructs which belong to A, and how their understanding of these, as revealed by the patterns of meaning in the FOCUSed grids, relate to A. This conversational exchange has proven to be enormously powerful. Similarities in

CONSTRUCT POLE RATED – 2

CONSTRUCT POLE RATED – 1	Code (1)	M14	M2	M3	M8	M10	M11	M1	M6	M9	M5	M12	M15	M13	M7	M4	Code (2)	CONSTRUCT POLE RATED – 2
FOGGY THINKER	C4	1	1	1	2	2	1	2	2	1	2	2	2	1	2	2	C4	CLEAR THINKING
LIKES A SECOND OPINION	RC15N	1	1	1	2	2	1	2	2	2	2	2	2	2	2	2	NRC15	CONFIDENT IN OWN ABILITY
INDECISIVE DECISION MAKER	C1	1	1	1	2	2	1	1	2	2	2	2	2	2	2	2	C1	POSITIVE DECISION MAKER
WEAKER PERSONALITY	RC6	1	1	1	1	2	2	2	2	2	2	2	2	1	2	2	RC6	STRONG PERSONALITY
INTROVERT NATURE	C10N	1	1	1	1	1	2	2	2	2	2	2	2	1	2	2	NC10	EXTROVERT
PEOPLE ORIENTED	C3	1	1	1	1	1	1	2	2	2	2	2	2	1	2	2	C3	TASK ORIENTED
DEMOCRATIC STYLE	RC2	2	1	1	1	1	1	1	2	2	2	2	2	1	2	2	RC2	AUTOCRATIC STYLE
DELEGATES WELL	RC14N	2	1	1	1	1	1	2	1	2	2	2	2	1	2	2	NRC14	DOES NOT DELEGATE WELL
NOT PROJECTING THIS NEED	RC9	2	2	2	1	1	1	2	1	2	2	2	2	1	2	2	RC9	NEED TO BE LIKED
SETS CLEAR OBJECTIVES	C7	2	2	2	1	1	1	1	1	2	2	2	2	1	2	2	C7	POOR AT SETTING OBJECTIVES
CONCERN FOR INDIVIDUALS	RC8	2	1	1	1	1	1	1	1	2	2	2	2	1	2	2	RC8	NO INTEREST IN INDIVIDUALS
GOOD COMMUNICATOR	C5	2	2	1	1	1	1	1	1	2	1	2	1	1	2	2	C5	POOR COMMUNICATOR
VERY DIRECT STYLE	C11N	1	1	1	1	1	1	1	1	1	1	2	1	1	2	2	NC11	RATHER DEVIOUS STYLE
LISTENS TO ADVICE	C12N	1	1	1	1	1	1	1	1	1	1	2	2	1	2	2	NC12	CANNOT TAKE ADVICE
ENCOURAGES OTHER PEOPLE	C13N	1	2	2	1	1	1	2	1	2	1	1	2	1	2	2	NC13	PUTS OTHERS OFF

Column elements (order left to right): MANAGER 14, MANAGER 2, MANAGER 3, MANAGER 8, MANAGER 10, MANAGER 11, MANAGER 1, MANAGER 6, MANAGER 9, MANAGER 5, MANAGER 12, MANAGER 15, MANAGER 13, MANAGER 7, MANAGER 4

BOLD Items (N) were introduced as a result of the change

R = Reversed

R = Reversed Construct 9

© The Centre for the Study of Human Learning

Figure 3.5 Change grid on 'Managers I Know'

their patterns of meaning will demonstrate their success in understanding A's world. Differences will show their own impositions onto A's world. The same process is then repeated, starting with the original grid of B and then C.

This rigorous mutual exchange among the learners is time-consuming, but the deep insights achieved are productive and long-lasting. It can also be very cost-effective, particularly in situations where a status quo, or even a destructive climate, has prevailed for, in some cases, months or even years. Areas of disagreement so identified can be deeply explored, leading to mutually creative shared understandings ending the stalemate for ever.

Pairs have also been known to use conversational grid exchange to end disputes and improve understanding. For example, an architect with a client, a manager with a deputy, the chief executive and chairperson of a company, learning partners, and husbands and wives in therapy. New insights and implications emerge. Emotionally the feelings associated with the topic may be reorganised, reconstrued and transformed.

Exchange procedures with the grid systematically take each person from his or her own position towards the other's position. The process highlights the nature of the moves that have to be made by each member of a pair or team, in attempting to share each others' world. Readers are referred to 'Self-Organised-Learning. Foundations of a Conversational Science for Psychology' (Harri-Augstein and Thomas (1985)) in the bibliography should they wish to investigate further.

Essentially *three forms* of conversational exchange can be explored:

1 The give over and take over, i.e. 'I'll fill in the grid as A sees the topic.'
2 The compromise, i.e. 'We'll identify precisely our areas of agreement and work on these, and agree to differ on our disagreements.'
3 The creative encounter, i.e. 'We'll pool all our elements and constructs and start again and produce one consensus grid which allows us to break into new ground.'

As with the CHANGE grid many variations are possible. Given the basic experience of eliciting, focusing and reflecting on individual grids, training practitioners with vision and commitment can take-off on these extended grid conversations in ways that suit them.

Table 3.4 summarises some of the topics that we have explored in our action research projects at CSHL. This gives some flavour of the range of possible uses for conversational grid procedures.

Table 3.4   *Topics for grid conversations*

Physical objects/products	*Living entities*
Breakfast cereals	Tennis players
Shoes	People in my life
Precision tools	Butterflies
Books I enjoy	Wild flowers
Project reports	Apples
Car paint finishes	Dogs
Sculptures	My customers
Perfumes	Footballers
Textures	Politicians
Faults on chocolates	Experts in one field
Whisky blends	Trainees
Temporal events	*Conceptual artefacts*
Appraisal interviews	Safety regulations
Job problems	Theories of learning
Lectures	Religions
Board meetings	Design criteria
Holiday trips	Learning myths
Management events	Work study techniques

Behaviours/processes
Air intercept control procedures
Operations in a manufacturing process
Bird song
Sequences in omelette making
Ice skating performances
Learning strategies

The Self-Organised Learner as a personal scientist: the SOL definition revisited

In this chapter we have introduced procedures for the achievement of greater awareness of those patterns of thoughts and feelings, i.e. personal meanings, which represent a person's construing of his or her world. This awareness empowers the person to change and grow. Personal meaning is constructed through experiences in life and such meanings can be systematically and purposefully reconstructed and exchanged. This takes us back to our original definition of SOL made in Chapter 1.

Let us now expand on this definition, introducing a *new dimension*. Self-Organised Learning is:

> The conversational construction, reconstruction and exchange of personally *significant, relevant* and *viable* meanings, with *purposiveness* and *controlled awareness*. The patterns of meaning we construct are the basis for all our actions.

By 'significant' we mean how the new meaning is valued in the person's life space. By 'relevant' we mean how it relates to the person's intentionality and specific purposes. By 'viable' we mean how it works for the learner in their actions in life. By 'purposiveness' we mean a deep understanding of how we motivate ourselves—how we channel our energies in particular directions to meet our needs. By 'controlled awareness' we mean deep personal conversations which tap inner processes in ways which open up the richness of personal experience.

Let us explain how this new dimension takes us further into the processes of SOL.

In Chapter 1 we referred to Kelly's metaphor of the 'person as scientist'. SOL uses this concept, and takes it further. In acting as a scientist—and, we would argue, as an artist—the learner builds 'theories' of his or her world and tests these out in subsequent actions on the world. 'Good' scientists revise their theories in the light of the consequences of their experiments (or actions). Such theories then form the basis of our plans, anticipations and actions.

Most of us suffer from pathologies of learning. One powerful explanation is that we are hardly aware of this 'person as scientist' process which underlies and conditions our learning. We all know that we strive to make sense of different aspects of our world *but do we know how we do this?* At the core of SOL is the idea that if we do not know how, how can we revise our 'theories' or partial understandings?

How can we generate feedback or knowledge of results of our actions so that we can effectively revise our theories?

The reflective tools and procedures of Learning Conversations are designed to enhance awareness of this meaning construction and action process, *so that we can model this for ourselves.* The training practitioner who chooses to act as a Learning Coach can enable this process.

Figure 3.6 outlines how the Self-Organised Learner uses tools and conversational procedures to act as an enlightened personal scientist.

Summary

In this chapter we have used the *repertory grid as the tool to help us to model the process of learning.* In Chapters 4, 5, 6 and 7 we offer an expanding repertoire of tools and procedures for conducting Learning Conversations both with ourselves and with others, to enable us to model our learning for the achievement of personal growth.

Learning is a process that we have to do for ourselves. If we allow others to organise our learning we become unthinking robots. We have to 'taste' the process, to experience it before we can reap the reward. No amount of description and vicarious explanation however lucid, poetic or erudite, will do! *The Self-Organised Learner is a sovereign learner.* The other-organised learner is reduced to being a helpless victim, an automaton unable to construct its destiny by seeking alternative futures. This victim travels on a fixed voyage through life, because robots are non-adaptive. They cannot learn; they perform routines more or less effectively

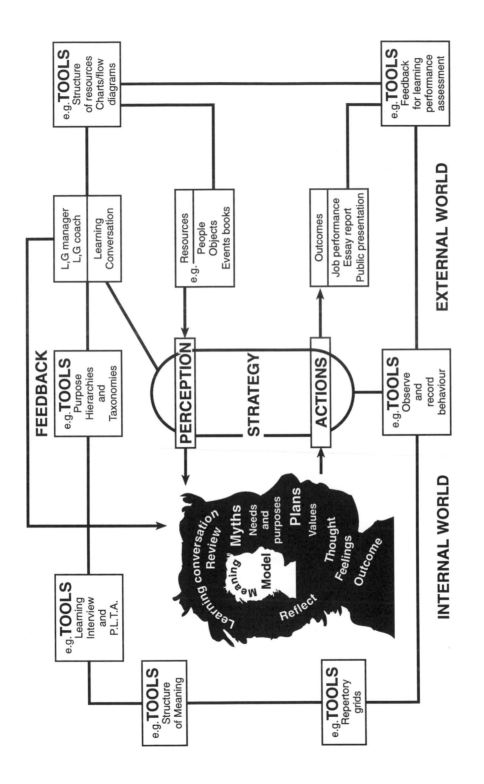

Figure 3.6 *Self-organised learner uses tools and conversational procedures*

in a relatively stable unchanging environment. *In a fast-changing environment, a blind and lurching robot is unable to switch itself off, puzzle out solutions to new problems, or understand itself.* Other-organised learners dangle like puppets on a string, creatures without responsibility for themselves.

Societies have been controlled, and some still are, by others who insist on pulling the strings—politicians, the military, police, theologians, scientists, educators and even trainers, to name but a few. In the ever-increasing unstable world in which we find ourselves, where flexibility, individual knowledge and skills and creativity are what is demanded at all levels of work and society, we depend on learners who know how to pull their own strings and to act with responsibility and total quality! Self-Organised Learning promotes a transformation of individuals from something 'base' and victimised into 'noble' individuals with sovereignty, empowered not only to shape their destiny but also to enrich the careers and lives of others. *In responding to change constructively, the learners initiate changes in their environment which open up new perspectives and destinies for all.*

Individuals, on their own, in pairs or in teams can be enabled through a system of Learning Conversations to develop their *capacity for learning*. This involves developing an *awareness of one's own processes*, the ability to *support oneself through periods of change* and the ability to *create one's own standards* by which to judge the quality of our achievements. Traditional training that is mainly concerned with the transmission of knowledge, skills and attitudes will not develop an individual's powers of SOL. The practitioner who takes on the function of a Learning Conversationalist can enable SOL as a life-long process.

We believe that learning organisations and societies composed of people who act as Self-Organised Learners will remain viable long after an organisation or society composed of experts and robots has disintegrated. *The disintegration is even more likely where the means of delivering training are standardised and packaged without taking into account the nature of the processes taking place in the learner.*

The next chapter describes the nuts and bolts of the Learning Conversation methodology; how personal meaning can be revised and actions on the world improved.

Suggested activity

Eliciting a personal model of managing people: construing the experience of managing people

Throughout this chapter we have invited you to carry out some exercises designed to familiarise you with the procedures. Now, you can put it all together and practise on yourself and with others in your team.

We have chosen 'Managing people' as the topic for this grid activity. This topic is chosen as it is likely to be familiar to all. You may be managing a team or working with clients whose business is concerned with managing people at different levels in an organisation. The activity will take you and your team half a day to complete. We guarantee you will find the experience challenging, revealing and personally rewarding.

The purpose of eliciting your model of managing people is to:

1 identify your attitudes underlying the ways in which you manage people;
2 explore how your attitudes influence your actions;
3 open up and extend the ways you think and feel about management.

Stage 1

Identify a representative sample of people that you may manage. These people can be anybody at work, home or any other social pursuit.

1 Think about the people you manage.
2 Write their names (or any other form of identification) on separate cards.
3 Add people until you reach 12. Should you consider more than 12, then select those that are representative of your ways of thinking and feeling. In other words, the maximum number of people should be 12.

Stage 2

Identify the dimensions of your construing.

1 Shuffle the cards so that they are in random order, then number them from 1 to 12.
2 Take cards 1, 2 and 3 and think about the people they represent.
3 Identify which pair are most alike to manage and which person stands apart.
4 On the grid form provided, write a short description on the left-hand side of what you find similar about the pair. Write a description of how the singleton stands apart on the right-hand side.
5 Repeat with additional sets of three. Refer to Table 3.1 for suggested combinations of three cards.

Stage 3

How do your constructs influence your actions?

1 Take your first description (construct). Consider the left-hand part of this (construct pole 1) in terms of how you manage someone described like this. Do the same for the right-hand description.
2 Repeat the process for each construct.

The aim of the technique is to re-order the columns (elements) and rows (constructs) to obtain the clearest display of the pattern of relationships implicit in the array of responses.

PROCEDURE

The following six figures show the key stages in hand sorting a repertory grid.

Transfer the results of your grid conversation onto the raw grid form (see Fig. A). In the example ✓ and ✗ are used to simplify the explanation, but the same procedure may be used with rated or ranked responses.

Pair ✓	E1	E2	E3	E4	E5	E6	Singleton ✗
C1	✗	✓	✗	✓	✓	✗	C1
C2	✗	✗	✓	✗	✗	✗	C2
C3	✓	✗	✓	✓	✗	✓	C3
C4	✓	✓	✗	✓	✓	✓	C4
C5	✓	✗	✓	✓	✗	✓	C5

Fig. A   Raw grid

Lay out your element grid strips as shown in Fig. B and enter the raw grid results.

Constructs	E1	E2	E3	E4	E5	E6	Constructs
C1	✗	✓	✗	✓	✓	✗	C1
C2	✗	✗	✓	✗	✗	✗	C2
C3	✓	✗	✓	✓	✗	✓	C3
C4	✓	✓	✗	✓	✓	✓	C4
C5	✓	✗	✓	✓	✗	✓	C5
Constructs	E1	E2	E3	E4	E5	E6	Constructs

Fig. B   Grid strips for elements

Compare patterns of responses on each element strip with every other strip. Find the pairs or groups that are most similar. Continue to put 'like' alongside 'like' until all the strips have been re-ordered. The element strips are now FOCUSed.

Constructs	E3	E1	F6	E4	E5	E2	Constructs
C1	✗	✗	✗	✓	✓	✓	C1
C2	✓	✗	✗	✗	✗	✗	C2
C3	✓	✓	✓	✓	✗	✗	C3
C4	✗	✓	✓	✓	✓	✓	C4
C5	✓	✓	✓	✓	✗	✗	C5
Constructs	E3	E1	E6	E4	E5	E2	Constructs

Fig. C   Element strips FOCUSed

Lay out the construct grid strips as shown in Fig. D and enter the element FOCUSed grid from your version of Fig. C.

Elements	E3		E1	E6	E4		E5	E2	Elements
C1	✗		✗	✗	✓		✓	✓	C1
C2	✓		✗	✗	✗		✗	✗	C2
C3	✓		✓	✓	✓		✗	✗	C3
C4	✗		✓	✓	✓		✓	✓	C4
C5	✓		✓	✓	✓		✗	✗	C5
C6									C6
Elements	E3		E1	E6	E4		E5	E2	Elements
Reversed									Reversed
Reversed									Reversed
Reversed									Reversed

Fig. D   FOCUSed elements entered on construct grid strips

Now proceed to sort the constructs but with one proviso. The constructs are bipolar so they may equally well be displayed with poles reversed. Extreme mismatch is therefore as significant as high match. Fig. E shows how in the example C2 and C4 are extremely mismatched. Reversing C4 allows C2 and C4 to match extremely well.

C2	✓		✗	✗	✗		✗	✗	C2
C4	✗		✓	✓	✓		✓	✓	C4
C4	✗		✓	✓	✓		✓	✓	C4
Reversed C4	✓		✗	✗	✗		✗	✗	C4 Reversed
C2	✓		✗	✗	✗		✗	✗	C2
Reversed C4	✓		✗	✗	✗		✗	✗	C4 Reversed

Fig. E   Reversing a construct

Continue to sort the construct strips transferring constructs to reversed strips where necessary until the grid is FOCUSed. See Fig. F.

Elements	E3		E1	E6	E4		E5	E2	Elements
C3	✓		✓	✓	✓		✗	✗	C3
C5	✓		✓	✓	✓		✗	✗	C5
Reversed C1	✓		✓	✓	✗		✗	✗	C1 Reversed
Reversed C4	✓		✗	✗	✗		✗	✗	C4 Reversed
C2	✓		✗	✗	✗		✗	✗	C2

Fig. F   FOCUSed construct strips carrying FOCUSed elements

Now transfer your FOCUSed grid onto a grid form to preserve a permanent record.

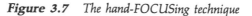

Figure 3.7   *The hand-FOCUSing technique*

Stage 4

Extend your attitudes towards managing people by exchange. Try to do this exercise with at least one other person.

1 Swap grid forms with your partner. Ask your partner to explain any descriptions you do not understand.
2 Repeat stage 3 using your partner's descriptions.

Stage 5

Highlight the meaning in your grid.

1 Taking each description in turn and using a two-point scale (i.e. $\sqrt{}$ and $\times$) rate each element on each construct. Refer to page 32, 'Stage 5: Generating the raw grid' to help you.
2 When you have completed your raw grid, analyse it by hand-FOCUSing it (see Figure 3.7) and page 33, 'Analysing and identifying the meaning in the raw grid'.
3 Use the reflect talkback procedure summarised in stage 7, page 35, 'Talkback conversation with the FOCUSed grid' to develop a model of your construing of managing people.
4 Begin to make an action plan for elaborating, modifying and improving your approach in the light of your discoveries.
5 Implement this by adopting the role of a 'personal scientist' acting as a Self-Organised Learner.

4 The morphology and anatomy of a Learning Conversation

Agenda board

- Learning conversations and the language
- Anatomy of a Learning Conversation
- Process dialogue
- Support dialogue
- Referent dialogue
- Three levels in the Learning Conversation
- Three suggested activities: developing a total quality approach using MA(R)4S, using MA(R)4S to reflect on enriching the learning process and managing Learning Conversations, developing a workshop to empower others to conduct Learning Conversations with their teams

Introduction

One of the major problems facing people when they are working towards improving their competence in learning is that they have no real operational language with which to analyse, reflect and evaluate their learning.

Imagine where the human race would be now if we were not sufficiently articulate to represent our thoughts, feelings, beliefs, values and ideas to ourselves and to others. Many of the artefacts, i.e. physical *products* or outcomes of some of our thought processes, may well exist from generation to generation and culture to culture, but the less tangible thought processes which have led to these do not.

The quality of these artefacts depends on the richness of the processes and languages involved in their production. Archaeologists who find artefacts of our ancient cultures have to infer how the artisans and literati of the time created them. We are left with the products of their thought processes but not the system of thought through which these products may be properly appreciated and faithfully replicated. Pause for a moment to consider *what are the products of our learning* in today's fast-lane culture? Do we have a rich language of learning to describe the processes involved? How can we develop this language to advance our capacity to learn? Today, in organisations all over the world there are very experienced individuals who are being retired early. They leave without a trace of the wealth of their *learnt experiences*. How can their 'on-the-job' experiences and processes be preserved as a resource for others in the organisation rather than, as with earlier cultures, be lost forever? Action Research shows that the language through which we think, feel and converse effectively about learning is very rudimentary, leading to low-level competences and capacities and to only partially effective employees in all industries. We are literally at the 'Stone Age' in understanding our learning processes. As with archaeologists we have a great deal of spade work to do to delve into the complex system of thoughts and feelings representing our language of learning.

Learning is a unique process. No one can learn for us. We all have to do it for ourselves. We have to self-organise our learning to empower ourselves for constructive actions in our world. To achieve this we need tools, the most important of which is a language to represent and communicate about our learning.

First, if learning is to become a consciously structured and controlled process, then this language needs to be *personally meaningful*. A personal language will help the reflective process when learners stand back and evaluate their processes and outcomes of learning. It is the means by which we can represent our learning and describe it to ourselves and share this experience with others.

Readers may well feel that any encouragement to have reflective conversations with ourselves about learning is a sign of self-indulgence or even frivolity. Some novice learners who were captivated by this activity initially saw this as the first sign of madness! The process was so new and so strange! However, this is a very necessary stage in developing learning competence. When stepping back from what we are doing to reflect on what is happening and to analyse the effectiveness of our thoughts, processes, feelings and actions we need terms and a structure to describe these processes.

Consider who or what is driving or controlling your own learning?

> Is it your robot?
> Is it someone else?
> Is it your faculty X (Colin Wilson)?
> Is it your internal executive?

How can you best model your personal process of learning? Building and rebuilding a better model of what is going on is essential for getting a grip on the process for achieving personal competence. Modelling our learning depends on the development of a personal vocabulary and system for describing our learning.

Learning Conversations

A language for developing our Learning Conversations which supports individuals' advance to greater degrees of learning competence must be based on their unique constructions and reconstructions of their learning processes. This 'Learning Conversation' involves:

1 A process of sustaining a conversation with oneself about learning, in order to be able to reflect on the processes involved and discover what works best and under what conditions.
2 A Learning Coach may temporarily externalise this Learning Conversation and describe certain aspects of it to the learner to improve its quality.
3 The Learning Coach makes the nature of the Learning Conversation more explicit to the learner *as he or she learns.*
4 The Learning Coach passes control of the Learning Conversation back to the learner as awareness of the language and the skills of learning are developing.
5 The Learning Conversation grows and spirals as individuals, pairs, and teams converse, initiating 'learning networks' and a whole system of Self-Organised Learning throughout the organisation.

The Learning Coach's function is not prescriptive. It involves developing precision in managing the Learning Conversation and channelling this within specific domains and tasks, helping learners to explore opportunities for on-the-job learning. So! How do we start? Let us introduce the three dialogues of learning.

The anatomy of the Learning Conversation

The Learning Conversation embodies three distinct but interwoven dialogues. Together these intensify the experience of learning, heightening awareness and enriching the ways in which the process can be understood and developed (Figure 4.1).

The *process* dialogue

This dialogue focuses on the individual's personal learning experiences. It helps the individual to reflect on these experiences, to examine his or her habitual patterns of thought and robotic behaviour, to challenge those characteristics and develop strategies for change. Tasks and activities that can be explored include processes of management, organisation of time, problem solving and various types of manual tasks. Any task, topic or skill can be the subject of personal exploration. Systematic and careful reconstruction of personal experience helps to raise awareness of fixed and limiting routines, and to develop a language for describing and explaining how learning progresses. Habits and personal myths (Chapter 2) can then be successfully challenged.

The process dialogue begins with the exploration of personal needs and purposes. These drive each learning event and to some extent allow the learners to converse about processes which underlie their motivation. Learning tactics, strategies, and outcomes are also analysed, refined and explored. The dialogue involves thoughts, feelings and actions relating to a learning event. Reviewing the processes and outcomes of learning enables the learners to examine and define their whole approach to learning a particular task or set of tasks or indeed their approach to developing and improving their general learning competence. Thus,

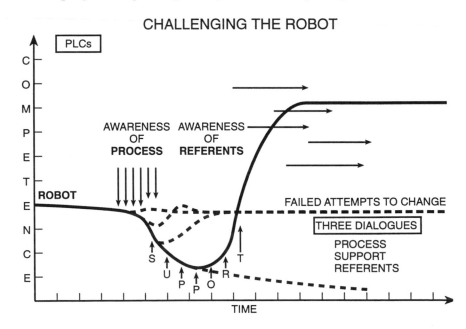

Figure 4.1　*The learning trough: challenging the robot*

Purpose–Strategy–Outcomes–Review are key terms in the developing process dialogue.

We shall go into a further description of this process dialogue when elaborating on Personal Learning Contracts, and illustrating how the Learning Conversation is used to develop such contracts in the next chapter. Here we shall explain in more detail the underlying structures that guide the Learning Coach as the process dialogue is introduced and managed in the Learning Conversation.

MA(R)4S: The deep structure of the reflective process dialogue

This represents a seven-step process, which is conversationally based, to enable the learner to model the unique processes of learning. We have developed a variety of learning tools that will help individuals work through this process. Some of these tools will be introduced and discussed, in the chapters that follow, with examples of previous learners' experiences to help enrich the reader's understanding of their use.

MA(R)4S stands for:

Step 1: M—Monitor

Mentally stand back from what you are doing, observe yourself in action, and observe or sequentially record what is happening as it is happening.

You can try this for yourself by monitoring any task you perform. Take a task such as making a cup of tea. This is often performed routinely while the mind is actively engaged on other matters, and may also be performed while doing other tasks, but *how well* is it performed? The Japanese tea ceremony is designed to emphasise the richness of the whole process.

This is not to suggest that we need to use the tea ceremony to meditate and challenge our tea-making skills at all times; rather that we have the capacity to do so should we choose! Next time you make tea and drink it, try to monitor the whole process *by observing it*. Picture it in your mind, get someone to observe you and describe what he or she sees, or make a video recording (see step 3)!

Step 2: A—Analyse

Run the record in your head, your notes or your observations of the event through your mind to identify and extract all those features that are essential to an adequate and rich reconstruction. It is important to include thoughts, feelings and perceptions.

What are the significant events? Go back to step 1 and try to identify these for your tea-making activities.

Step 3: R—Record

Make an *external record* which summarises sufficiently to make an adequate reconstruction of the activities and intentions. The video record of making tea would be one example. Your notes and sketches of the same process would be another example. An observer's notes or visual record would be another.

Step 4: R—Reconstruct

Run the record compiled in step 3 through your head to *relive* the total original experience *in its purest form without evaluation*. No judgements at this stage; just a replay in the mind.

Step 5: R—Reflect

Having reconstructed the experience as realistically and as holistically as possible, the learner is then able to begin to make judgements, i.e. to evaluate the actions in terms of what they were trying to achieve.

How successful were they? The learner is encouraged to explore and evaluate the way in which the event flowed, any mismatches in expectations and results, poor timing, wrong emphasis, or badly distributed effort.

The term 'realistic' is used because during the preceding steps, an individual may well be influenced *by what was thought to have happened* and not *what actually happened*. When teaching his wife to reverse into a car park space, a husband explained in detail what he was going to do. His wife, a novice learner, then observed him in action, and told him once the car was parked that his actions were totally different from his explanatory account. They then had a Learning Conversation which focused on the explanations for the mismatch. He saw that his model of how he thought he drove and his model in reality, were very different. This proved to be a most valuable insight to the teacher/driver, and in this instance the external observer, his wife, provided him with valuable information with which to reflect and converse truly (rather than argue!) about his driving skills. His wife confessed that she learnt more from this reflective Learning Conversation than weeks of mundane car driving instruction! So who was learning from whom?

Again a video or some other external record provides a protocol against which a more realistic account can be reconstructed. This reflective step includes a consideration of both positive and negative aspects of the process.

Step 6: R—Review

Begin to take the whole process apart, identify criteria for improvement, amend and reconstruct it so that it will more effectively enable you to achieve your desired outcomes.

This stage enables the learner to remodel ways of performing and thinking and planning. Many learners at this stage feel overwhelmed, but gradually become more in control of their actions and cannot wait to test out their new model to see whether or not it enables them to better meet their desired outcomes. Success at this stage sows the seeds of transforming learning from a ubiquitous, vague process into an exciting and ever-changing personal journey.

Step 7: S—Spiral

Try another learning event and go through the cycle again *with a fresh look*, new purposes and with expectations for more competent outcomes. Iterative cycles of the MA(R)4S process leads to a total quality approach to learning. Once the learner's model of the task has been tested in action, the learner goes back to step 1 in the MA(R)4S process and progresses to step 6, the review of the model in terms of original or developing outcomes. If the model of the process has met the learner's needs and total quality approach, the process is then exited with this particular learning need satisfied.

MA(R)4S allows the whole of the process dialogue to be driven forward into an all-spiralling activity.

You could now develop our tea-making and drinking example by going through this process (Marsing) for yourself. Try this out on the family, or with colleagues at work. Who knows, you may invent a new vogue in tea ceremonies! You may also learn a great deal about the language of learning.

Some training practitioners may hold the view that encouraging employees to discuss their *learning needs and processes* would lead to a wide range of activities on the job that could not possibly be satisfied, and that this could lead to a breakdown in organisational control towards achieving corporate goals. Some hold the view that it could possibly lead to anarchy! We have found in our extensive experience of working closely with a wide range of organisations that this is definitely not the case. We find that encouraging active learning on the job results in greater commitment to work and greater striving to find innovative ways of improving performance. Job satisfaction significantly improves as a result. Local training, preferably on the job, then becomes a valuable option, and instead of being passive receivers of imposed training, individuals learn to diagnose their needs, and identify appropriate training support. The important point to make here is that learning will start before any training has been formally arranged and continue afterwards until the desired learning outcome and new standards have been achieved. We also find that encouraging the learner to take responsibility for learning leads to learning outcomes being continuously revised and developed.

This approach transcends the job into a 'whole life activity'. Therefore, to sum up, this process dialogue of the Learning Conversation is to establish exactly the 'why' and 'how' of the learning process as this relates to any topic, task or skill. The Learning Coach engages in the process dialogue of learning, and works with the learners to challenge their skills and develop their capacity to learn.

The *support* dialogue

The support dialogue helps the learner to cope with the *effects of awareness and of experimentation with learning processes leading to change*. When learners strive to improve their competence, there comes a point—through greater awareness of learning—when their performance nearly always becomes worse (see Figure 4.1). There are a variety of reasons for this: the learners are now concentrating not only on carrying out the task in hand but also on trying out *strategies for improvement*. Observing ourselves in action and experimenting with change instead of robotically performing a task is not an easy skill to master; it takes time and practice until a learner becomes more aware of the processes (see stage 2 of SOL awareness in Figure 1.1, page 8). Through the process learning dialogue our performance will temporarily suffer; however, once this 'Marsing' skill has been developed and given support, performance will dramatically increase and continue to do so.

The Learning Coach needs to help the learners detect and become sensitive to this crucial phase in the learning process and to recruit an appropriate support strategy to encourage the learners to see the sometimes traumatic process through. When no external support is present, the learners would have to provide their own support. Failing this, learners will quickly abandon the process altogether and return to their old robotic habits, or they may even lose confidence altogether and experience a breakdown in learning which may, in extreme and rare cases, have catastrophic personal effects.

What, then, are the ingredients of support? Learning involves explaining the unknown, and that leap into the dark void can be unnerving for many. The Learning Coach works with learners so that they can develop ways of supporting themselves, thus internalising the support dialogue. This dialogue involves ways of developing *trust* in the learning situation, for greater risk-taking and experimentation, and for banishing anxieties and unnecessary tensions which reduce learning potential. Learners learn to trust themselves more and to take bigger leaps into the dark void. Learners need to learn how to *buffer* their increasing tensions as they move into the unknown and unexplored territories of learning, so that those energies locked up in anxiety are refocused into personal experimentation and growth.

In Chapter 1 we referred to Rogers' therapeutic dialogue involving 'empathy', 'congruence', and 'unconditional positive regard'. These processes are recruited into the support dialogue, and the Learning Coach works with the learner to heal the learning traumas that may develop. Often this begins by simple encouragement, a friendly chat, a sharing of learning difficulties. It is not to be confused with traditional counselling. The skills in conducting a support-learning dialogue can be effectively learnt by novice Learning Coaches and passed on to learners themselves.

Additional, more practical, forms of support will include, for example, creating ample opportunities for learning on the job, offering shared peer learning support, and managers who actively support on-the-job learning by creating space and resourcing learning experiments at work. All too often participants on a training course off the job, rapidly lose their new skills, because they fail to get support to develop these newly acquired skills on the job. Often learners who have begun to explore their learning and who are effectively supported, fail to enhance their learning skills because *they do not know how to assess themselves and to set new standards.* The referent dialogue serves this purpose. It helps in the identification of benchmarks for learning.

The *referent* dialogue

For the purposes of Self-Organised Learning we define a referent as a *set of criteria against which learners can begin to assess their competence.* Engaging in a Learning Conversation by focusing on the referent dialogue allows the learners to appraise their own performances by identifying appropriate criteria. The learners need to have confidence in exploring as wide a range of referents as possible. Gradually learners are encouraged to consider such referents as others' standards: for example, those set by the learners' direct bosses; standards set by an acknowledged expert in the specific area under review; and a combination of standards used by experienced staff. Such standards are only used as referents against which to develop personal standards.

Within the work setting, learners are encouraged to review their own criteria of performance before they converse with their direct bosses. Only then should they engage in progress debrief about how their learning relates to organisationally set and external standards, which usually emphasise contributions to organisationally valued objectives relating to systems, output and quality.

This referent dialogue links to self-appraisal and personal development plans, career development, training needs analyses and management development audits.

Thus, to summarise, *the Learning Conversation can be said to have three interwoven strands of dialogues: a conversation about the process of learning, support during the learning and subsequent reflection; and a conversation regarding the system of personal evaluation in terms of learning competence and observable performance.*

These dialogues then contribute to the language of learning to be developed and personalised by each learner: they enrich the experience of learning. A major function that the Learning Coach needs to manage is the successful internalisation of these dialogues by learners themselves.

Case study 1: The three dialogues

This case study involves a newly appointed supervisor at a factory-based organisation, and starts at the point when the learner has requested a meeting with the Learning Coach.

The learning need

Learner: I have just finished my supervisor's course, and was particularly impressed by the theories put forward on more democratic styles of management. I am taking charge of my section on Monday and want to show them that we are very much a team and their views will be listened to and respected by me.

Setting the scene: an exploratory Personal Learning Contract.

Learning Coach: Why are you particularly impressed with this form of management?
Learner: This organisation, particularly at the shop floor, has always been very autocratic—not allowing individuals to think for themselves. I have never been comfortable with this myself, and I know that my staff could be a lot more effective if they thought they were doing a worthwhile job and were respected by management.

The learner then talks through a strategy for learning to introduce a more democratic style of management by taking staff to one side for five minutes and talking them through the new style of management. During the contract phase the learner and Learning Coach contract to work together, with the Learning Coach observing the learner's actions.

'Marsing' the learning event

The first step is to stand back and make observations on what happened while it is happening, and the learner was encouraged to do this during the planning phase of the learning event.

Analysing the event

Learning Coach: We were both present when you had a meeting with your staff. Talk me through your observations of the event.
Learner: Some of my staff looked genuinely pleased when I spoke to them as a group, but the majority started laughing at me as if I was some kind of 'softy'.

The external record was kept in note form after the event, and now the Learning Coach is encouraging the learner to reconstruct what happened.

Learning Coach: Would you try to recreate exactly what happened in your head and talk me through the event?
Learner: Yes. I asked them all to come in ten minutes before the shift started for the meeting, which they did. They all looked interested when I started the meeting by telling them about my new responsibilities. Then, when I talked about my new style, three looked genuinely interested and eight started laughing.

Now the learner is encouraged to reflect on what happened.

Learning Coach: Why did you think that happened?
Learner: I have carefully considered this. I think that I tried to change too many things at one go. First, I was a new supervisor and they needed to get

used to that; then I immediately told them about a change in management style. The previous culture was very much autocratic and tough, and I feel that they now saw me as a weakling manager. They may find this threatening and feel that working with me may threaten their future. So now I have to be careful that they do not try to undermine my authority in order to get rid of me. I am beginning to feel very frustrated after trying so hard to be a more effective manager than most of my colleagues.

The learner is suffering from the effects of a dip in performance and needs support from the coach.

Learning Coach: When I was first learning to become a Learning Coach, I found that it took much longer to help people who were experiencing performance problems compared with my previous work as a trainer. This frustrated me greatly, and I would have given up were it not for my own Learning Coach who supported me at the time. I now see that I was looking for instant solutions to performance problems, rather than empowering individuals to learn for themselves. So as your initial strategy for communicating with staff did not work as you expected, can you reconstruct the event in a way that would make it more effective?

The learner is being encouraged to take the process apart and reconstruct it in a way that would more successfully meet the desired outcomes.

Learner: Yes, I need to address directly their concerns about being a weakling manager and show them how my new and fresh approach would benefit them as well as the organisation.
Learning Coach: Would you run me through exactly how you would take the meeting if you could hold it again.
Learner: Yes I would ...

Spiral. Now the learner is encouraged to take another learning event and go through the cycle again.

Learning Coach: Do you think that it is worth while holding another meeting along the lines we discussed, or are you going to work on another learning event?
Learner: I do not think another meeting would solve the problem, so I am going to develop my skills at democratic management by concentrating on breakdowns —we have at least three minor mechanical failures a week, and I am going to encourage the machinists to think through what needs to be done when the situation arises. The supervisors' course included using counselling skills to get individuals to take responsibility for decisions. They basically know what to do but are not used to using their own initiative.

Another Personal Learning Contract is about to be planned; however, the Learning Coach needs to make explicit to the learner what was happening in terms of the Learning Conversation and Marsing.

Learning Coach: I think it would be useful to reflect on what has been happening over the last half an hour, when I asked you to stand back and observe what was happening.

The Learning Coach shows how each stage of the MA(R)4S process was tackled during the Learning Conversation so that the learner may carry out the process independently.

This is an example of an early dialogue. As the process continues we get more support and referent dialogues taking place. The Learning Conversations would continue until the learner suffers a plateau in performance. Here the conversation would centre around giving support during a time when the learner feels he or she is getting nowhere. The support dialogue moves from being task based to being learning focused and considering what happens with various learning strategies: what went well, what did not work and why. The last few learning events are reviewed. The Learning Coach also encourages the learner to look at the negative aspects of learning and try to reframe, converting anxiety and worry towards a more creative and positive outcome.

The support dialogue is so important and is one of the many reasons that apparently highly professional traditional training results in very little real change in learner behaviour on the job, because this dialogue is not part of the process. From this dialogue the Learning Conversation may well move to the referent dialogue.

Learning Coach: How will you know when your style of management has been effectively introduced?
Learner: Well some of my criteria for effectiveness include: less moaning, more initiative used on routine simple problems, and an increase in productivity.
Learning Coach: How does your manager view your effectiveness as a supervisor?

THIS MAY REQUIRE SOME RESEARCH INTO APPRAISALS AND SO ON.

Learner: My manager bases my effectiveness on productivity and wastage figures. I need to raise productivity by 1 per cent and reduce wastage by 10 per cent.
Learning Coach: Do you know how the organisation overall judges the success of its management team?

THIS MAY ALSO REQUIRE FURTHER RESEARCH.

Learner: Staff turnover figures, sales, profit and so on.

The Learning Coach then encourages the learner to consider his or her learning and work quality in terms of learner-based outcomes, manager-based criteria for success and organisationally valued criteria for success.

Levels in the Learning Conversation

The Learning Conversation inevitably starts by being task oriented, and by focusing on needs and purposes. That is to say, the conversations focus on learning the task in hand (see stage 2, Figure 1.1, page 8). This was illustrated in our earlier example. After several tasks have been conversed about in this way the Learning Coach and sometimes the learner independently can begin to converse about the perceived connections in ways of learning (stage 3, Figure 1.1, page 8). Thus a series of *task-*

focused and *learning-focused* 'tutorial' conversations develop. These emphasise the strategic aspects of learning and form the basis of *personal learning contracts* to be described more fully in the next chapter. Such Personal Learning Contracts, based on the tutorial level of the Learning Conversation, may falter for two reasons: lack of skill in performing the task or in reflecting on the processes of learning involved. This will shift the conversation to emphasise the development of specific task-based or learning-based skills. This is the *'learning to learn' level of the Learning Conversation*.

Once these skills are acquired through a series of micro-experimentation and reflection based on the three dialogues, the conversation reverts to the central 'tutorial' Learning Conversation. On the other hand, a drop in motivation to continue learning will highlight the need to refocus on individual needs and personal relevance, so the conversation shifts to the 'life' level—that is, to the individual's 'life space' as a whole.

At *each level of the conversation*, all three *dialogues* can be brought to bear to advance Self-Organised Learning (Figure 4.2). The Learning Coach needs to have a feel for timing, to know when to move the conversation into learning to learn if the learner demonstrates lack of skill, or to the life level if motivation dips. The Learning Coach needs to manage the dialogues, sometimes emphasising one more than the two others as the Learning Conversation develops. Such skills come with experience and detecting the responses from the learner after making the moves. If the learner is not ready the Learning Coach simply moves back to the central tutorial Learning Conversation which drives the Personal Learning Contract (next chapter) until the time is right to shift levels.

Gradually a figure-of-eight pattern evolves, involving all three levels of the Learning Conversation and all three dialogues (see Figure 4.2). Generally, after a short period of SOL coaching, the skills in conducting such Learning Conversations are acquired by the learner. Once this happens our action research shows that the individual is likely to become a long-term Self-Organised Learner

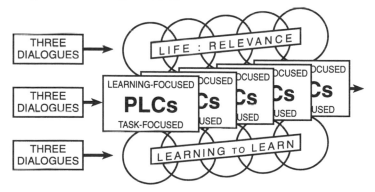

Figure 4.2 *The three dialogues and the three levels of the Learning Conversation*

One real example of how the different levels of Learning Conversation work and interact is given below. This example has been considerably shortened for illustrative purposes.

Case study 2: The three levels in action

A manager has identified a need for developing an ability to become more persuasive at work.

Initial life level conversation

Learning Coach: Why do you feel you need to be more persuasive?

ASKED TO CLARIFY THE LEARNER'S NEEDS FOR LEARNING.

Learner: There are several situations at work where I would like to be able to persuade people to take a particular course of action without them dismissing me and my ideas before they have given me a proper hearing.
Learning Coach: Why is this important to you?

ASKED TO PROBE LEARNING NEEDS IN MORE DETAIL.

Learner: It is important to me because I have pride in my work and want others to respect this, and also I want to make a career for myself in this organisation. If people will not give me a fair hearing, urgent actions will not be carried out, and this can lead to all sorts of failures, eventually affecting my promotional prospects.

Tutorial task-focused conversation

Learning Coach: Describe one situation you have experienced in the recent past that you would have liked to have handled differently.

ASKED TO ENCOURAGE THE REFLECTION ON THE LEARNER'S CURRENT MODEL OF PERFORMANCE, RELATING TO PERSUASION SKILLS.

Learner: There was a situation last week when I wished to persuade my senior manager on improvements in the way in which I do my job. This would have involved me in making major changes in daily duties which would have saved over an hour a day and made considerable financial savings. I put this to my manager but hardly got a hearing.
Learning Coach: Try to reflect on exactly what happened when you approached your manager.
Learner: I simply went in and said I had a good idea about how the job could be done better at considerable savings. My manager immediately retorted that when I am in a position to do my job as it stands now more effectively, then any changes would be listened to.
Learning Coach: What I have started to do here is encourage you to Mars the learning event.
Learner: Ah, yes, I see what you mean.
The Learning Coach then asks the learner to self-debrief by using the MA(R)4S process.
Learner: OK. It seems that my strategy was to tell my manager that I had a good idea for improving my job and I did not achieve my desired result. I think my manager failed to respond because ...

The conversation focuses on the precise strategy that was used and why it did not work. The Learning Coach then tries to encourage the learner to elicit an improved model and this forms the basis of the next learning event when it is actioned, reflected on, and if necessary further refined until the quality of competence meets the learner's needs. Where the learner does not have the internal resource to refine the model an external referent is sought. This referent may well be the Learning Coach if this is appropriate in terms of what can be offered, or may be other suitably qualified people in the organisation. Where the Learning Coach temporarily acts as an expert referent, there is a change in role and this needs to be made explicit to the learner in the conversation. In other words, at this point the coach is temporarily concentrating more on content than on process.

Assume that there have now been a number of task-focused tutorial Learning Conversations which, when fully developed, take the form of Personal Learning Contracts. The learner's competence has been developing, but a new plateau is being reached and further learning opportunities do not appear to be bringing about any significant improvements. This is a signal to the Learning Coach to move to a different level in the conversation and concentrate on learning to learn.

Learner: I was really pleased with the way in which I have improved my ability to persuade other people, or at least get a fair hearing, so that ideas may be exchanged and considered. But despite working really hard I seem to be getting stuck and I am not improving as I would wish.
Learning Coach: OK. So let's move from looking at specific learning tasks to reviewing your learning so far. When you reconstruct your learning to date, what would you say were the significant landmarks in your learning?

WE ARE NOW ENCOURAGING THE LEARNER TO GO THROUGH THE MA(R)4S MODEL DESCRIBED EARLIER IN THIS CHAPTER.

The Learning Coach will move from *what* was significant to identify *why* it was significant. Significant lack of skills and possibly motivation may be identified despite attempts to improve.

The learner has become despondent with personal actions at work, because of a lack of relevance. A life conversation is then initiated by the Learning Coach.

Life conversation

Learner: I really have become quite disillusioned with my progress in persuading people at work. I suppose I just wonder about the point of working hard to improve when there is all this change going on. Change at work, change at home and I don't seem to have any control over what is going on.
Learning Coach: What major events would you really like to bring about in your life?
Learner: Oh that is too complex a question for me to answer. I really do not know.
Learning Coach: If you like we could initially concentrate over a period of, say, the next two years.
Learner: Well I would like to do something worth while.

Learning Coach: When you say worth while would you elaborate on what would be worth while to you?

The conversation continues at the life level to make clear what the learner would like to happen. Events at work or in social life can then be linked by the learner to overall life needs and, in our experience, learners are able to remotivate themselves as a result.

Self-Organised Learning definition elaborated

In Chapter 1 we briefly referred to the relationships between self-organised learning, chaos theory and complexity theory. We suggested that it is useful to conceive of processes of learning operating on the 'edge of chaos', between chaos and order, i.e. between provisionality and equilibrium, and the status quo. Here we see that during learning, as well-practised or unfamiliar skills are challenged and brought into conscious awareness, learners often experience a temporary *drop* in competence. The worst scenario is that this could lead to disintegration of competence and so to chaos. A person who, in the first instance, is keen to improve computer skills, management skills, or sales skills by trying to improve and learn new skills, could at worse become temporarily so unskilled that all motivation to continue would be lost and that person may well lose interest completely. This is why it is so important to monitor the process and to understand what is happening. The support dialogue in the Learning Conversation is designed specifically to see the learner through this stage. Chaos theory does play a part in learning!

Again 'learning robots' often prove very obstinate and unwilling to change! Certain routines or skills which are often repeated, are temporarily lost to conscious control! They are what we call 'ultra stable', in absolute equilibrium, trapped within a fixed pattern of behaviours. Challenging such 'robots' is crucial to developing learning competence. This is why the process dialogue in the Learning Conversation is so very important. It is the way to melt down the frozen conversations that have led to fixed routines of behaviour and to fixed ways of thinking and feeling. Through the Learning Conversation learners maintain themselves constructively 'on the edge of chaos', occasionally skirmishing with chaos, as they construct new skills, new understandings, and evolve themselves towards greater 'complexity' as human beings. This way of approaching learning is radical; it allows the *learner* to appreciate what is happening during learning and, supported initially by the Learning Coach, he or she learns how to operate effectively 'on the edge'. This method allows learners to develop their capacity to learn and to continue to improve their learning, in changing job and life situations. The process can be as exhilarating and as fulfilling as windsurfing or gliding. It gives richness and meaning to living.

The process, support and referent dialogues of the Learning Conversation become the vehicle for the construction, reconstruction and exchange of personally significant, relevant and viable meanings with greater awareness and purposiveness.

The three dialogues in the Learning Conversation also support the learners when 'testing out' new meanings, i.e. the pattern of meanings they construct during learning. Thus the *viability* of their learning is constantly checked out in real life. In Chapter 5 we explore how the Personal Learning Contract (PLC) supports learners to experiment practically with their learning so that this becomes a personally significant, relevant and viable activity.

Summary

In this chapter we have introduced a *process-based language* for developing Learning Conversations and we have described the overall form of the Learning Conversation. This differentiates into *three levels*: **life, tutorial** and **learning to learn**. We have illustrated with examples how each level is characterised by *three dialogues*: **process, support** and **referent.**

The Learning Conversation advances Self-Organised Learning and the individual's *capacity to learn*. The SOL Coach conducts Learning Conversations with each and every learner in ways that enable them to *internalise the conversation* so that they may conduct such conversations with themselves and with other learners.

Suggested activities

1 Developing a total quality approach using MA(R)4S

1 Select a task that you perform regularly but feel you do only fairly well and consider your performance could be much improved. For a pilot trial you might select a mundane, everyday task, such as cleaning your teeth, opening a tin can, boiling an egg or dressing the children. Then proceed to select some work-based task ranging from problem solving, decision making, interviewing, time management, running meetings, etc.

2 Next time you have to perform the task try to monitor and record what you do and when you do it, then ask yourself why you do it. Use the MA(R)4S reflective process. Engage in a process dialogue with yourself. With 'problem solving' you may decide to take an area that you find particularly frustrating and part of the commentary could try to identify the cause(s) of the frustration and how to overcome this. With 'recruitment' or 'appraisal interviews' you may decide to reflect on how your model of interviewing differs for different types of people and whether the model successfully meets your needs. The possibilities are endless.

3 Having used the MA(R)4S process you will inevitably have identified an area you wish to develop. This may be a new skill or the dismantling of unwanted robotic behaviour. If it involves remodelling, check performance during learning and see if there is a dip. If there is a dip in performance ask yourself how you feel about the task and assess the build-up of anxiety, tension and stress. Start a support dialogue with yourself which will help you out of the dip. Recruit another person who might carry on a Rogerian-based dialogue with you. Record what it was in the support dialogues that helped you mentally over the dip. Now engage in conversations with your boss about new learning opportunities. This can provide useful feedback measures of your performance.

Work with peers, boss, Learning Coach or mentor to identify, first, your own criteria for evaluating your success. Next, use external criteria from others against which to evaluate your own, then try to expand your criteria. Develop a total quality approach.

2   Using MA(R)4S to reflect on enriching the learning process and managing Learning Conversations

1 Once you have personally experienced the process take someone else through a similar type of Learning Conversation. While you are acting as a Learning Coach and helping them to become a Self-Organised Learner, use the MA(R)4S model to reflect on how the learning process can be enriched and work with them to learn about managing Learning Conversations, involving all three dialogues and all three levels.

3   Developing a workshop to empower others to conduct Learning Conversations with their teams

1 Once you have acquired some degree of competence in managing Learning Conversations, try to develop a workshop that will empower others in the organisation to conduct Learning Conversations with their teams.

5 Personal Learning Contracts for change: SOL in action

Agenda board

> - The learner's commitment to learning
> - The anatomy of a Personal Learning Contract
> - An example of the Personal Learning Contract in action
> - The Personal Learning Contract as an iterative process
> - Recording what happened during the progress of the contract
> - Reviewing the Personal Learning Contract
> - A complete PLC, including the review, in action
> - Suggested activity: setting up Personal Learning Contracts

Introduction

Towards the end of the last chapter we introduced the concept of three levels in the Learning Conversation. We referred to the central 'tutorial' Learning Conversation which moves to the 'life level' and to 'learning to learn' as this becomes appropriate in the Learning Conversation. In this chapter we focus on the Personal Learning Contract (PLC) as a vehicle for driving the tutorial Learning Conversation.

The term 'learning contract' is now widespread in the training world. Generally, this takes the form of a written agreement between the learner, trainer or tutor. The learner records a set of rules which he or she agrees to follow, i.e. be on time for workshops, do all the prescribed pre-workshop reading, carry out pre-set activities (which may include project workload) and self-assessment. The same process applies to the trainer, i.e. be on time for the agreed learning event, do the necessary preparation, have professionally prepared hand-outs and visual aids, prepare and meet training objectives and so on. Both parties are expected to sign the contract which is mutually agreed, and if one party reneges on any part of the contract, the document is produced to encourage the individual to abide by the rules.

This type of contract is neither intended nor structured in ways that will enhance a learner's capacity to learn and go on learning continuously. It is an organisational commitment involving the completion of certain tasks within an agreed schedule. In practice, this type of contract is known as 'other organised', but leaving the learner with some responsibility as to how and when the tasks will be completed. It is important to stress at the outset that our term 'Personal Learning Contract' represents a totally different concept, and is not in any way connected to an agreed code of conduct. Basically, it is a contract that learners make with themselves. The tutor's function is solely to support the learners in eliciting, actioning and reviewing their own contracts. The Personal Learning Contract (PLC) is generated by the learner and is completely under his or her control. The development of this tool (PLC) arose from studying the degree of commitment and skill that learners require to fulfil learning events of their own choice.

The learning commitment

The level of commitment learners have to learning is closely connected to, and largely driven by:

Purpose

1 The sense of purpose that drives their learning. Why do the learners wish to learn about or learn to do a particular task?

To be successful, their purpose for learning needs to be connected operationally to their strategy for learning.

Strategy

2 How do they intend to go about learning this particular topic/task. What actions may be involved and in what order will these be carried out?

Their strategy needs to be closely connected with their expectations about a satisfactory learning outcome.

Outcome 3 How will they know when they have completed the task successfully?

We then find that commitment becomes on-going when the learners stand back and review what has happened.

Review What has worked? What has not worked? Why? What remains to be learnt?

This process was discussed in the last chapter when we examined Marsing a learning event. The PLC is specifically designed to enable learners to develop their capacity to learn and acquire the skills of learning that endure and continue to develop long after the learning event has ended. Thus, the PLC is not only a practical tool for learning that has been well tested in a variety of circumstances, as we shall show in Chapter 6, but it is also firmly based on a deep psychological methodology, as we have pointed out in the General Introduction and referred to and built on in each subsequent chapter. It is a major tool for Self-Organised Learning. As such it enables learners to converse with themselves about the processes of learning, and to review the quality of their learning competence. It has the power to record the content and the process of learning. Later we show how it can be used as a tool for a Learning Conversation between the learner and the tutor, and between groups of learners as they exchange their experiences of learning.

The anatomy of a PLC

The PLC has been specially developed with the following structure:

- Topic and overall task for learning
- Purpose
- Strategy
- Outcome
- Review

The PLC is structured *over time* into planning, action and review phases. Within *each* phase the topic and task, purpose, strategy and outcome are reflected upon as part of a developing process. When the learner is provisionally satisfied with his or her PLC action *plan*, the contract is executed. During the *action* phase the learner is encouraged to 'remember' the plan, to use it to monitor the process, and to constantly revise the plan as the predetermined strategy develops and the learning resources are accessed. This is what we mean by the iterative process. Finally, the learner *reviews* performance in the light of the contract, and re-examines the whole, completed, PLC. Occasions when certain aspects of the PLC have not been successful are regarded as particularly significant *learning opportunities*: they confront the learner with inconsistencies in the internal models of the topic and task in hand.

The comparison between the before- and after-task action phases of the PLC is used by the learner to identify the direction of development and the formulation of the next PLC. *The PLC empowers the learner to think positively and constructively about his or her learning competence.* In the early stages the Learning Coach supports learners as they complete their PLC. As learning skills develop, learners initiate and complete PLCs for themselves.

Figure 5.1 shows one format of the PLC. This is a useful method for recording a simple written version of the contract. As familiarity in its use is acquired, the PLC can be elaborated to allow for hierarchies of purposes, strategies and outcomes, a wide variety of *learning resources*, and different technologies for recording actions as the contract is carried out. It can also be refined in the self-debrief activity upon completion of the action phase of the contract and before the final review.

The PLC in action

Figure 5.2 (c) shows a completed example of a PLC on management Group Team Building. In this example there are three purposes for learning, two strategies for planning actions, and four desired outcomes.

In order to illustrate the *planning phase* of a PLC (Figures 5.2(a)–(c)), we have included an extract from a Learning Conversation concerned with the topic of 'word processing'. The overall task was concerned with improving a learner's ability in specific aspects of word processing.

For the purpose of this illustration of the Learning Conversation the initials LC denote the Learning Coach and L the learner.

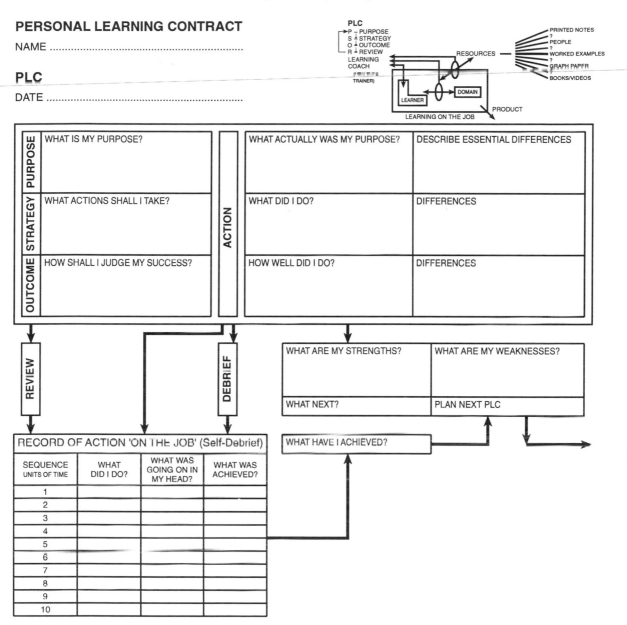

Figure 5.1 *A basic form of the PLC*

THE PERSONAL LEARNING CONTRACT FORM
PLAN – Negotiating the contract

	BEFORE

NAME

TOPIC AND TASK FOR LEARNING

P
U
R
P
O
S
E

PURPOSES FOR LEARNING: What is my purpose?

S
T
R
A
T
E
G
Y

INTENDED STRATEGY: What actions?

O
U
T
C
O
M
E

DESIRED OUTCOME: How shall I judge my success?

Figure 5.2(a) *The planning phase of the PLC: Form*

THE PERSONAL LEARNING CONTRACT FORM

PLAN – Negotiating the contract

NAME A. Learner	**BEFORE**

TOPIC AND TASK FOR LEARNING

To develop my skills n designing reports and brochures using WordPerfect

P U R P O S E

PURPOSES FOR LEARNING: What is my purpose?

WHY DO I WISH TO LEARN THIS TOPIC?
1 To prepare better reports for my increased personal competence and job effectiveness.
2 To develop these skills which will help a career move into Marketing Management, which has long been my ambition.

S T R A T E G Y

INTENDED STRATEGY: What actions?

HOW DO I INTEND TO GO ABOUT DEVELOPING THE NECESSARY KNOWLEDGE AND SKILLS?
1 To attend a company workshop and focus particularly on opportunities for practising formats for reports and brochures.
2 To locate other word-processor users in the company by enquiry with the Management Information Services Department.
3 To discuss and observe and question some experienced software users.
4 To negotiate with my boss time on the job to carry this out.
5 To consult my manager for coaching on report formats.

O U T C O M E

DESIRED OUTCOME: How shall I judge my success?

HOW WILL I KNOW WHEN I AM SUCCESSFUL?
1 When I use the features of WordPerfect to produce professional-looking reports.
2 When I know what these should look like and when I know what format to use for each type of report.

Figure 5.2(b) *The planning phase of the PLC: Example A*

THE PERSONAL LEARNING CONTRACT FORM

PLAN – Negotiating the contract

BEFORE

NAME Arthur Timothy

TOPIC AND TASK FOR LEARNING

Management Group Team Building

PURPOSES FOR LEARNING: What is my purpose?

P
U
R
P
O
S
E

1 To help Nigel, Ray, Dave, Alan, Steve and Pete to develop personally and to support their efforts in introducing SOL to the team.
2 To improve the quality of the appraisal of the managerial team by collecting specific evidence of actual performance on the job.
3 To win the support of team members in achieving Sorting Office objectives.

INTENDED STRATEGY: What actions?

S
T
R
A
T
E
G
Y

1 Regular, pre-scheduled, individual meetings. Probably once a month but shift managers may meet each time they perform an early shift. I shall use the learning conversation and commitment on a regular basis and the repertory grid, task interview/analysis and charting as necessary.
2 Team meetings to pool ideas, review general progress and agree action.

DESIRED OUTCOME: How shall I judge my success?

O
U
T
C
O
M
E

1 Monthly learning commitments and their outcomes.
2 Learning activity going on throughout the team with feedback via my meetings.
3 Specific appraisal evidence.
4 Achievement of office objectives.

Figure 5.2(c) The planning phase of the PLC: Example B

Negotiating a PLC

LC: You wish to be able to improve your competence in word processing?

L: Yes, I can produce simple documents such as memos and letters, but nothing more complex.

LC: What would you like to be able to do and why?

L: Well, I would like to be able to produce well-structured reports and even brochures, because I feel I could progress better in my job.

LC: Are you concerned with the layout of these documents as well as their format?

L: Yes, both layout and format using WordPerfect.

LC: So if I understand you, your learning topic and overall task are to develop your skills in designing reports and brochures using WordPerfect?

L: Yes.

The first stage of the learning topic has been elicited. The conversation continues and the Learning Coach encourages the learner to explore the purposes for learning in more detail. The reason for exploring purposes at this point is that purposes are tied up with an individual's motivation to learn, and strategies for going about the desired learning.

LC: Why do you wish to develop these skills?

L: From time to time I produce reports for my department. I am not entirely happy with the finished report and think it could be done better. I also feel that more professionally finished reports will enhance my credibility and help my promotional prospects. Eventually I would like to progress into Marketing Management, and report design is an important skill for Marketing Managers.

There are now two defined purposes for learning: (1) to prepare better reports for increased personal competence and job effectiveness; (2) to develop this skill which will eventually help a career move into Marketing Management. For an experienced learner who can use the PLC as a reflective tool for learning, the Learning Coach may extend the conversation to broaden the range of purposes and explore in more depth the details of implicit nesting purposes within these more broadly defined purposes. But for a novice learner, the Learning Coach now steers the conversation towards the development of a strategy for learning the skills required.

LC: How do you intend to develop the skills you require to design reports/ brochures more professionally?

L: The company has an internal course on the advanced features of Word-Perfect and this does include some time spent on reports/brochures.

LC: Will the course meet your needs completely?

L: No, I don't think so, but it will go some way towards helping me with general design features, but there are some issues regarding presentation of figures that I will need specifically to improve on and are not covered on workshops.

LC: Can you think of any ways you can go about developing these specific areas?

L: I suppose I could find out if anyone else uses the software on documents with similar sets of figures, discuss my needs with them, and also if possible observe them in action to see what they do, and how they do it. Hopefully this could give me an opportunity to ask questions too.

LC: How will you find out about other software users in the company?

L: I can find this out from the Management Information Services Department.

LC: Are there any other learning activities that you can think of now that will help you meet your learning needs?

L: No, not at the moment.

LC: Have you given time for the WordPerfect Tutorial, which is available on Microsoft Software?

L: I did not know this existed.

LC: Perhaps you could look into this possibility.

The initial learning strategy has been elicited: to attend an internal company workshop which is likely to meet some of the needs of the learner, and to discuss, observe and question experienced software users who process similar data. The conversation is now steered towards encouraging the learner to define learning outcomes—in other words, how will the learner know when his or her learning has been successful?

LC: I'd like you to think about how you will know when your learning activities have successfully met your needs?

L: I'm not sure I can do this! I suppose when I can use the features of Word-Perfect to produce professional reports and brochures, but I don't really know what this means yet. Also when I know what these professional documents should look like, and when I know what format of report to use to suit each type of occasion.

LC: OK. That's a start! Now check your learning strategy against those outcomes you intend for your learning. Are you likely to be successful?

L: Yes, the strategies will meet all but the last learning outcome, which is, when I know what format of report to use to suit the occasion. I really need to consult my manager and he could coach me on the most appropriate formats of report. I'll have to negotiate this very carefully. My manager is very busy.

Now the Learning Coach needs to encourage the learner to update and modify the Personal Learning Contract to include the additional strategy of consulting and being coached by the manager on appropriate formats for reports (see section 5, Figure 5.2(b)). The process of generating a PLC is iterative in nature; that is, it does not always flow logically from 'learning topic' to 'purposes for learning' to 'strategy' and then exiting after defining learning outcomes. The process of eliciting purposes for learning may mean that the learning topic has to be modified, and so on. Let us now consider the iterative nature of the PLC.

The PLC as an iterative process

We discussed the fact that the PLC rarely moves sequentially from stage to stage, but that it often involves iterative loops back to previous stages once purposes, or strategy or outcomes are carefully considered and analysed by the individual. In our previous short example of a Learning Conversation we can see how the conversation involved an iterative loop back to add a further strategy, that of consulting and being coached by the manager.

Figure 5.3 shows a flow chart of the PLC as an iterative process. Looking at the figure you can see that, once in stage 2, a conversation about purposes for learning may well lead to an elaboration of the learning topic. Once the learner has progressed to stage 3 (the strategy stage), an iterative loop back to amend purposes may arise as the learner explores deeply how learning is going to be planned and the strategy chosen is tested against purposes for learning.

The PLC undoubtedly encourages learners to plan structure into their learning, but also acts as a catalyst enticing learners to go much deeper into their real purposes for learning and be honest and critical about their anticipated outcomes from successful learning. On completion of the planning phase, this iterative process continues during the action phase and is again reviewed during the final phase of the PLC.

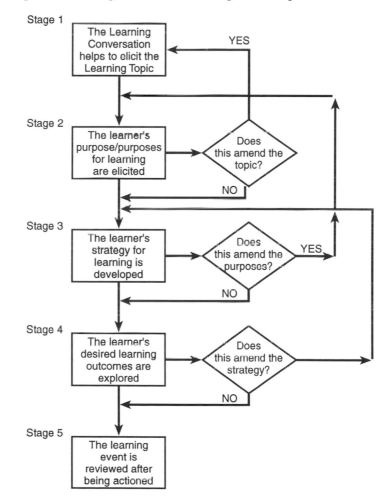

Figure 5.3   *The PLC as an iterative process*

At first glance the PLC may seem to be a fairly simple procedure that really does not need to be completed in written form, but only committed to memory; however, the act of completing it starts the process of deeper reflection and analysis. Most learners find that the iterative loops make the process very satisfying as they discover hidden and deeper reasons for learning which increase their personal commitment to learning and the effectiveness with which they plan their learning.

After many PLCs have been committed to paper and discussed with the help of a Learning Coach initially, the experienced Self-Organised Learner will have no need to go through the process of planning and recording a PLC on paper every time. This is because the model of the process has become *internalised*. In other words, the learner has internalised this aspect of the Learning Conversation. However, when a PLC becomes very complicated, even an experienced Self-Organised Learner may need to commit the PLC to paper to help clarify his or her thought processes. When this happens the learner will want to reflect on the processes for generating a PLC as this may well need to be revised in order to meet the needs for more complex learning issues, and so may form the basis of another PLC in itself. Thus, nesting sets of PLCs may develop which relate to certain topics and tasks.

Recording the action phase　　The personal learning record may seem fairly simplistic as far as forms go, but it has proved most useful to learners in helping to record what happened when they took an objective view of themselves in action. Figure 5.4 illustrates one type of personal learning record for noting *what happened during the learning events*, in order to help reflection during the review process. The next chapter will illustrate how the PLC procedure and recording format have been used by learners and show how this has helped the learning process.

Although the personal learning record appears simple, we find it a highly effective tool for reflecting on the progress of the PLC while it is in action rather than leaving the review until after much of the planned learning events have taken place. The best analogy to use here is that of time management. When individuals complete a time diary in retrospect (how they think their time was spent) it is often quite different from reality. Again, much of the individuals' processes of learning may be overlooked when the learning is performed robotically, and the personal learning record helps the learners to be more aware of what, and how, they learn and the record needs to be completed *as the learning progresses*.

As individuals become more aware of their evolving model of learning, reviewing the learning can be performed without physically recording each step of the process.

Let us now look at a slightly more complex example of a PLC in action, and see how the complete process takes place, including the review.

LEARNING RECORD

NAME:

PERSONAL LEARNING CONTRACT TOPIC:

DATE STARTED:

DATE FINISHED:

UNDER EACH TACTIC IN YOUR STRATEGY DESCRIBE WHAT ACTIONS YOU TOOK	WHAT ARE YOUR COMMENTS? Which actions were helpful and which were not? Reflect on why this should be. How have the actions affected your learning?

Figure 5.4   *A personal learning record*

The review phase The learner puts his or her plan of learning into action, and uses the record sheet (see Figure 5.4), which is a simple form, to record the actions taken and impressions of how the learning event progressed.

Once the PLC has been planned and put into action, the process needs to be reviewed. Figure 5.5 shows an appropriate framework for talking the learner through the planning, action, and review of the learning event.

In our first example of how a PLC is generated, you can see an example of two purposes for learning being generated: to prepare higher quality reports for increased credibility; and to develop this skill, which will eventually help a career move into Marketing Management. The learner is now ready to action this plan and be prepared to flex the structure according to any emergent needs, purposes, strategy and outcomes that may be generated during the learning process. Reviewing the contract (Figure 5.5) encourages the learner to reflect on what was originally the purpose, strategy and defined outcome of planned learning and compare those original statements with what has actually happened since. The PLC forms a basis for the learner to act as an internal observer so that he or she may 'Mars' the process of going through the learning event. The Learning Coach may also use this PLC as a tool to help learners converse about their learning.

We now proceed to illustrate a complete PLC, including the review, in action.

A complete PLC in action Think of a PLC on the topic of *Assertiveness*. The theoretical steps towards becoming assertive are easy to comprehend but very difficult to put into practice. Many individuals have attended assertiveness workshops and undoubtedly have benefited from a greater understanding of what they need to do to be more assertive when the occasion demands it. Unfortunately, putting theory into practice is not easy as there are often deep underlying reasons for not being assertive and a knowledge of the theory and experience of using that theory in a workshop-based role-play situation is simply not effective enough for real life.

Negotiating the PLC L: I would like to become more assertive, and so need to develop skills in this area.

Assertiveness is a very broad area, so the learner needs to analyse the topic in greater depth.

LC: When you say assertive, can you give me some examples of when you were not assertive, but would have liked to be assertive.

THE PERSONAL LEARNING CONTRACT FORM
AFTER – Reviewing the contract

NAME

Before and after differences		
TOPIC AND TASK FOR LEARNING		
P U R P O S E	What actually was my purpose?	Compare purpose	What are my strengths?
S T R A T E G Y	What did I actually do?	Compare strategy	What are my weaknesses?
O U T C O M E	How well did I actually do?	Compare outcome	What shall I do next? Make plan for learning

Figure 5.5 The review phase of the PLC

L: Yes, only last week my boss asked me to take on an extra task, and I felt compelled to do so, even though I knew it would mean yet more work, late nights and aggravation from my wife. The worst thing is, I did not even have enough guts to tell her how busy I am.

LC: Why did you feel compelled to accept the extra task?

L: Well, it is hard to say. I suppose I do not like letting her down . . . and it looks as if my job is stretching me to the point where I cannot cope.

LC: Are there any examples outside work where you need to be more assertive?

L: Yes. The other day I was at a restaurant with friends, and was served coffee in a cracked cup. I knew that this would not be hygienic but could not bring myself to complain.

LC: Why?

L: Because I did not want the possibility of entering into an argument that I might lose, in front of my friends.

LC: I see, so you would like to develop your ability for dealing more assertively with certain situations, both at work and socially?

L: Yes.

Topic for learning has now been elicited from the learner.

LC: A little earlier you said that you took on an extra task from your boss despite more work, extra late nights, and aggravation from your wife. Are these side-effects of taking on the extra task related to your purposes for learning to be more assertive?

L: Yes, I want desperately to work fewer late nights and spend more time with my wife. I also feel annoyed with myself for not telling people what is on my mind. The silly thing is that I know people would respect me more if I were more assertive and I would like that, but even that does not make it any easier for me.

The purposes for learning are to gain greater respect from people by being honest and open, have a more realistic workload with fewer late nights and spend more time at home.

LC: OK. Now, how are you going to become more assertive? How will you develop the skills needed?

L: It would help if I knew what skills need to be developed. I suppose I could read a book or attend some course, but I never seem to change my behaviour just by reading books. I need the stimulus of other people, so I really want to attend a course to start with.

LC: Can you think of any other learning activities?

L: No. I really do not believe that assertiveness can be learnt by copying others, and whatever I learn from any course needs to be fully adapted to suit my personality.

LC: Have you considered recording how you handle situations where you wish to be assertive, before and after the course? Recording what happened, the actions you took, the result and reflecting on how you could have improved will help you to selectively use the assertiveness techniques learnt on the course you plan to attend.

L: Yes, I would like to do that. I would also like to know why it is that I find assertiveness so difficult, whereas others do not appear to experience such mental anguish.

LC: You could work on a repertory grid, which may help you discover the underlying reasons for your difficulty with assertiveness. I suggest you consider some situations where you are assertive, and some where you are not, as the basis for the grid.

L: Yes, I would like to do that. Thinking about it there are some situations and people I am assertive with. Actually, thinking about it I would also like promotion, and feel strongly that being more assertive would help me tremendously in this respect.

Iterative loop to purposes, now amended by including promotion. The purposes for learning are to gain greater respect from people by being honest and open, achieve promotion, have a more realistic workload with fewer late nights and spend more time at home. Learning strategy is to attend an assertiveness course, recording situations where the learner wishes to be more assertive before and after the course, and to complete a repertory grid on assertiveness.

LC: How will you know when you have been successful with your learning?

L: I will be successful when I can be assertive when I wish without unduly offending others in the process and regretting my actions later. I know I will feel better about myself as well.

The learner has now defined the criteria for learning success in personal terms. This is now recorded under expected learning outcome.

Let us consider the sequential steps of the planning phase of the PLC.

Topic for learning   To develop your ability for dealing more assertively with certain situations, both at work and socially.

Purposes for learning   The purposes for learning are to gain greater respect from people by being honest and open, have a more realistic workload with fewer late nights and spend more time at home. *Iterative loop*: **I want promotion and assertiveness will help.**

Strategies for learning   To attend an assertiveness course, recording situations where the learner wishes to be more assertive before and after the course, and to complete a repertory grid on assertiveness to examine the reasons behind non-assertiveness. *Iterative loop back to develop purposes by including promotion.*

Outcome   I will be successful when I can be assertive when I wish without unduly offending others in the process and regretting my actions later. I know I will feel better about myself as well.

The action phase   This has been recorded on the learning record form, see Figure 5.8.

The review phase LC: Let us review what has happened so far. Would you start by talking me through your original purposes for learning, and then elaborate on any changes to those purposes during learning?

L: Yes. My original purposes were to do with gaining greater respect from people by being honest and open, achieve promotion, having a more realistic workload with fewer late nights and spending more time at home. These purposes remained strong but what also emerged for me during my learning was that I also wanted to reduce the high levels of stress and tension caused by being too passive.

LC: What about strategy?

L: My original strategy was to attend an assertiveness course, record situations where I wish to be more assertive before and after the course, and to complete a repertory grid on assertiveness. I did attend a one-day workshop on assertiveness which covered no less than eight techniques for becoming more assertive. I then took part in role-playing using these techniques, which I found less daunting than I imagined, and received very positive feedback from my partner in the role-play. The role-play was videoed and a personal copy of the video given to all workshop delegates. I have since reviewed my performance on role-play several times and found the experience very encouraging. I was also able to experience my partner using these techniques on me—they certainly do work but I am not entirely happy.

LC: Why is that?

L: Because when I left the course I knew *what* techniques and skills I needed to use but still cannot make a start on using them in a real-life situation.

LC: Why is that?

L: For two main reasons. The first is that I feel uncomfortable using the techniques. I do not feel that they suit me or my style. The other reason is that when I try to use them I experience the sensation of playing games with people and this adds an element of falseness to my relationships.

LC: What about recording those situations where you would have liked to be more assertive?

L: Yes, I have done this, and when I finished I stood back, reflected and came to the conclusion that in each case the factor that has inhibited me before the workshop and indeed even after it is the fear of causing others offence. The strategy that helped me above all others to understand more deeply about these non-assertive situations is the repertory grid. [*Readers may wish to briefly review repertory grids in Chapter 2.*] When I looked at my FOCUSed grid [see Figure 5.6] on situations I can handle assertively, and those I feel I do not handle assertively, I saw a most interesting pattern emerging, which, I must admit I understand now that I have seen it, was not apparent without the help of the grid. I suddenly see that all those situations in which I am assertive, involve the following factors: I would not offend the other party, I feel I am credible in their eyes—I rated appraising staff 3 (in fact some staff I would rate 1 and others 3 and 4— I am working on this as another area for learning). I enjoy having arguments in these situations, I feel comfortable, and with the exception of appraising staff I have fun. With those situations in which I am not assertive I am worried about causing offence, with the exception of restaurants, I am not too worried about my credibility, but I do fear losing arguments,

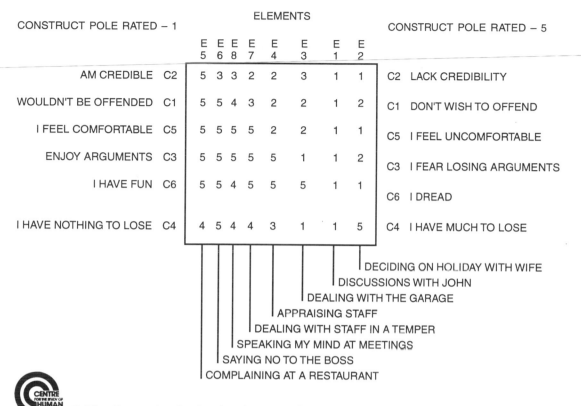

Figure 5.6 on assertiveness grid:

CONSTRUCT POLE RATED – 1   ELEMENTS   CONSTRUCT POLE RATED – 5

Construct Pole 1		E5	E6	E8	E7	E4	E3	E1	E2	Construct Pole 5
AM CREDIBLE	C2	5	3	3	2	2	3	1	1	C2 LACK CREDIBILITY
WOULDN'T BE OFFENDED	C1	5	5	4	3	2	2	1	2	C1 DON'T WISH TO OFFEND
I FEEL COMFORTABLE	C5	5	5	5	5	2	2	1	1	C5 I FEEL UNCOMFORTABLE
ENJOY ARGUMENTS	C3	5	5	5	5	5	1	1	2	C3 I FEAR LOSING ARGUMENTS
I HAVE FUN	C6	5	5	4	5	5	5	1	1	C6 I DREAD
I HAVE NOTHING TO LOSE	C4	4	5	4	4	3	1	1	5	C4 I HAVE MUCH TO LOSE

Elements:
- DECIDING ON HOLIDAY WITH WIFE
- DISCUSSIONS WITH JOHN
- DEALING WITH THE GARAGE
- APPRAISING STAFF
- DEALING WITH STAFF IN A TEMPER
- SPEAKING MY MIND AT MEETINGS
- SAYING NO TO THE BOSS
- COMPLAINING AT A RESTAURANT

Figure 5.6 *The first repertory grid on assertiveness*

I feel uncomfortable (thinking about this, I feel uncomfortable because of the fear of losing arguments and causing offence) and I dread these types of situations. What I must do now is to set up another PLC to find out why I do not wish to cause offence and why these situations should ever result in an argument.

If a repertory grid is used as part of the learning strategy for the first time, it is likely to help the learner focus on emerging learning needs and form the basis of another PLC. Also, if this Learning Conversation was being carried out in real life, the Learning Coach would encourage the learner to reflect more deeply into each personal construct and its relationship with every element. In addition, in our example the constructs 'I feel comfortable/uncomfortable' and 'I have fun/dread' appear to be closely related with the exception of appraising staff and dealing with the garage. These two constructs would be discussed with the learner to examine the links between them. If they were rated identically the Learning Coach would probe to see whether there is one superordinate construct that would cover both. If the learner was unhappy with this, the Learning Coach would ask the learner to consider what additional elements would receive different ratings from the two constructs.

LC: To what extent have your learning outcomes been met?
L: I need to do far more work before I reach my original learning outcomes, and this PLC (my FOCUSed grid) has resulted in more learning outcomes.

The PLC documentation recording this learner's progress towards assertiveness is illustrated in Figure 5.7 (planning the PLC), Figure 5.8 (the personal learning record) and Figure 5.9 (the review).

The Learning Coach then encourages the learner to develop another PLC which is focused on those outcomes of learning not yet met by previous strategies. Should the learner get stuck at this stage, by not knowing how to meet the learning outcome or if the previous strategies have been unsuccessful, then the learner is encouraged to develop a PLC on learning to learn.

To summarise the PLC procedure, Figure 5.10 shows in diagrammatic form the time/structure of the PLC.

Definition of Self-Organised Learning and the PLC

The PLC and the tutorial Learning Conversation forms part of the figure-of-eight dynamic of the Learning Conversation as a whole (see Figure 4.2, page 65). The PLC is a systematic, practical tool for raising awareness of the task-focused and learning-focused Learning Conversation (see Figure 1.1, page 8). It is organised by the learner and is under that person's control. When recorded fully, it becomes a record of both the *content* and *process* of learning. By its use, learners develop a richer language to describe their own learning (Chapter 3) and to enrich their learning skills and competence. When practised over time, learners can advance their capacity to learn on many topics and tasks. The PLC is a learning tool for empowering self-constructed change.

In Chapters 1, 2 and 3 we developed a definition of Self-Organised Learning. Let us now draw your attention to this definition so that we can explain how the PLC relates to it:

> The conversational construction, reconstruction, and exchange of personally *significant, relevant,* and *viable* meanings, with purposiveness and controlled awareness. The patterns of meaning we construct are the basis for all our actions.

The PLC allows learners to record and reflect on their construction of meaning as this relates to any given learning event. The *relevance* of the learning taking place relates to the learners' *purposes* recorded in their PLCs. The *viability* of their learning relates to a review of how their strategies have worked to produce effective outcomes. The *personal significance* of the learning relates to how the topic and task of the PLC relates to the life level of the Learning Conversation, i.e. the overall needs and goals of the learners. By working through a sequential series

THE PERSONAL LEARNING CONTRACT FORM

PLAN – Negotiating the contract

BEFORE

NAME A. N. Other

TOPIC AND TASK FOR LEARNING

To develop my ability for dealing more assertively with certain situations, both at work and socially.

P U R P O S E	**PURPOSES FOR LEARNING**: What is my purpose? WHY DO I WISH TO LEARN THIS TOPIC? My purposes for learning are to gain greater respect for people by being honest and open, have a more realistic workload with fewer late nights and spend more time at home. I also want promotion.
S T R A T E G Y	**INTENDED STRATEGY**: What actions? HOW DO I INTEND TO GO ABOUT DEVELOPING THE NECESSARY KNOWLEDGE AND SKILLS? To attend an assertiveness course, recording situations where I wish to be more assertive before and after the course, and to complete a repertory grid on assertiveness to examine reasons for non-assertiveness.
O U T C O M E	**DESIRED OUTCOME**: How shall I judge my success? HOW WILL I KNOW WHEN I AM SUCCESSFUL? I will be successful when I can be assertive, when I wish to be without unduly offending others in the process and regretting my actions later. I know I will feel better about myself as well.

Figure 5.7 Planning the PLC on assertiveness

LEARNING RECORD

NAME:
PERSONAL LEARNING CONTRACT TOPIC:
DATE STARTED:
DATE FINISHED:

UNDER EACH TACTIC IN YOUR STRATEGY DESCRIBE WHAT ACTIONS YOU TOOK	WHAT ARE YOUR COMMENTS? Which actions were helpful and which were not? Reflect on why this should be. How have the actions affected your learning?
1　I attended a one day workshop on assertiveness run by my company	I found the workshop less daunting than I had imagined. I found the techniques taught to be fairly easy to implement. Much easier than in real life. It was comforting to learn that other people were having similar problems with being assertive. Positive feedback from my partner was very comforting. I often watch the video we were given, and this gives me hope.
2　My boss asked me to work on a short-term project and was very 'flattering' about my work. I tried to be assertive but just mumbled YES!!	Here was an ideal opportunity to use my new found techniques. I had practised them at the workshop, but it seemed that I was playing 'silly' games, and it just did not seem to be me. I felt as if I had hands, but they were tied behind my back, and I was greatly frustrated.
3　I worked on a repertory grid on assertiveness	I can now see why I am not assertive. It is like a curtain being unveiled, the problem now is relating to people without causing undue offence. I need to look at my credibility problem, and why I feel inferior to certain people.

Figure 5.8　*Personal learning record on assertiveness*

Learning Resources
Centre

THE PERSONAL LEARNING CONTRACT FORM
AFTER – Reviewing the contract

NAME A. N. Other

Before and after differences

TOPIC AND TASK FOR LEARNING

ASSERTIVENESS

	What actually was my purpose? / What did I actually do? / How well did I actually do?	**Compare**	**What are my strengths? / weaknesses? / next?**
P U R P O S E	**What actually was my purpose?** Gaining greater respect from people by being honest and open. Achieve promotion. Have a more realistic work load. Fewer late nights. More time at home.	**Compare purpose** Original purposes remained strong, but a new purpose emerged: to reduce the high levels of stress caused by being passive.	**What are my strengths?** My strengths lie in my ability to see why I am assertive with some people and non-assertive with others.
S T R A T E G Y	**What did I actually do?** I attended the one-day workshop on assertiveness and worked on a repertory grid. I had an opportunity to supplement my strategy by practising my skills on my boss.	**Compare strategy** I did not foresee the opportunity for practising my skills on my boss.	**What are my weaknesses?** My desire not to cause offence and feeling inferior towards some people.
O U T C O M E	**How well did I actually do?** My original outcome was to be assertive without causing offence to others. This I did not achieve, but I am most pleased with the result so far. I now have an appreciation of why I am not assertive.	**Compare outcome** The actual outcome fell well short of my original aspirations. But I feel quite elated at being able to see the 'root' cause of being non-assertive. I suppose, secretively I thought this was a fixed trait.	**What shall I do next? Make plan for learning** I will work on a new PLC to find out why I do not wish to cause offence to some people and why causing offence should result in an argument.

Figure 5.9 Reviewing the PLC on assertiveness

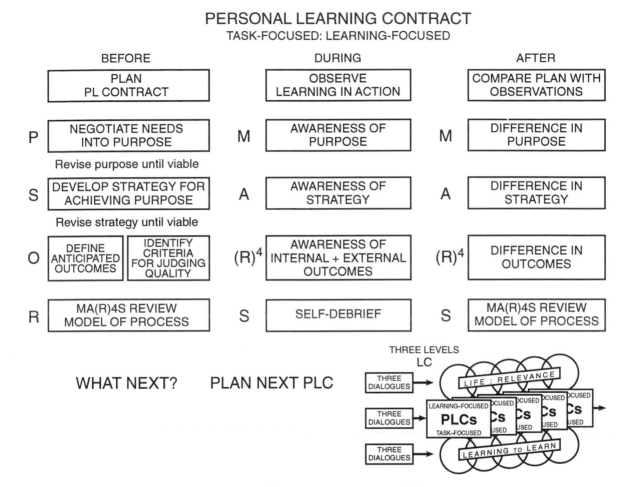

Figure 5.10 *The time/structure of the PLC*

of PLCs, the learners become increasingly *aware* of both the *process* and the *content* of their learning. By using the PLC to engage in Learning Conversations with the Learning Coach, the learners can exchange their experience and develop their skills and competence in SOL.

For those who may be interested, the CSHL has computer software for using PLCs: this is known as CHAT-TO-LEARN.

Summary

In this chapter we have used two fairly simple examples to illustrate the procedure of conducting a tutorial Learning Conversation using the PLC as the major tool. There are a myriad of adaptations and variations on the core procedure. Some of these are illustrated in the next chapter. Essentially, the PLC is the vehicle for conducting the tutorial level of the Learning Conversation. As learners engage in a series of PLCs on a given topic and task, it may be useful to shift to the life level of the Learning Conversation when motivation appears to lose momentum, so that learners can reassess their needs, life goals, and reflect on how the particular PLC in hand relates to these. Again, it may be useful to shift to the learning-to-learn level if detailed aspects of relevant skills need to be developed.

In the following chapter we aim to give you practical insights into all of these processes by showing how PLCs have been used in the world of industry and commerce.

Suggested activity

Setting up Personal Learning Contracts

1 Take an area of personal learning, this could be from work or home life, and set up a PLC. Areas you may consider could include, appraising staff, chairing meetings, evaluating personal development programmes, making presentations, running discussion groups.
2 While developing the PLC note any iterative loops that arise and write up the planning phase of the PLC.
3 Complete the action phase of the PLC.
4 Record the progress of the actions on a record form. Reflect on these comments and note how they affect the PLC. Some learning experiences may alter the strategy, and noting how and why this happened will help enrich the talkback process.
5 Carry out the final review phase. Review the whole process using the framework we suggested in this chapter. Mentally, stand back and reflect on what has happened, and what you can learn about your own learning processes as a result.
6 Plan your next PLC either on the same topic and task or a very different one.
7 Try to reflect on how the PLC may help you to challenge robotic ways of tackling tasks, and to reflect on the nature of your 'learning robots'.
8 Now, refer to the figure-of-eight dynamic of the Learning Conversation (Figure 4.2, page 65). How can you use a series of PLCs to shift into the life level or the learning-to-learn level of the Learning Conversation? What have you gained from this?
9 Reflect on your developing Learning Conversations with yourself. Jot down the terms, your ways of thinking and feeling about learning processes. How much richer is your language of learning as a result?
10 Now, in the light of your own experience, assist someone else to set up, record and review his or her own PLC.

6 Applications of Personal Learning Contracts on the job

Agenda board

Introduction

In this chapter we aim to consolidate Chapter 5 by illustrating the practical application of Personal Learning Contracts on the job. In order to give the training practitioner as wide a picture as possible we offer a range of situations that may be faced by a Learning Coach and we conversationally take the reader through each case study in turn. The examples which follow show a range of PLCs and include mainly short-term process-based task-focused contracts. The reason for this is that these are the most likely PLCs that the Learning Coach will work with when initially enabling individuals to become Self-Organised Learners. We have included an example of PLCs that give more emphasis to the learning-to-learn and life level of the Learning Conversation so that the training practitioner may see the application of these tools, in a real-life setting.

PLCs in industry

The first series of case studies are taken from industry and include our work with the Post Office. Obviously we can only offer readers 'snapshots' of the example PLCs. We have chosen not to include the detailed logs of each PLC, as we wish to convey the 'flavour' of the Learning Conversation.

Newly appointed supervisor

This first example of a PLC in action concerns a young, newly appointed acting supervisor who had attended a training course in management techniques. Bold sections signify the development of the PLC from learning topic to anticipated learning outcomes.

Planning phase

L: I have just attended a course for acting supervisors and was impressed by the session on management styles. I have always experienced autocratic management in the past, and yet I knew there had to be another way. The workshop really opened my eyes to another method of management, and I want to be more consultative in my approach. So this is the topic of my next PLC.

Topic and task is to be more consultative as a manager.

LC: Let's explore why you wish to become more consultative.
L: Because all my life I have resented those people who have told me what to do and how to do it without asking my opinion. This happened at school and throughout my working life. I really do feel that my managers and teachers could have got a lot more out of me if they had involved me in decisions and actions. You could say that I wish to become more consultative because of my previous experience of people being autocratic towards me and the feeling of negativity that this aroused in me, and if I feel like this I am sure others do as well.

Purposes are related to personal negative experience of autocratic management.

LC: How do you intend to show your staff that you are going to be consultative?

L: I have thought long and hard about this, and I think I shall simply tell them I have been on a course, learnt about these two styles and will adopt the consultative style.

LC: Try to imagine that you are a member of your team. How would you feel if you were on the receiving end of that message?

L: Ah, yes, I would probably think that the supervisor was going to use some new fangled theory on me and treat me as a guinea pig. I would resent this. I shall organise a short meeting on my first day as a supervisor and share with the staff my experience of people being over-bossy with me and say in jargon-free language that I really am interested in their ideas and intend to consult them both individually and as a team in future. When applying the test of me as a team member I would be happy with that course of action.

Strategy: I shall organise a short meeting on my first day as a supervisor and share with the staff my experience of people being over-bossy with me and say in jargon-free language that I really am interested in their ideas and intend to consult them both individually and as a team in future.

LC: How will you know when you have been successful?

L: When the staff have accepted this new approach at the meeting.

LC: At some point you need to consider carefully how you come to the conclusion that your staff have accepted the new consultative approach. Also your initial learning topic was to become more consultative and yet your measure of success only covers the result of your first meeting with staff and not the actual application of a consultative style.

L: Yes, I shall take this a step at a time. This PLC will only concern my first meeting with staff. In talking through this PLC I can see that management style is probably a long-term issue.

Amended topic: 'Introducing my style of management to my team at an initial meeting.'

Action phase   During this phase of the PLC the actions were recorded on a personal learning record similar to Figure 5.8 on page 92. This tool was used by the learner and Learning Coach to review the PLC.

Review phase   **LC:** How did you get on at your first meeting?

L: Well, my learning topic and purposes for learning remained more or less unchanged, but before the meeting my actual strategy included writing down how I would structure the meeting and writing down what I intended to say. I wrote my comments on cards and committed the notes to memory so that I would sound sincere.

LC: What happened?

L: About half the team looked genuinely interested. The others sniggered, so I decided to speak to two of those who expressed cynicism discreetly and individually. They said that they felt the formality of the meeting was 'over the top' but although they fully supported me they had the impression I was going 'soft'.

LC: Are you happy with the outcome of your PLC?

L: Although there was not 100 per cent acceptance of my approach, I think my initial expectation was not unreasonable. I must now work on putting a consultative style of management into action.

LC: What have you learnt about you as a learner?

L: I shall have to think more about this and think about my strategies in general.

This learner then went on to develop her style of management and views this as a long-term task.

Establishing a common way of operating the shift

The next example shows how SOL may be used by more than one person to refine the way the job is done. The supervisors run a 24-hour operation with some staff who work part of their shift under one supervisor and part under the other.

Planning phase

L: I am a little worried about the way the work is done on this job.

LC: Why is that?

L: Well, for two reasons really. One is that I am not entirely happy about the way work is left for my shift to complete. The other is that I overheard some of the workers in the canteen say they work in one way for my colleague and another way for me because they know we like the job done in different ways. That is not right—there should be a common approach to work and everyone ought to know the standards of operating. So I want to establish a common method of operating.

Learning topic and task is to establish a common method of operating the shift. The purposes for learning have already been expressed: 'I am not entirely happy about the way work is left for my shift to complete. The other is that staff work in one way for my colleague and another way for me because they know we like the job done in different ways. That is not right—there should be a common approach to work and everyone ought to know the standards of operating.'

LC: What are you going to do about this?

L: I do not know—I have spoken to my boss who seems to be disinterested.

The Learning Coach may now refer the learner to an expert referent for advice on how to move forward. In this case the Learning Coach was able to help.

LC: Consider writing down how you think you operate your shift and allocate work among the staff. You could then stand back and reflect on how you carry out your shift by keeping a diary for one shift, noting what happened, what you did, and why you did it. You could persuade your colleague to do the same, and finally ask your boss to write down his view of how the job is carried out. You could then hold a meeting between all parties to discuss a common model of the job.

L: I might have problems convincing my colleague but I shall have a go. I shall also try to plan more of a 'hand-over' period so that we can discuss how the diary is going and any problems that have arisen in the shifts. I suggest we complete a diary over one week's shifts as a single shift would not represent the range of work or pressure situations we are involved in.

Strategy: For both supervisors to keep a diary of one week's shifts noting what happened, actions taken and the reasons for those actions. The learner to compare his diary with his view of how he thinks he operates and to note the differences. To discuss the maintenance of the diary during 'hand-over' periods and ask the boss to note down what he thinks the shift involves. To discuss the action models of the supervisors with the boss's view and determine a model of running the shift that would accommodate individuality with common work standards of performance.

LC: How will you know when you have been successful?

L: When my colleague, myself and boss have a common understanding of how we carry out the job, and when the staff reporting to us work towards similar standards. This will mean that staff will be working towards a common set of standards for both shifts.

Learning outcome: 'When my colleague, myself and boss have a common understanding of how we carry out the job, and when the staff reporting to us work towards similar standards. This will mean that staff will be working towards a common set of standards for both shifts.'

Action phase   The learner recorded the actions taken for subsequent reflection in the form of a large notebook and in diary format.

The learner requests an interim review

L: I wanted to see you because I am amazed at the difference between how I think I work and how I actually work. I wrote down faithfully how I thought, and indeed was convinced, I operate but in actual reality there are some striking differences between what I think I do and what I do. For instance I was convinced that I simply allocated the shift tasks evenly among staff at the beginning of the shift. When I kept my diary and noted who was given what task, and reflected on this I noticed that the tasks were not evenly allocated and that there was a complicated structure in my mind which led me to allocate tasks on the basis of ability, staff who moan about certain jobs and reliability. Later in the week I found that this structure changed when we had a pressure situation. In fact I am not happy that my method of allocating tasks is entirely right as it does not help the staff to develop and work with a range of tasks in a variety of pressure situations.

This led to the learner starting a PLC on allocation of tasks while still working with the original PLC. This particular supervisor was close to retirement but still became highly committed towards changing and improving the way the job was done.

Review phase   LC: How have you got on since our last interim meeting?

L: I managed to convince my colleague and the boss to be involved, and was surprised how keen they were. First, my colleague and I were able for the first time to look at what we are doing objectively and then we were in a position to converse about why we took the actions we did, and it was this conversation that really helped us both to see what we did and why we did it from the other's standpoint. We then went to the boss, and to be honest he was so surprised at the way in which we talked openly about the job that he became very open with us. We have a clearer under-standing of how we see the job and we have both learnt from each other in the process. All three of us are going to hold a short meeting for the workers on our shift to talk about the tasks and how they are carried out as well as our measures for assessing the effectiveness of the shift.

Both learners then went on to work on their methods of managing their shifts for many months. Also, communication improved as a result.

PLCs initiated without assistance

In one organisation a number of supervisors were initiating PLCs with-out involving a Learning Coach. This happened because the Learning Coach had made explicit the nature of what they were doing during the elicitation of the PLC and also made explicit the nature and structure of the Learning Conversation so that the learners were able to function without assistance. During our time with this organisation the company moved from fairly old buildings to premises that were purpose built. A team of planners was responsible for ensuring that the accommodation would be adequate for every function, and the planners were working largely without consulting the shop-floor workers. A large number of workers had been using SOL in their work, and were so concerned about their performance that they requested permission to enter the new premises before they were completed and be shown their space allocation and any new machinery they may have to use. They then attempted to recreate their actions and tasks and were able to make some very significant observations that led to important changes. The point is that SOL has the effect of enabling staff to become pro-active rather than simply to stand back and wait for events to take place. Quite a number of staff used PLCs for learning at home and improving relationships with the family after experiencing the beneficial effects of PLCs and Learning Conversations at work.

Examples of PLC topics

Personal Learning Contracts in this industry covered a very wide area. The range of topics involved included: dealing with staff who turn up improperly dressed for work; meeting work-based deadlines; improving quality of service; teambuilding; time management; dealing with crises on the shop floor; running meetings; appraising staff; promotion inter-views; interpreting statistics; report writing; work procedures; effec-tively using new machinery; improving effectiveness by observing performance at other sites; handling disciplinary situations; machine breakdowns; detecting faults on vehicles; presentations.

One acting supervisor started as a Learning Coach and as well as enabling others to work with SOL, he used SOL himself, working through a range of PLCs which involved task-focused, learning-to-learn and life conversations. He progressed rapidly from acting supervisor to a position of seniority in a short space of time. We shall consider measuring the process of change in the next chapter.

PLCs in business

Familiarisation with a new spreadsheet

This example is quite straightforward and is concerned with a clerk who has recently joined a company that uses a different type of computer-based spreadsheet software.

Planning phase

L:　I am used to using a spreadsheet package which is quite different from this company's, and although I understand how spreadsheets work I cannot use this spreadsheet without constantly having to refer to the manual.

LC: Your learning topic then is to know and be able to use the different commands necessary for this spreadsheet.

L:　Yes and I do not know how to do this.

Learning topic and task is to know and be able to use the different commands necessary for the spreadsheet currently used at work.

LC: Why do you wish to be able to do this?

L:　Because the majority of my work involves the use of spreadsheets, and if I do not get the hang of the different commands my new employer will not be impressed.

Purposes for learning: 'The majority of my work involves the use of spreadsheets, and if I do not get the hang of the different commands my new employer will not be impressed.'

LC: How are going to overcome this problem?

L:　I do not know. I could speak to the Information Services Manager and see what she says.

Learning strategy. 'Speak to the Information Services Manager and see what she says.'

LC: How will you know when there is a satisfactory outcome to your learning?

L:　When I can operate the spreadsheet without constantly having to delve into the manual.

Learning outcome: 'When I can operate the spreadsheet without constantly having to delve into the manual.'

Action phase

The learner intended to make notes on his discussion with the Information Services Manager, but found that a wall chart existed with the different commands for varying spreadsheet packages, allowing translation from one package to another without endless time spent delving into manuals.

Review phase

LC: How did you get on?

L:　Tremendously. The Information Services Manager had a wall chart which shows the differing commands of most of the popular spreadsheet packages. I put this up on the wall and because I am constantly using the software I am becoming rapidly familiar with the new commands. I am really very pleased.

LC: What have you learnt about yourself as a learner?

L: I am not sure what you mean?

LC: Has this experience taught you anything about how you learn?

L: Oh. I suppose I tend to get very frustrated when I cannot find instant solutions to my learning needs. In this case I needed prompting to think about someone in the organisation who could help me. Next time I need to learn something I shall spend more time planning it and thinking about it.

Impromptu meetings

This example comes from a senior administration manager who was having problems with impromptu meetings.

Planning phase

L: I wish to manage my time more efficiently by spending less time on impromptu meetings.

Learning topic and task: 'To manage my time more efficiently by spending less time on impromptu meetings.'

LC: Why do you need to do this?

L: I need to have more time at my disposal in order to tackle important tasks that have to be done by me and should not be delegated.

Purpose for learning: 'I need to have more time at my disposal in order to tackle important tasks that have to be done by me and should not be delegated.'

LC: How are you going to do this?

L: The informal and impromptu meetings arise when staff feel that they wish to discuss something important with me. This may be on a one-to-one basis or may involve a group of people. What I intend to do is:

1 Determine whether or not the meeting is serious and demands my time as a top priority task. If the answer is 'yes' I shall tackle it straight away. If the answer is 'no' I shall decide whether it can be delegated or left until another time.

2 If the meeting runs, then keep it to the absolute minimum (providing it does not feature a personal problem). I intend to keep the meeting to a minimum by gaining information rapidly through careful questioning. I shall control the amount of talking by summarising and confirming action points.

Strategy:

1 Determine whether or not the meeting is serious and demands my time as a top priority task. If the answer is 'yes' I shall tackle it straight away. If the answer is 'no' I shall decide whether it can be delegated or left until another time.

2 If the meeting runs, then keep it to the absolute minimum (providing it does not feature a personal problem). I intend to keep the meeting to a minimum by gaining information rapidly through careful questioning. I shall control the amount of talking by summarising and confirming action points.

LC: How will you know when you have been effective?

L: When I can control impromptu meetings more effectively. In fact I shall also keep a book which records each impromptu meeting and my comments on how I handled it.

The strategy needs to be updated to include the book which records meetings and reflective comments.

LC: How will you know that the meetings are being controlled more effectively?

L: At this stage all I can say is that when I feel we have discussed the salient points and decisions can be made and actions planned.

Outcome: When impromptu meetings can be controlled more effectively, this will be when they are closed down after the salient points, decisions have been made and actions have been planned.

Action phase   The learner kept a large notebook, with the heading of each impromptu meeting, how long it lasted, the salient points discussed, decisions made and actions planned. The learner also recorded his reflective comments on his handling of the meetings—what he did and the results. This notebook formed the basis of the review phase and was used by both the learner and the Learning Coach.

Review phase   **LC**: How have you got on with your PLC?

L: I can cope with some informal meetings in a far better way now, but the act of recording what I am doing has highlighted that others are still a problem.

LC: Which are those?

L: I can manage informal meetings with junior staff and peers but I am unhappy about the way in which staff who are senior to me just drop in for long periods of time. I really feel that they are wasting my time but I feel powerless to do anything about it.

LC: Talk me through a meeting with someone junior that you felt you managed effectively.

L: Well, I established that it was urgent. I then set about establishing the facts and not wasting time in irrelevant chit-chat. I took notes and was able to clarify each stage of the meeting and this seemed to focus the attention of the other person.

LC: Have you tried doing this with senior staff?

L: No. The reason is that I have been using questioning and control techniques that were covered on a workshop for handling meetings. Well, most of the senior staff have attended that workshop and they will know that I am using the techniques on them.

LC: Do these senior members of staff use the questioning and control techniques with you?

L: Yes. Thinking about it, I suppose some of them do. The problem is that I shall have to adapt the way in which I use the techniques—perhaps use them in a more subtle way.

Further PLCs were elicited to address the issue of senior managers and directors, in fact a separate PLC was developed for learning to work with each of the directors.

Time Management for a senior manager

This is quite a long example and comes from a finance manager who wanted to manage time more effectively. The first meeting with the Learning Coach simply threw up Time Management as a learning topic; however, further probing during the initial Learning Conversation revealed that the manager had been on two Time Management workshops with little appreciable difference in the way he managed his time.

Planning phase

LC: You say that you have been on two Time Management workshops; what would you like to improve on most of all?

L: I work to a set of deadlines, and sometimes I am not able to meet those deadlines because staff have not given me the necessary information or made the necessary reports.

LC: Why is this?

L: Mainly because I do not have sufficient time to hold some of the necessary meetings.

LC: You said some of the necessary meetings. Does that mean that some meetings are held by you and some not?

L: Yes.

LC: Can you tell me about those meetings you do not hold in time?

L: Yes, they are work-in-progress, and feasibility study meetings with my staff.

LC: Why do these meetings in particular get held back?

L: They can be difficult and time consuming.

LC: Why?

L: Staff will often have conflicting views and as the manager it is my responsibility to ensure the work gets done to agreed targets. The problem is that if I am unable to handle the conflict my own manager may lose confidence in me and I may lose my job.

LC: So you really need to be able to handle differing opinions and any conflict that may arise?

Learning topic and task: To be able to handle differing opinions and any conflict that may arise.

L: Yes. Somehow I instinctively knew this was the case but felt that Time Management is something we all have problems with here and somehow people do not get sacked because they have too much to do. My position is becoming serious though. I need to get to grips with this—my job depends on it. Still I do also waste time on non-important tasks; they give me a sense of achievement.

Purposes for learning: 'My position is becoming serious though. I need to get to grips with this—my job depends on it.'

LC: Wasting time on non-important tasks would form the basis of another PLC—shall we start with handling differing opinions and conflict?

L: Yes, definitely.

LC: Talk me through a time when you experienced differing opinions and conflict.

L: There was the time when we held a meeting on the progress of a contract. A number of people held differing views on what should be done next and some were having heated exchanges. I made a couple of suggestions but they were ignored, I was becoming very annoyed and lost my temper. I then told people what I expected them to do and by when. They then went away and did as I asked but grudgingly.

LC: How could you handle the meeting differently?

L: I just do not know.

LC: What made you lose your temper?

L: Staff ignoring my suggestions—I am the boss after all!

LC: How do you start your meetings?

L: By asking people to report on progress, and letting them discuss what needs to happen—I just feel I am losing control especially when conflict arises, then I have to be autocratic.

LC: How could you have run the meeting differently?

L: I could have run the meeting on a formal basis, declare the time available and issues to be discussed. I suppose I could also ask staff for items for the agenda so that they feel that important issues will be addressed. This will also give me forewarning of possible contentious issues. Then I could make sure that all comments are through the chair so that I am seen to be in control and the meeting is unlikely to slip into anarchy.

LC: How will you prepare yourself for possible contentious issues?

L: All that I can say is that I shall think them through beforehand, work out how I think people will stand on the issues and look at the pros and cons of various approaches. I shall update my analysis as the meeting progresses and as fresh information is at hand. This will allow me to put a reasonable course of action to the team in the event of disagreement.

LC: To summarise then, your learning strategy is to run the meeting on a formal basis, declare the time available and issues to be discussed. Ask staff for items for the agenda and note possible contentious issues. Once possible contentious issues have been identified you will work out how you think people will react and look at the pros and cons of various approaches and update your analysis as the meeting progresses and fresh information is at hand. This will allow you to put a reasonable course of action to the team in the event of disagreement. Once the meeting is running you will make sure that all comments are through the chair. Have I got that right?

L: Yes, I cannot wait to get started.

Learning strategy: To run the meeting on a formal basis, declare the time available and issues to be discussed. Ask staff for items for the agenda and note possible contentious issues. Once possible contentious issues have been identified he will work out how the learner thinks people will react and look at the pros and cons of various approaches and update his analysis as the meeting progresses and fresh information is at hand. This will allow him to put a reasonable course of action to the team in the event of disagreement. Once the meeting is running he will make sure that all comments are through the chair.

LC: How will you know when you have been successful?

L: When the meeting is held and we have constructively agreed on a course of action without futile arguing.

Learning outcome: 'When the meeting is held and we have constructively agreed on a course of action without futile arguing.'

Action phase   The learner seriously considered recording a meeting using closed circuit television, but after careful reflection felt that the act of recording may have affected the way those attending the meeting would have behaved. So he opted for recording his recollections in note form.

Review phase   LC: How did you get on?

L: The meeting went well, and I did meet my original learning outcome, but I felt strange. I felt that the way I was conducting the meeting wasn't really me.

LC: Why was this?

L: It just felt strange and a lot of effort. I think I am going to have to repeat this PLC until I feel 'at home' with this new meeting structure and my behaviour.

The next PLC was then planned and a new learning outcome was identified that did not emerge before:

New learning outcome: To feel 'at home' with the new meeting structure and change in behaviour.

This example has been selected purposely as it illustrates how complicated it can be to elicit a PLC when the learner has been trying to hide what is going on, in this case even to himself. There were times when the learner had no idea of what to do as a strategy for learning, and where there is an impasse and the Learning Coach does not have the expertise, then an expert referent may be sought to help with the learning strategy. This may be a personnel manager or someone else appropriate in the organisation or even outside it.

Interviewing for appraisal   This example concerns a branch manager of a city-based office who had attended a workshop to improve her skills at interviewing for appraising staff. The example illustrates a learning-to-learn PLC, and the learning dip explained in an earlier chapter:

Planning phase   L: I feel very depressed indeed.

LC: Why is that?

L: Because I have been appraising staff for years, and although I knew that I could be doing this better I felt relatively happy with what I was doing. Our organisation then ran a series of workshops for planning, organising, carrying out and recording appraisals. I really felt that the workshop was worth while when we were discussing our roles in the appraisal process, and I do feel that all round I plan more effectively and know how to record the results unambiguously. My interviewing, though, is another matter.

LC: What is concerning you about interviewing?

L: I think that I used to be a passable interviewer, but having attended this workshop I find that there is a whole new world of questioning technique, paralinguistics, body language, neuro-linguistic programming, interview plans, creating rapport and so on. While I am concentrating on all these things I find that it is difficult to be myself with the appraisee. To cut a long story short, I am now convinced that I am worse at interviewing than I was before, with all these newfangled techniques.

LC: What would you like to do about your interviewing?

L: I do believe that if I can only use these techniques naturally, and be myself, then I really will be good at appraisals. I really need to ask myself why I am having so much difficulty in improving.

Here the Learning Coach discusses the effects of the learning dip, and that this experience is common among learners who go through a learning event with some previous ability. Readers may wish to refer to our earlier chapter where the learning dip is discussed.

LC: Looking back over your previous Personal Learning Contracts, have you noticed anything about how you go about learning new skills?

L: No, I would like to know more about how I learn so that I can become more effective at learning, and not look stupid in front of colleagues and subordinates.

Learning topic and task: 'To know more about how I learn.'
Purposes for learning: (1) 'so that I can become more effective at learning'; (2) 'and not look stupid in front of colleagues and subordinates.'

LC: Why don't you analyse all of your previous PLCs and the reviews to see if there is anything you can learn about how you learn?

L: Yes, I shall do that.

Strategy: To analyse all of the previous PLCs and the reviews to see if there is anything that can be learnt about how the learner learns.

Some learners may need help from the Learning Coach when reviewing previous PLCs; this learner was quite happy to carry out the analysis for herself.

LC: How will you know when you have been successful?

L: When I discover enough about my learning to help me plan to develop my skills in interviewing.

Learning outcome: 'When I discover enough about my learning to help me plan to develop my skills in interviewing.'

Action phase   The learner decided to complete a personal learning record, listing each PLC and what subsequent reflection has revealed about her learning strengths and weaknesses in that PLC. The learner then said she would write her overall reflections after each PLC had been considered as a separate entity.

Review phase   L: I have analysed my PLCs and it has struck me that I learn best when I concentrate on one thing at a time; also, much of my valued learning I see as a challenge. What I want to do now is to concentrate on my interviewing skills by tackling them one at a time rapidly because of the appraisal deadlines. What I would also like to do is to discuss a PLC with you regarding developing my skills at learning without having to focus exclusively on one skill at a time.

LC: How will you use the fact that much of your valued learning is seen as a challenge?

L: As far as interviewing is concerned, I shall set weekly deadlines for reviewing each major skill such as questioning, summarising and note taking. This will challenge me to concentrate and work within time constraints.

The learner then goes on to set a series of task-based PLCs which will be reviewed for learning outcomes connected with specific task-based skills, and will also form the basis for on-going learning to learn PLCs.

PLCs in healthcare

A chiropodist without job satisfaction

This example involves a chiropodist who was unhappy with her work, and was considering changing her career. This is an example of a PLC at the life-level. She appeared to be uncertain of which elements of the work she was unhappy with, stating only that the job was not giving her the satisfaction she expected from it.

Planning phase

L: I would like to learn why I do not like my job.
LC: Are there any parts of the job you feel you like?
L: No, not really.
LC: Have you at any time enjoyed chiropody?
L: I have enjoyed it more than I do now, but I really do not know why and I want to find out. There may be something I can do to increase my job satisfaction or I may need to change my career, depending on what I discover about my views of the job I do.

Learning topic and task: To find out why the learner does not like her job.

Purposes for learning: To enrich job satisfaction and to know whether a change in career would be beneficial.

LC: What are you going to do to discover more about your job and whether you derive job satisfaction from any elements of your work?
L: I have wondered about this for some time, but just thinking about the job does not seem to help me.

The Learning Coach was able to act as expert referent and suggest the use of the repertory grid. This is an established tool for Self-Organised Learners and so Learning Coaches should be in a position to offer help in this area without needing to refer the learner to another expert referent.

LC: I suggest you use the repertory grid to reflect on the various elements of the job. First I would like you to think about your main job-based activities, and put each activity on a separate card.
L: OK.

Strategy for learning: To complete a repertory grid on the main elements of the job for subsequent reflection and talkback.

LC: How will you know when you have been successful with your learning?
L: When I can discover what it is that is making me unhappy at work.

Learning outcome: 'When I can discover what it is that is making me unhappy at work.'

Action phase   This involved the Learning Coach working with the learner on her strategy of using the repertory grid. She made a record of her thoughts when she stated each construct, and when rating the grid, she made a brief statement as to why she rated the grid in the way she did. This helped her revisit the grid on subsequent occasions and know why she rated it in the way she did. She may well have wished to re-rate the grid later (this did not happen) and writing her reasons for the re-rating would help her to see how and why her thinking had moved on.

Repertory grid procedure   The Learning Coach asked the learner to triad the job activities and suggested a set of bipolar personal constructs (readers are reminded that Chapter 3 contains guidelines on the elicitation of repertory grids).

The job elements were identified as:

Obtaining patients list from the clerk
Admitting patient for treatment (this includes helping infirm patients
    and removing footwear)
Establishing symptoms and health
Conducting appropriate treatment
Rendering appropriate aftercare (including medication and dressings)
Giving appropriate advice on self-help
Arranging domiciliary help (home visits)
Writing record cards
Sweeping the floor (clearing up dressings and debris from treatments)
Laundering overalls
Checking stocks and re-ordering
Liaising with district chiropodist
Liaising with appropriate personnel (district chiropodist's assistant, the
    receptionist, etc.)
Listening to patients' private problems

After triading the bipolar constructs were:

Interest	No interest
Enjoy	Dislike
Job satisfaction	Job dissatisfaction
Smooth running	Aggravation
People	Things
Amusing	Depressing
Exciting	Boring

A repertory grid was then elicited and is reproduced (see Figure 6.1). The Learning Coach pointed out that the following elements were rated identically:

Domiciliary help   Conduct treatment
Appropriate aftercare   Advice on self-help
Establish symptoms

All these elements were rated as involving people, smooth running, to some extent exciting, interesting, enjoyable, and giving a degree of job satisfaction, and neither amusing nor depressing.

Review phase The learner was invited to reflect on this and make observations.

L: I am absolutely amazed, I can see from this grid that my main interest and enjoyment in carrying out the job is from work associated with treatment. The whole job appeared to be getting me down, but I can see that the parts of the job I hate were clouding my view of the parts of the job I do enjoy. Liaising with the district chiropodist leaves me frustrated and annoyed, and having to launder my own overalls, I find quite aggravating. The grid has made me more aware of the fact that I only feel that things run smoothly when I have control over them. This is borne out by my experience of leaving tasks for other people to perform, such as cleaning the medicaments trolley after treatments.

LC: I see that liaising with the district chiropodist you have rated a 4 on aggravation, job dissatisfaction and depressing.

L: Yes, I have. This is because I have little confidence and trust in him as a manager.

LC: Why?

L: I feel that he is constantly checking up on all his staff with regard to appointments and he intends to check the quality of our treatments. However, he also treats patients himself and patients have complained about the delay and sometimes non-arrival of appliances. I suppose I feel that there is one set of rules by which he operates and another by which he manages his staff and I do not happen to think this is fair. Reflecting on all this I can see that I would be much better off being my 'own boss'.

LC: How could you go about doing this?

L: I could apply to do far more domiciliary work (home visits to patients who are not mobile).

LC: What about liaising with the district chiropodist?

L: That would be greatly reduced and sweeping the clinic floor and clearing up the mess on the trolley left by others would be reduced.

This learner was able to change the balance of her work to more domiciliary visits and reported that she was a great deal happier as a result. The repertory grid had helped her to focus more sharply on the elements within her job and her attitude to each element. She had achieved her desired learning outcome and was very pleased with the result.

112

ELEMENTS

CONSTRUCT POLE RATED – 1   CONSTRUCT POLE RATED – 5

		E10	E09	E11	E08	E01	E07 E05 E03 E04 E06	E02	E12	E11	E14	E13		
PEOPLE	C5	5	5	5	4	3	11111	1	1	1	1	1	C5	THINGS
SMOOTH RUNNING	C4	4	3	2	1	1	11111	2	3	3	3	4	C4	AGGRAVATION
INTEREST	C1	5	5	3	3	1	22222	2	3	3	3	3	C1	NO INTEREST
ENJOY	C2	5	5	3	3	3	22222	2	3	3	2	3	C2	DISLIKE
EXCITING	C7	5	4	4	3	2	22222	2	2	2	2	3	C7	BORING
JOB SATISFACTION	C3	5	3	2	3	3	22222	2	2	2	3	4	C3	JOB DISSATISFACTION
AMUSING	C6	4	3	3	3	3	33333	3	3	3	3	4	C6	DEPRESSING

Elements:
LAUNDER OVERALLS
SWEEP FLOOR
CHECK FLOOR
WRITE STOCK
CHECK STOCK
OBTAIN LIST FROM CLERK
DOMICILIARY HELP
APPROPRIATE AFTERCARE
ESTABLISH SYMPTOMS
CONDUCT TREATMENT
ADVISE ON SELF-HELP
ADMITTANCE FOR TREATMENT
LIAISE WITH APPROPRIATE PERSONNEL
LISTEN TO PATIENTS' PROBLEMS
LIAISE WITH DISTRICT CHIROPODIST

Figure 6.1   *A chiropodist's repertory grid*

PLCs in education

Personal Learning Contracts have been used by Self-Organised Learners in education for a number of areas of learning. Here we aim to show how the PLC was used to help trainees on an International Training Management programme become more autonomous during a one-week self-managed project. We are not reproducing individual PLCs or the text of the Learning Conversation; instead we aim to show the reader how a group of individuals benefited from using this tool.

The programme included eight trainees who were, in the main, managers from countries all over the world, and part of their programme involved identifying a suitable topic related to training and to the work they perform within their organisations, and then carrying out the research themselves. They were given one week to carry out the research and present their findings to the course tutor and their peers for evaluation. During the research week a rota of tutors was drawn up to whom trainees could refer when they encountered problems and needed advice. This programme had been run for a considerable number of years, and past experience had shown that the tutors were in high demand throughout the week. Time constraints were such that I was unable to introduce the trainees to much more than the Personal Learning Contract before their project week, and so I spent about two hours familiarising them with this tool alone. They then presented their project proposals to the tutors under:

- Learning topic
- Purposes for learning
- Strategy
- Identified learning outcomes.

An interesting point to note here is that most of the proposals were accepted. Often trainees can be quite ambitious in what they hope to achieve during the week, but this framework helped them to think through their projects in a more systematic and carefully considered manner. Another interesting observation was that very few trainees asked for tutorial support during the week, and those that did mainly requested help in preparing visual aids for presentations. All the trainees used the Personal Learning Contract review framework when making their presentations. Finally, the course tutors remarked on the sound structure and high quality of content in the presentations.

This example has been selected to show the reader how the PLC can be used as a valuable tool to enable the learner to structure and reflect on learning, become rapidly independent with the learning, and obtain a quick return on the time invested in the process.

Definition of SOL: MA(R)4S and the PLC

The PLC is an all purpose vehicle which allows the MA(R)4S learning conversation to proceed (Chapter 4). It encourages the learner to *monitor* and *analyse* at each of the three phases of the PLC: the planning phase, the action phase and the review phase. By inviting the learner to make comparisons between the planning and the review phases, it encourages the individual to *reconstruct, reflect, record* and *review* the whole learning sequence. Finally, it invites the learner to make constructive assessments of current competences, attitudes and skills and to plan directions for personal growth. By actioning a series of PLCs on the job, learners are empowered to *spiral* onwards and upwards, developing their capacity to learn. The whole procedure is content independent, allowing any topic, task, and areas of skill, however complex or simple, to be explored and developed.

Summary

These examples are intended to give readers a feel for PLCs in action over a broad area of work-based situations. They have predominantly been examples of task-focused PLCs, but also included an example of a learning-to-learn PLC and a PLC at the life-level. In each case we have endeavoured to show how the different types of PLC have been triggered. Learners are invited to experiment with the suggested activities in Chapter 5 for initiating PLCs on yourselves and with at least one client.

Learners from within industry, commerce, as well as education and social services, have frequently remarked how revealing and rewarding the PLCs and the tutorial Learning Conversation can be. The conversational process illuminates the power of the PLC procedure, its eliciting and recording facility and its self-debriefing and comparison facility. This is the resource which nourishes the learners' development of Learning Conversations with themselves.

In this chapter we have tried to show how the PLC is used in the different habitats of work. Supported by the SOL Coach, the PLC functions for the achievement of Self-Organised Learning, and measuring the processes of change arising from SOL will be dealt with in Chapter 7.

Suggested activity

Applying the PLC for job improvement

1 Take one situation in which, as training practitioner or manager, you may be involved.
2 Map out a plan of action for making some improvements.
3 Identify the nature of the problems in that specific situation which, if worked through with the relevant individuals or the team as a whole, would make a significant impact on the productivity, quality of service, or cost-effectiveness of that situation.
4 Identify the key people involved, and consider carefully how you might introduce these to the practical benefits of the PLC and to the idea that they can significantly improve themselves as learners, which will benefit them personally as well as the organisation.

5 Keep a careful log of *your own* purposes, strategies and expected outcomes.

6 Use the iterative procedure referred to in Chapter 5 and log the changes in purposes, strategies and outcomes as you progress.

7 In this activity we have invited you to elicit and complete a PLC on *yourself*, as you work with others, helping them to familiarise themselves with SOL and the PLC as a vehicle for conducting Learning Conversations. Try to work with at least three clients in a particular situation, so that each completes at least two or three PLCs. Record what they have learnt about themselves: their strengths as well as any skills, attitudes and competences they may need to develop. Record what you have learnt in carrying out this project.

The next chapter shows how you can log progress as a learner.

7 Self-Organised Learning and evaluation: how to measure the process of change

Agenda board

- The expert-based and the pluralistic value systems: two conflicting evaluation approaches
- Feedback-for-Learning and conversational evaluation
- Conversational evaluation in practice
- The PLC as evidence for learning from the learner's perspective
- Other perspectives on learning
- The Personal Learning Biography: a multi-perspective evaluation tool
- Suggested activity: identifying your assessment model of learning

Introduction

In the General Introduction we introduced Self-Organised Learning as a radical approach, and this is especially true of the conversational method developed at CSHL for assessing the effectiveness of learning. In this chapter we introduce a 'conversational evaluation model' developed and tested within SOL action research projects. We explain some of the techniques and procedures which are addressed within this model.

To better understand the philosophy underlying this model it is necessary to examine the value system predominant within current education practices, and to compare this with the value system intrinsic to SOL. This brings us face to face with two different philosophies, two different value systems which uncomfortably coexist in our education and training culture.

Conflicting evaluation approaches

Traditionally, the evaluation of learning remains largely within the framework of the EXPERT'S VALUE SYSTEM. This is so well established and accepted that seldom has it been questioned, despite the progressive trend particularly in the world of vocational training, for 'open learning', 'distance learning', 'learning contracts', 'project work', and the NCVQ accreditation of prior learning through experience. There exists a growing recognition that for learning to be effective *it must be owned or controlled by the person doing the learning*. SOL goes further; it accepts that if learners are to develop their capacity to learn, then not only must the method and content of their learning be under their control, but also the evaluation system within which their learning is to be assessed. If learning is a process of self-defined change, it must be justified within these parameters and merge out of this process.

Many of the problems in education and training emerge from a failure to grasp the implications of this philosophy. The majority of learners are formally evaluated within an expert-based system, which disregards the criteria and values of those involved in the learning, and in many cases, such as public examinations, those involved in teaching and training. This is incompatible with self-development, personal growth and self-controlled change.

The problem is not insurmountable, once a pluralistic paradigm, i.e. a relativistic framework, is accepted. This implies that learners' own values, the values of those responsible for supporting them—teachers, trainers, parents, advisers, those within a chain of command in an organisation—as well as the values of professional bodies and experts can all be integrated within a relativistic framework. *These are all legitimate perspectives which together provide evidence to evaluate learning.*

The 'conversational evaluation model' integrates:

   topics and tasks
   purposes and strategies
   skills and competences

outcomes
criteria for assessment

into a multi-perspective system, which operates over the short, medium and longer term. *This model also combines feedback-for-learning and assessment into an on-going system designed to support self-controlled change.*

Feedback-for-Learning and conversational evaluation

The provision of good-quality feedback is an essential component of a Self-Organised Learning environment. The conversational evaluation model embodies two functions of assessment:

1 To provide feedback of progress, in terms which learners can understand, so that they can direct their learning activities.
2 To appraise learners' levels of achievement against 'objective' measures, in whatever form these may be represented.

However, the conversational evaluation model goes beyond this. It also allows for all the criteria falling into (1) and (2) to be part of an integrative system of feedback-for-learning. Within this system 'subjective' judgements and 'objective' measures become complementary sources of evidence for individual, team and organisational learning, and for strategically planned growth.

Figure 7.1 outlines this system, how it works, and how it has the capacity to evolve continuously. Columns 1 and 2 contain the date and a diary record of all the learning activities in which each learner/learning team has participated. In our various projects, this is usefully recorded in some shorthand or agreed coded form. The model anticipates that the chain of 'cause and effect' leads first to changes in perception, attitudes and understanding in the learner's own view. Columns 3 and 4 show this first evidence of learning. The Learning Conversation as a whole, and the completed Personal Learning Contract (PLC) with its records of performance (Chapters 3, 4, 5 and 6), the conversational repertory grid (Chapter 3), and structures of meaning (Chapter 2) are all reflective tools designed to encourage personal experimentation, and inevitably provide evidences for learning. *Only learners themselves can really know if their thoughts, feelings and ways of seeing the world have changed.* Only they have direct access to their own experiences and values. Column 3 records the evidences of the learner's own experiences, often summarised from the representation of experience as recorded through the various SOL tools used in a Learning Conversation.

More obvious evidences exist in changes in the way learners perform their tasks in their various situations; the way they do their jobs, interact with colleagues, complete and present their assignments, and so on. *Thus, others can observe and, if possible, keep records of the learner's behaviour* (column 4), in the short, medium and long term.

The conversational evaluation system is itself part of the SOL tool kit

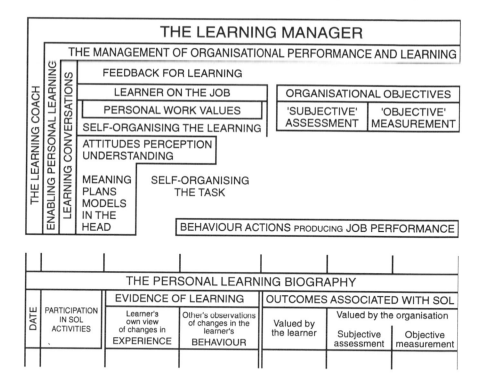

Figure 7.1 *The conversational evaluation model*

and is used within the Learning Conversation. Learners are invited to reflect on their on-going learning activities (column 2) and on their EXPERIENTIAL evidences for learning (column 3), as well as other evidences of their learning BEHAVIOURS (column 4). *They are then invited to record those* OUTCOMES *of their learning that they* VALUE *(column 5), and to try to seek causal links and explanations.* Initially, they may find this difficult and this is one part of the Learning Coach's role, to work with each learner, eliciting personal explanations for the learning that is taking place.

Evaluations by others are recorded 'subjectively' (column 6) and 'objectively' (column 7). Subjective assessments include weekly/monthly assessments carried out by the learner's immediate boss or tutor. These may be informal commentaries. They may take the form of assessment schedules, tests, performance records and so on. In the medium term they may include data such as appraisal records and project assessments. Objective measures include those used by an organisation to calibrate its overall performance, such as productivity, quality of service and cost-effectiveness. They may also include examination results expressed as grades on 'norm-based' or 'criteria-referenced' terms.

Together, the learner's own view and the evaluations of others are the evidences which corroborate the effects of learning taking place in the short, medium and long term. As the learning becomes more self-organised within a developing SOL environment, then the evaluations of the outcomes of learning from the various perspectives will become more and more synchronised. *This is particularly the case when the learner is involved in this whole evaluation process as part of an on-going Learning Conversation, involving several nodes in the hierarchy of an organisation.* This important issue is taken further in the next chapter.

In practice, the conversational evaluation model takes on the form of the Personal Learning Biography (PLB). In a superficial sense, this is analogous to 'student profiles' or 'trainee profiles', although even as a log of progress it is a much more refined tool than those generally available. At a deeper level, however, when used *conversationally* the PLB embodies all the characteristics of an SOL tool (see the General Introduction) and generates evidences to be used as feedback-for-learning in the short, medium and long term. Unfortunately, in educational and training practices, the evaluation of learning made by others rarely synchronises with the learner's own. The problem basically lies in the unresolved paradigm debate, the clash of the two value systems—traditional 'expert' values and learner-generated values—referred to earlier. The former is concerned exclusively with assessment from the top down, while the latter, when conceived of within the SOL approach, embraces values concerned with offering a coherent feedback-for-learning *and* appraisal. Having explained the conversational evaluation model, we shall now show how the effects of SOL can be measured for feedback and for assessment, to promote self-organised change.

Conversational evaluation in practice

Self-organised learners seek valid meaning as part of their study and work. In all cases this involves working productively to achieve quality results by cost-effective means. To move a system of Learning Conversations from an exclusive learner-centred base towards organisationally or professionally valued objectives requires an adaptive and enlightened shift in values within an organisation. *For the Self-Organised Learners this is no effort; they seek evaluations from significant others in their lives, as a resource against which to benchmark their own development.* For the organisation or profession, however, it often involves a considerable struggle, much new insight is demanded and a preparedness to evolve towards a pluralistic paradigm of values and out of an expert-bound mode of thought. The onus is on these 'others'—bosses in a chain of command, teachers, trainers, top management and experts—to ensure that assessment information can be provided that delivers specific feedback which relates to the outcomes achieved. The terms in which the feedback is offered, and its timing, defines the quality of learning. This should provide a real context for learning to continue, on the job, on the course or workshop or at college. The effectiveness of a worker, supervisor or manager 'on the job' depends on how their tasks are performed. This performance needs to be correlated with the goals and objectives of the enterprise. Generally, they inform themselves on these issues by using all the evidences at their disposal, such as their day-by-day experiences and information they receive from others. Often the information they receive is vague and sometimes erroneous. *Experience of SOL projects in many organisations has shown that unless and until something radical is done to generate valid, consistent and reliable feedback-for-learning, Self-Organised Learners should not rely on being able to obtain it easily!* But they can engage in Learning Conversations 'on the job' with colleagues, bosses and experienced elders, and use a myriad of other resources to detect and work out for themselves the often implicitly held subjective judgements and the incredibly coarse and inadequate objective measures that do exist in some form within the organisation.

The training practitioner involved in supporting learning on the job should be concerned with this. There are many ways in which that person can create a better learning environment within which consistent, relevant and good-quality feedback is more readily available. There is much that can be done by taking a hard look at the information systems available, what these are used for, by whom, and how they are made available to learners. Within a learning organisation there is much they can do by working closely with others to up-date, refine, reform, and transform this welter of information for feedback-for-learning.

These issues are taken further in the next chapter. Here we concentrate on what a Self-Organised Learner can do proactively, given some degree of support, within an environment of intermittent, inconsistent, unreliable, invalid information and often misleading and confusing feedback. Such ill-controlled information makes it difficult to learn to become more effective, particularly in terms which 'the enterprise' or the 'profession' will value. But for a Self-Organised Learner this can be perceived as a challenge!

The PLC as evidences of learning from the learner's perspective

In Chapter 4 we introduced the three dialogues which combine to structure the discourse of the Learning Conversation. We explained that these dialogues become integrated within the three levels—the central personal learning contract (PLC) or 'tutorial conversation', 'the life or relevance conversation', and the more intensive 'learning-to-learn conversation'. We described the figure-of-eight pattern of the three levels within the flow of the Learning Conversation as a whole (see Figure 4.2, page 65). Given this dynamic organisation, *records of the process dialogue in action within a series of PLCs become indicators of the evolving 'language of learning'*. For instance, the degree of precision and elaboration of purpose in a nesting set of purposes, of strategies and tactics and the range of identified criteria for defining the quality of outcomes are some of the indicators that *learning itself is a developing skill*.

Each completed PLC can be examined in terms of the 'syntax and semantics' of its 'language of learning' represented in the learner's responses. How the learner thinks and feels in process terms will be partly reflected in this recorded language. Thus, *within the PLC structure, evidences of learning from the learner's point of view are revealed*. As the figure-of-eight flow of the Learning Conversation shifts to the life-relevance level or to the learning-to-learn level, the quality of the support dialogue required to shift the conversational flowback to the central PLC becomes an indicator of the tensions and inner struggles involved in 'challenging the robots' (Chapter 3), in attempting to break into new ground, and in coping with a temporary drop in skill followed by spurts of growth. *An analysis of the support dialogue reveals the otherwise hidden evidences of processes of learning.*

As learning at this deeper experiential level is explored, attempts to *calibrate personal standards of skill begin to reveal themselves*. Initially, the referent dialogue in the Learning Conversation can be very rudimentary, as revealed by the type and limited range of criteria identified in the PLC. But as Self-Organised Learners become experienced in identifying their own criteria for evaluating the effectiveness of their learning, it becomes possible to track progress with the degree of control they exert on evaluating their own learning process.

Thus, the PLCs that have been completed through the use of all three dialogues and carried out by the learner with the Learning Coach, or by the learner alone, represent the first evidences of learning. If such sessions have involved a Learning Coach or a peer learner working in partnership, then such external Learning Conversations can be recorded with video or audio equipment, providing a rich source of evidence for the personal processes of learning.

The self-debrief One can look further into the PLC activities for evidences of learning. In Chapter 5 we referred to the three temporal perspectives built into the PLC heuristic—the negotiating learning phase, the action phase and the retrospective review phase. During the action phase of the PLC, learners are guided to reflect on and to review their learning as this is taking place. We explained how the MA(R)4S heuristic can be used to guide this activity. In the best possible scenario learners are offered some facility to record their actions (video records, computer logs, time charts, or human observer). These are then used for self-debrief sessions, to heighten awareness, and Chapter 6 offered some examples. Self-debrief carried out in this way is a very different process to an 'expert-debrief', which is often practised in traditional training situations. Micro teaching is one such example. 'Sitting by Nellie' and being told what to do, how to do it and what was done wrongly is another. Self-debriefs of actions within Personal Learning Contracts provide behavioural explanations of learning from the learner's point of view. *These sessions form a rich source of evidence of learning.*

The review phase of the PLC

As part of the PLC heuristic, the retrospective review phase elicits in structured form a comparison between 'before' and 'after' learning. Purposes, strategies, and outcome evaluation criteria are compared. The differences in these temporal perspectives, centred around a particular learning event, provide a source of evidence about how the learning process is progressing. The learner's summaries of these in assessments of his or her strengths and weaknesses (areas of skills and knowledge which are in need of development) become indicators of personal evaluation.

Thus, the Learning Conversation methodology with its built-in reflective tools offers abundant sources of evidence of learning from the learner's own point of view. Through personal experimentation Self-Organised Learners discover how to become responsible for using themselves as the primary referent for evaluating the quality of their learning. Our reference to Carl Rogers and his concept of freedom-to-learn in the General Introduction can now be better appreciated as part of the SOL approach. The learners learn to place trust in themselves and use the whole experience with all their senses as a test bed for judging the quality of the learning process and the learning outcomes. The criteria must arise from each individual's own process.

The accumulating evidences of learning, as revealed within a series of PLCs, form a very useful resource within the conversational evaluation model. Evidences of learning from the learner's point of view are entered onto columns 2, 3, 4 and 5 of Figure 7.1. In practice, the SOL Coach or the Learning Manager can work with individual learners to record this information.

Other perspectives on learning

Individuals and teams learn in some social context, whether it be in education or on training courses and workshops, in the work situation, or in the professions. *Self-Organised Learners are able to work out and identify for themselves the values and criteria behind the judgements of others, who may be significant observers and participants in their learning activities, and may be involved in assessing their learning outcomes.* These external referents become sources for feedback-for-learning. Such referents are accustomed to calibrating their own learning, once they recognise their value and they fall into place as part of the learner's own evolving evaluation system. This is partly what is meant by the 'conversational' evaluation model. This process begins with a self-assessment, but this is based on the criteria of others.

Self-assessment and the criteria of others

The 'self-debrief' referred to earlier is not the same procedure as self-assessment. In the former case, the Self-Organised Learners rely exclusively on the referents generated from within their deeply personal processes of learning. The learners' needs and purposes, tactics and strategies, knowledge and skills, beliefs and values combine to identify criteria for evaluating the quality and outcome of learning arising from within their process. In the latter case, the *learners look outwards, seek criteria beyond their own boundaries and explore how any or all of these can be integrated into their own evaluative system so that they are enabled to expand their horizons.* This is a very different process to that of submitting to the criteria of 'experts' as an authority which must be obeyed, thus inevitably divorcing their own value systems from those in the public, outside world.

Self-organised learners can use the formal assessment situation—i.e. the junior supervisor or manager being appraised on a weekly or monthly basis by a boss—as an opportunity to better integrate their self-assessment with others' assessments of their performance and achievements. For example, in our Post Office project, every supervisor within trial offices were given copies of the weekly assessment sheets and asked to assess themselves on the criteria listed on the schedule. Having completed this with their own notes and explanations, they proactively introduced this assessment into the formal session with their second-line manager. This proved to be an extremely successful activity and a learning experience for both parties. The second-line managers often reported that they were 'put on their mettle' and had to rethink their own judgements, sometimes in ways leading to significant shifts in their own value systems. *This process was not one way*, in many cases the more junior supervisors were positively challenged to defend their positions, and to justify their own stands in detail overall. It was very interesting to observe that the junior supervisors involved in this project were much more differentiated in their use of grades on all the criteria within the assessment schedule, being prepared to use all five classes of grades in assessing themselves. Their bosses, on the other hand, were much more cautious, and the distribution of their grades clustered very densely in the middle grade range, that is Band C. This is hardly an assessment situation to generate a detailed and refined feedback for a self-development programme.

Figure 7.2 offers an example of three assessment sessions, illustrating a learner's self-assessment attempts and his bosses' assessment using the same criteria. Where they disagreed, the SOL site coach was invited to act as arbiter, and to work closely with the learner to resolve what should be done. Supervisors reported this to be an extremely productive experience, which enabled them to rethink their own position and to better understand their bosses' values.

Supervisors within the same dedicated teams were also encouraged to work together, exchanging with each other their own self-assessments before they were assessed by their boss. The Learning Coach on site supported this on-the-job learning activity, and liaised with the team leader, i.e. the second-line supervisor, bringing this leader into the exercise as an additional resource.

FEEDBACK FOR SELF-ORGANISED LEARNING

ACTING P.E.D. .... 'JOHN' ....

RECORD OF DUTIES AND APPRAISALS

DATE: JAN – MARCH (WEEKLY)

DUTY (P.E.D. OR P.H.G. + TRAINING)

CRITERIA:

Filled in by P.E.C.S. 'PEARSON'	7 SELF	7 BOSS	11 SELF	11 BOSS	7 SELF	7 BOSS
01 Knowledge of work area	D	C+	C+	C+	B	B+
01 Knowledge of other work areas	E	D+	C	C+	C+	B–
02 Quick to grasp essentials	C	D–	C	B–	B	B
03 Receptive to new ideas	C+	D+	B	B–	B+	B+
03 Provides constructive criticism	C	D	B+	C	B+	B+
04 Acts/works well under pressure	C	C	C	C	C+	B
05 Welcomes responsibility and advice	E	C–	B	C+	B+	B
06 Gets cooperation and respect	E	C	D–	C+	B	B+
07 Applies rules sensibly	D	D–	D	D	A	B
08 Guides and informs other staff	C–	C	C+	C	A	B
09 Encourages staff skills	E	B–	B+	B–	B	B–
09 Firm, tactful fault correction	C	C	B	B–	B	B–
010 Good verbal expression	C+	C–	C+	C+	B–	C+
010 Good written expression	E	D–	D	D–	C–	C+

| Overall performance of higher duties | D | D+ | C | C+ | B | B |

RECORD OF LEARNING CONVERSATIONS

Purpose	✓	✓	✓	✓	✓	✓	✓	✓		
Strategy	✓	✓	✓	✓	✓	✓	✓	✓	✓	
Outcome	✓	✓	✓	✓	✓	✓	✓	✓	✓	✓
Review		✓	✓	✓	✓	✓	✓	✓	✓	✓

Figure 7.2 Conversational assessment sessions at the Post Office

One example of assessment concerns a Self-Organised Learner who was working in an industrial setting, had just been promoted to a junior supervisory post, and was given weekly appraisals before being confirmed in his post. One of his duties involved working a night shift, where he was the most senior person in the post at a particular location. His boss, who did not work at nights, thought it was reasonable to give the supervisor a 'C' rating for his week of night duty on the grounds that he was unable to check the supervisor's work and could therefore only give him an average grade. The learner said that he would not accept the grading as he felt that such an appraisal was misleading. The two had a Learning Conversation about the value and purpose of appraisal as well as the possible effects of rating a member of staff without seeing any evidence of performance. The boss then attended the shift, for the first time, one night, stayed, assessed and had Learning Conversations with the supervisor. This resulted in a much more effective appraisal from the learner's and the organisation's point of view, and a far more positive working and learning relationship between the two. The learner said that he felt that without SOL he probably would have grudgingly accepted the 'C' grades because he would not know how to handle such a situation and would have accepted that the boss 'knows best'. Another example involved a sales representative who used two repertory grids to represent her evolving learning on team work; the first grid was completed at the outset of her learning and the second, CHANGE grid, reflected how she had developed after learning to be a more effective team player for four weeks. She used the grids to have a Learning Conversation with her sales manager who, although she noticed a distinct difference in the improvements in communication and support by the representative towards her colleagues, had no idea how comprehensive and sophisticated her learning in team working had become. The sales manager was able to alter her criteria for assessing the quality of team work as a result.

Charting a learner's progress

As part of his PhD thesis, Ian, one of the co-authors, produced a conversational evaluation chart for encouraging learners to discuss and chart their progress in becoming self-organised. A simple version of the chart with 30 steps is illustrated in Figure 7.3. The chart was based on the three stages towards becoming a Self-Organised Learner (see Figure 1.1, page 8) and shows 30 sub-steps towards the goal of becoming a fully effective Self-Organised Learner. This, of course, is a lifetime's work and no one is ever likely to claim that they cannot improve their competence at being a Self-Organised Learner, still it was helpful to identify that as a goal.

It is important to point out that the steps between base and 20 are considerably easier than between 20 and the ultimate goal of 30. This is highlighted in the chart by the first 20 steps being tightly compacted and the remaining 10 being spread much further apart. In the true self-organised manner, the author did not set criteria for each step; instead

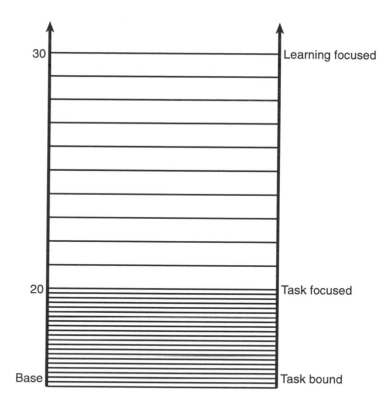

Figure 7.3 *Conversational chart for evaluating progress as a Self-Organised Learner*

he invited learners to rate themselves on the scale of 1 to 30 and converse about why they felt they were at this step. The importance of this approach lies in having a framework for conversing and validating competence in learning, not in defining the criteria for competence based on 'expert' values. Learners will also find that they are likely to rate themselves at one point on the chart and later in time, although they have progressed in competence, may rate themselves at a lower point in the chart. Learning conversations on this are very important as the learner will have developed a more sophisticated framework for validating competence in learning, and it is important for the learner to stand back and reflect on how this shift in values has taken place. *As learners become more and more sophisticated in their approach to validating learning, they will define a range of criteria within each step of the chart.*

The Personal Learning Biography

The conversational evaluation model referred to earlier forms the basis for the Personal Learning Biography (PLB). The Learning Conversation evolves from an initial centring on the learner's own personally generated criteria for evaluation towards the perspectives of 'significant others'. Basically, this requires no more than a social, educational, or work context and a good information system, and allows learners to extend their horizon of values. The self-assessment and expert-assessment conversational examples already referred to illustrate this.

Anchored within their own evaluative system learners can converse with others (peer learners in learning partnerships, bosses, tutors and experts) who may be responsible for making judgements on their performance, i.e. outcomes of learning. The effectiveness of each learner (worker, supervisor, manager, student, teacher and trainer) depends on how their model of the tasks, duties and skills, and 'job' works in practice. This is assessed primarily by themselves, and then by each of those in the 'chain of command' responsible for providing adequate feedback. The terms and timing of the feedback defines the evaluation system.

Two major problems that confront learners are:

1 Individuals have rarely been given opportunities to assess their own learning, and they often do not know how.
2 As individuals attempt to expand their frame of reference, they need feedback, and seldom is the information system structured in ways that are operationally helpful.

If Self-Organised Learning is to grow, and if a pluralistic evaluation system is to be allowed to develop, then others in the social and organisational setting making up the learner's world must also learn to change their paradigm of values. The examples already given show that a conversational evaluation process involves a learning experience for the evaluators as well as the learners. As Self-Organised Learners seek increasingly valid feedback, so the whole assessment system has to be sharpened up. Criteria vary from person to person, from department to department, from one institution to another and from one examining body to another.

The function of the PLB is to support and record this multi-perspective evaluation process. *The PLB is specifically designed as a tool for extending the Learning Conversation by inviting the learners and others who may be involved in making judgements about them, both informally and formally, to participate in a Learning Conversation which focuses on exchanging the value systems involved in performance assessment.* These values can all be represented within the format of the PLB.

Definition and evaluation of SOL

Now, to return to the definition of SOL. In this chapter we have been concerned with referents for learning; how progress in learning can be measured. As learners CONSTRUCT, RECONSTRUCT AND EXCHANGE their PERSONALLY SIGNIFICANT, RELEVANT AND VIABLE MEANINGS they need a *referent system* to calibrate their learning processes. The conversational evaluation model and the PLB introduced in this chapter provides this. Figures 7.4(a) and (b) and 7.5 give two examples of PLBs. Comments from the manager detailed in Figure 7.4 are given on page 133.

DATE	PARTICIPATION IN SOL ACTIVITIES	EVIDENCE OF LEARNING		OUTCOMES ASSOCIATED WITH SOL		
		Learner's own view Changes in attitude and understanding	Others' observations Changes in the learner's behaviour	Outcomes valued by the learner	Outcomes valued by the Post Office	
					'Subjectively' assessed	'Objectively' measured
June	Feasibility L. ints	Awareness of personal problem-solving algorithm		Able to think more about planning	Produced a chart (1) for planning a project	Used on national coaches course & seminars for LM's.
Feb	Ind. L. Conv. – 'Looking at sections with a planning eye'	Two problems identified: (I) Tidy vs messy How this affects the floor (II) Need for incentives at the grass roots	Began to have sleepless nights. Began to talk to himself silently at home about job in P.O.	Began to keep an SOL diary. Deep insight gained on process of reflection	National steering committee welcomed a project on tidiness. P.O. did not respond to report (II)	REPORT (2) to head postmaster & to boss 'The P.O. & reorganisation – the broad horizon'
March	Ind. L. Convs. – 'How to set up a tidy project'	Developed a method and learnt SOL techniques, e.g. L. int. & rep. grid int.	Started L. interviews with selected staff in delivery	Dev. skills in L. int. Got staff thinking about tidiness – on the job	Produced a provisional plan for project, approved by SOL team (I)	
	Ind. L. Convs. – 'The job of the PEC'	Consolidation of his views & expansion in thinking about staff development	Confidence gained – greater participation in L. Conv's & in SOL coach learn meetings	Helped him in his planning project for MLO manager. Thought more about idea of 'coaching'	Report to MLO manager on return letter branch PH6 insp. very well received; & some suggestion made about becoming (organisation) chief in due course. Produced a chart (3) for the job of a PEC.	
April	Ind. L. Convs. – 'How can I involve myself as SOL coach'	Able to distinguish more clearly between training & learning	Attended SOL coach lunchtime meetings and became more supportive of acting PES(D) course.	A new way of thinking about learning – from 'the hard way' to SOL support. Produced a paper (4) on 'Reflections on SOL'. Saw coaching as part of his job	Produced a learning biography (4) of personal learning in P.O. Made useful suggesting re acting course. Ray's paper (5) circulated to L. coaches national network.	
May	3-day SOL coach workshop plus 2-day follow-up	Is talking to oneself 'a bit of madness' – insight into reflection and review of one's process	Negotiated coaching time with boss – first 4-6 hrs which later reduced to 2 hrs p.w.			
June	Ind. L. Convs. – Re 'SOL-tidy project' and continuing	New insights into:- (I) SOL approach (II) Casualties of disorder/untidiness on the floor	Improved interview techniques	Staff interviewed became more aware of tidiness on the floor	Delivery area generally tidied Flow chart (6) on his plan for P.O. reorganisation re PM & PHG grades produced	Less 'bad take overs' – from shift to shift – effect on throughputs? No response to date

© The Centre for the Study of Human Learning

Figure 7.4(a)   A senior manager (Planning): a Personal Learning Biography

		EVIDENCE OF LEARNING		OUTCOMES ASSOCIATED WITH SOL		
DATE	PARTICIPATION IN SOL ACTIVITIES	Learner's own view — Changes in attitude and understanding	Others' observations — Changes in the learner's behaviour	Outcomes valued by the learner	Outcomes valued by the Post Office — 'Subjectively' assessed	Outcomes valued by the Post Office — 'Objectively' measured
June / July	Ray SOL's PESD, acting PESD & PESC in delivery (and elsewhere where possible – individual ints / paired ints)	Developed a structured understanding of effects of untidiness through exploration with staff	Tried to negotiate more coaching time but failed because of pressures on planning. More participative in SOL activities in Reading P.O.	Notion of a learning coach more and more appealing. Other coaches and PESC got involved in his 'tidy' project, e.g. in OLO & station.	Produced summary (7) sheets (8) concluding causes & effects relating to tidiness & medium–long-term planning of project. OLO & station generally tidier, including offices. Produced report (9) on his project.	Effects on throughputs. on safety on morale to be checked?
July	Attended PESC Basingstoke wkshop	Became more optimistic – thought his pessimism about PESC taking on SOL unjustified	Tried to talk more to his boss about SOL (who also came to Basingstoke)			
Sept / Oct	Ray's contribution to substantive PESD workshop on his tidy project	Greater awareness of resistance to change amongst older supervisors	Carried out some more ind. L. Convs informally with substantives re tidy project when possible	Some PESD begin to think more about consequences untidiness and apply themselves to be tidier & keep areas tidy. They requested more bins (e.g. P. Treasure in delivery) Unsure of 'planning' response so far	Some PESD begin to incorporate notion of orderliness in personal work plans.	
Nov			Ray quietly places bins in delivery & OLO. Ray starts making notices to display information re his project	Felt unsure of Xmas arrangements	Produced a paper (10) on 'The enemy of SOL – fear'	Cost-effective changes to be expected as a result? Post codes in town area (to formulate up to date records). Report is now being used by P.O. constructively.
Sept / Oct / Nov	Attending ind. L. Convs with Sheila regularly	Continues to develop his thinking about planning, e.g. (1) alternative problem solving; (2) how cost-effectiveness methods and quality of service relate to planning. Early planning for Xmas arrangements made with P. Hood informally, Ray to learn more about PESB responsibilities re Xmas, stats, etc. (expecting PEB temp. post). Discovered that 'Management plans for Xmas not well thought out.' Got worried about his own progress if taking B post on board with a novice team. Got worried too for P.O.	More critical and rigorous in his analysis of planning briefs. Started negotiating with P. Hood but told he was off soon to parcels. Enquired about Xmas plans. Refused PESB temp. 'To shake management to think more about planning Xmas arrangements' & to ensure that there would be no drop in Q of S re Xmas. Ray applies for D. Simpson B post. Thinks he can apply coaching skills in this job	Lost opportunity to learn & practise at B level for Xmas but P. Hood brought back for Xmas, good for P.O. Intends to learn more from Hood this time'. Doesn't think he'll get it but would welcome it as a challenge	Produced a report to his boss sharply critical of current practices in an office. Thinks that he probably (Ray) 'deserves to lose out as a result of his behaviour'. Not usual not to accept Temp. B opportunity. Waiting for response	Xmas arrangements expected to go off smoothly with 'old team' back again P. Hood — B R. Watson — C † usual — D staff

© The Centre for the Study of Human Learning

Figure 7.4(b) Extract from a personal learning biography

DATE	PARTICIPATION IN SOL ACTIVITIES	EVIDENCE OF LEARNING		OUTCOMES ASSOCIATED WITH SOL		
		Learner's own view — Changes in attitude and understanding	Others' observations — Changes in the learner's behaviour	Outcomes valued by the learner	Outcomes valued by the Post Office — 'Subjectively' assessed	Outcomes valued by the Post Office — 'Objectively' measured
March – April	SOL meetings with LOM (LM) & 2 other chiefs re SOL policy, organisation and resources	Very gradual shift from seeing staff dev. as task-centred and training resourced to learning-centred with resources for learning 'on the job'	More positive actions to support SOL activities as these affected his area		Still a hard directive chief	
May	SOL & staff appraisal elicitation of chiefs criteria for dev. of SOL feedback/ appraisal package. Results of 1st round of computer analysis of PEB & PEC responses fed back	Gradual dev. of understanding of function of learning in staff. dev. More sympathetic to SOL approach. Learning from experience on the job less to do with time, i.e. no. of years, and more to do with learning skills & dev. of task expertise	Less confrontal oral in promotion meetings. More useful comments re staff competence	New insights gained into other chiefs and PESC views on acting men	More sensitive approach to staff (annual counselling and daily briefs)	
June	SOL support in annual counselling/appraisal sessions: confidential	Considerably enhanced confidence in conducting annual appraisal interviews, especially 'tricky ones'	More frequent follow-up dialogues with PESC concerned – better rapport with individual PESC re job competence and incompetence and 'personal problems'	Better daily working relationship with his men		
July	Attended Basingstoke encounter weekend and participated in L. Conv role-play exercise	Increased confidence in SOL approach for himself	Much more sensitive to others' needs and purposes	Sees 'change' as something relevant to him – a mind-blowing experience	PESC began to see him in a new light	

 © The Centre for the Study of Human Learning

Figure 7.5 Personal learning biography of a chief inspector (*continues*)

DATE	PARTICIPATION IN SOL ACTIVITIES	EVIDENCE OF LEARNING		OUTCOMES ASSOCIATED WITH SOL		
		Learner's own view — Changes in attitude and understanding	Others' observations — Changes in the learner's behaviour	Outcomes valued by the learner	Outcomes valued by the Post Office	
					'Subjectively' assessed	'Objectively' measured
Sept	Attended national LM seminar (CHSL)	Began to appreciate national significance of managing staff learning	More supportive of SOL activities at Reading – especially in relation to a PESD. Used results of feedback for learning/appraisal package for decision making re promotion of acting men	Sees SOL within an ever-increasing perspective	PESD & PESC value 'personal' changes in chiefs' approach to them – a transformation. Offers more feedback & advice to CHSL team re operations. Makes more use of the learning coach system	
	Involved in on-going SOL meetings with M. – SOL 318 & locs project. (with G.D. & CHSL TEAM)	Greater understanding of a theory of a control as a feedback for individuals' performance on the job	Used SOL 318 project as a resource for review of 318 duties in his area and created his own special duty project recruiting a newly promoted acting man to complement this	Began to recognise a chief's function as a learning manager	Control proformas in OLO in process of revision	
	Visited Tonbridge with PED on 318 special project to inspect their software					
Oct Dec	Supported SOL substantive PED workshops	More confidence in tasks as chief. More skill in managing control data	Made sure his men were available for SOL workshops. More discussions with MLO manager re SOL. Called his men to thank them for the way they responded during Xmas period. Goes on developing new ways of dealing with staff on operations on his floor		New control forms developed for his area. MLO manager recognises and values improvement in his management skills. Three named PESC comments:- Before SOL – he was loud in instructions on the floor and a bit of a bully. After SOL – more adult, more thinking, more dedicated, more confident, more appreciative of his staff	

© The Centre for the Study of Human Learning

Figure 7.5 Personal learning biography of a chief inspector (continued)

Reflections on a PLB by a senior planning manager

— A lifetime of learning in the Post Office.
— From PM to PHG through the BARRIER to Supervisor is a *very hard jump.*
— Acting man is in 'no man's land'.
  Postmen and PHGs have their own Union.
  Supervisors have their own Union.
— No open shop.
— No support.
— No instruction/training.
— Had to learn *on my own* against a background of resentment from PM and PHGs; very much a Service-type model—out of the ranks.
— PEsD and PEsC (i.e. my managers) not too forthcoming.
— I learnt *the hard way* and it took a long time
  — by always watching
  — asking when I could.
— Learnt to take responsibilities on ME as I could.

I found it all quite hard

and now

SOL—has removed some of the *obstacles to my own learning*
—no longer so hard
—I *do* enjoy it
—I've learnt new thinking skills
—responsibility can now joyfully grow.

I would stay on another five *years* if they gave me a chance.

The SOL spreadsheet

In an action research project with the Post Office, the SOL spreadsheet was developed as a procedure for collecting the relevant data, which was later summarised and recorded within the PLB as shown. The spreadsheet includes relevant evidences collected from within each learner's PLCs but is represented in coded form. It also includes evidences from the evaluations of others. These evidences are first agreed with each learner, with due regard to confidentiality. The spreadsheet also includes self-assessment records, regular assessments by the learner's boss or bosses, and the annual appraisal. Such assessments are based on criteria issued by the Post Office headquarters. Later we introduced the feedback-for-learning system which elicits criteria based on local values, and analyses the judgements made on these criteria to maximise feedback. This is described in Chapter 8, which explains how this SOL tool was used to drive the engine of change in a learning organisation.

The SOL spreadsheet and the PLB are used by the learners, their SOL coach and the Learning Manager, to coordinate a series of Learning Conversations on the job, creating a systems approach to SOL. This is also described in Chapter 8.

Summary

In this chapter we have introduced a pluralistic conversational evaluation system for charting the progress of a learner and we have shown how this works. The Personal Learning Biography (PLB) and the SOL spreadsheet are powerful tools which provide Feedback-for-Learning on the one hand, and evidences for the evaluation of learning on the other. This approach allows the values of learners, the coaches and professional experts to be integrated into a fully-functioning evaluation system.

Suggested activity

Identifying your assessment model of learning

To challenge you to reconsider some core issues that need to be resolved before learning can be effectively measured, we now summarise some of these and invite you to carry out an evaluative exercise. This is divided into three stages.

Stage I

Read through the questionnaire on learning and mark your responses to each question by ticking one of the boxes, either yes or no, as most appropriate to you. Should you feel that you almost agree with a statement BUT there are aspects with which you are uncomfortable, then, in the spirit of SOL, rewrite the statement in your own terms in the spaces below each question.

Stage II

When you have completed the questionnaire, cut out those statements with which you are in agreement, sort them into groups, and give each group a descriptive heading as you have done previously in the structures of meaning activity (Chapter 2). As you sort, consider 'which question goes with which'. This structure will represent your model of learning, at least in part. Consider how your model influences the manner in which you set about assessing learning.

Stage III

Take any assessment questionnaires or any other assessment systems with which you may be familiar and put them into two piles: one pile represents those with which you are in broad agreement, the other represents those you do not feel are adequate assessment measures. Now, take those assessment measures you agree with and see to what extent they compare with the statements you agree with in the questionnaire. Similarly, take those assessment measures you are unhappy with and see how they measure up to the statements you rejected.

Now, consider the evidences before you and ask yourself if you fall into the 'pluralistic' evaluation camp or the traditional 'expert'-based evaluation camp.

Note

The questionnaire has been developed by CSHL who owns the copyright. Should you find it useful, we give you full permission to use it as a reflective tool on your own courses or workshops. You could also use it as a pre- and post-'test' course evaluation device. The Statistics Package for Social Scientists (SPSS) can be used to help you analyse your results. You will be able to see if there are any significant changes in the values of your clients/learners as a result of the events on your course.

CSHL questionnaire on learning

Yes   No

1 The acquisition of appropriate knowledge, skills, attitudes should be measured against publicly/ professionally acknowledged standards.

2 The achievement of valued standards in behaviour should be assessed against a predetermined *norm*.

3 In learning, the construction of personal experience is the most important factor.

4 Learning involves conversing with oneself and others about personal processes of development. This involves as much feeling as thought.

5 Learning involves the construction, reconstruction, exchange and negotiation of personally significant, relevant and viable meanings with awareness and controlled purposiveness.

6 Meanings generated from our experience are the basis of our anticipations and actions.

7 All learning may be measured in changes of behaviour and any other so-called forms of learning are without value as they cannot be measured.

8 Learning involves a change of behaviour which is observable evidence to an external observer as well as a development in experience which is only directly accessible to the learner.

9 'Cause and effect' as understood by the behaviourists cannot be appropriate for explaining learning. A stimulus does not control a response. It is the meaning given to a stimulus which guides the response.

10 Within a paradigm of conversational science, events in the outside world do not produce predictable consequences; it is the meaning attributed to events which become the 'conversational cause'.

11 Learners are like empty vessels, pour in the knowledge, skill and develop the right attitude and you will have an effective learner that will pass a predetermined test.

12 If you find a top performer, then you will find a top teacher/trainer.

13 Learning involves process, content and outcomes. Each perspective is of equal importance.

14 Learners should have the inner freedom and skills to define their own learning and assess its quality.

15 Individuals develop their own 'theories' about everything they experience.

16 The most socially useful learning in the modern world, according to Carl Rogers, is the learning of the processes of learning, a continuing openness to experience and incorporation into oneself of the process of change.

17 Evaluation by others is of secondary importance.

18 Learning involves successfully submitting to being taught, trained and instructed, in accordance with clearly defined behavioural objectives.

19 When workshop/training event behavioural objectives are agreed by an employing organisation, and have been tested successfully by a trainer, then the learning event has been a success.

20 Behaviour modification of the learner by the trainer is a vital part of learning.

Yes No

21 Learning requires reflectivity and awareness.

22 Reliability involves repeatability and consistency of results.

23 Validity must be judged according to predetermined norms, involving statistical averaging and testing within large samples of populations.

24 Objectivity depends on statistically valid, and well-tested measures. These relate to absolute criteria of truth.

25 Reliability as defined traditionally is an inappropriate measure of learning, since learning involves personal change.

26 Validity can only be defined within the learner's own processes, the way purposes are defined, resources explored, and meaning is represented based on prior knowledge and experience.

27 Objectivity is only valid when the criteria are agreed by learners and teachers/trainers.

28 Questionnaires that offer profiles of behavioural performance give a valid measure of learning.

29 Questionnaires that offer profiles of styles of management/teamwork/decision making, etc., give a valid measure of performance.

30 Serialist, holist, lateralist, conservationist and gambler are best seen as some of the identified strategies of learning, rather than as style of learning.

31 Cognitive schemata, as defined by Piaget, are appropriate measures of learning.

32 Bloom's classification of knowledge provides useful and educational training objectives with benchmarks for measuring progress in learning.

33 Personal Learning Contracts are useful and systematic devices for measuring learning.

34 The only valid experience of learning is measured through performance tests.

35 Personal experience of learning is best measured conversationally.

Yes   No

36 Control groups are essential to calibrate the effectiveness of learning.

37 The only valid control is that defined by the Self-Organised Learner who conversationally sets the parameters for personal change.

38 The learner supported by a tutor, Learning Coach, counsellor, etc., negotiates multiple criteria which can be used as measures of learning from different points of view.

39 The learner is in active conversation with the learning resource as part of the domain of learning, and is personally involved in researching his or her own meaning constructing process.

40 An 'expert's' primary role is to resource the learner, offering tools, procedures and personal involvement in this process.

41 The experimenter, researcher, teacher and trainer must be in control of the learning.

42 The learning situation must be pre-planned and the tests for measuring learning must be determined in advance.

43 The learner must be in control of learning as an open-ended creative activity.

44 The experimenter, tutor, trainer and the learner together act as full participants in a joint enterprise.

45 Learners recognise that learning involves a unique action research expertise centred on themselves, their learning projects and their learning skills.

46 Researchers implied contracts with learners mean that the data is analysed according to the objectives set by the researcher.

47 Researchers should involve their clients in the processes taking place, sharing purposes and resources, and mutually cooperating in the data analysis so that everyone learns from the experience.

Please add any statements about assessing learning that you may feel have been left out of the questionnaire but are important to you.

8 Installing a system of Learning Conversations

Agenda board

- Individuals, teams and a system of Learning Conversations
- The SOL Systems 7: an environment for change
- Feedback-for-Learning: the engine of SOL
- A new role for the training practitioner: to empower learning organisations
- The conversational evaluation of SOL
- Suggested activity: constructing, deconstructing and reconstructing your job description

Individuals, teams and a system of Learning Conversations

Learners who are enabled through SOL to develop their capacity to learn, on the job, in college, and in life become more competent, involved and motivated. They perform more effectively because they are able to bring their better evaluated experience to bear on each new situation and every learning event. *They have learnt how to sustain a Learning Conversation with themselves.*

A Learning Coach may initiate a Learning Conversation with individuals in whom this process has either become dormant, or is in need of improvement in power and quality. Those individuals who are already reflecting on their experience and reviewing their progress, can always continue to improve. Throughout this book we have introduced reflective techniques and tools, which augment the power of the Learning Conversation. Over time and through personal experimentation and support, an individual's capacity for learning continues to develop, resulting in improved skill, competence and creativity.

In Chapter 2 we explored how personal myths, rigidly held beliefs, values, attitudes and prejudices can be challenged to open up an individual's horizons for learning. In Chapter 3 we showed how the various conversational uses of the repertory grid can be used for modelling the experience of learning. A better understanding of how one learns becomes a major stepping stone for personal change. Chapters 4, 5 and 6 addressed the method, techniques and procedures of the Learning Conversation. The Personal Learning Contract was introduced as a major tool for Self-Organised Learning. Chapter 7 dealt with issues and procedures for measuring learning, how an individual progresses and how changes in thoughts, feelings and actions can be evaluated for effectiveness. A conversational evaluation model was introduced, which is discussed again in this chapter.

The increased capacity for learning that is released through 'challenging personal robots', on-going reflection, and reviewing personal skills and competences is the 'fuel' that drives the SOL process forward to produce changes that result in improved performance. Released in this way, the SOL process continues to develop through life.

Where an organisation is concerned, it becomes necessary to ask the question: How can this capacity for learning at the individual level be harnessed into a system, enabling the development of SOL for the benefit of working groups, teams, and the organisation as a whole?

This last chapter deals in the issues concerned with creating a system of Learning Conversations. Unless this system is effectively installed and managed, SOL will remain, at best, a series of *ad hoc* experiences within isolated pockets of the organisation. *Effectively led and managed, the SOL system gradually evolves and has the power to transform at the leading edge of a learning organisation.*

SOL can be applied to activities in a group. Any group who share a common purpose—a family, a sports team, a project group, or even a whole enterprise—can function as one integrated learning unit. Through group Learning Conversations members of a team can share their 'personal knowing'. All the techniques and procedures we have described in this book can be used in a group situation. A 'learning group' becomes more than 'the sum of its parts'; its learning power is augmented and its effects can be dramatic. Such a group becomes a 'learning entity'. Gradually the idea of an SOL enterprise emerges. Let us examine this further.

An environment for constructive change— Systems 7

Learners become more effective as they work with the SOL coach and with each other to identify what it is they should be learning. It is here that a tasks supervisor who is a *Domain Expert* begins to contribute. This function is concerned with creating better opportunities for learning, beyond those of offering expert instruction. These opportunities must be concerned with 'real life', 'on the job' or 'project type' events, so designed to extend, refine and elaborate the experiences of learners. *The domain which forms the substrate of the intended learning is enriched and manipulated to enhance feedback about learning, as learning is taking place.* It is the Domain Expert's job to generate the information which provides learners with 'knowledge of results'. Such results can take the form of both 'subjective measures' and 'objective measures', as discussed previously in Chapter 7.

Mini-activity

Readers might usefully pause here and imagine at least two or three scenarios in which a Domain Expert can effectively intervene to enrich the learning environment, by creating a wider repertoire of opportunities for learning. Once the idea of an SOL Domain Expert is understood, readers will be astounded at how easy such opportunities are to construct, and how infinite the possibilities can become. Training practitioners should consider what their role might be in learning situations involving a Domain Expert.

Towards a fully fledged SOL Systems 7

As the SOL Coach and the Domain Expert liaise with each other, and work with individual learners to enable them to become more effective, the Learning Conversations can be extended to groups of individuals learning as a team. Group Learning Conversations employ the same content-free reflective techniques, allowing all members of the group to not only explore their own learning but to exchange their learning experiences. The group becomes the 'learning entity' to be supported and enabled by the SOL

Coach and the Domain Expert. A production team experimenting with new procedures on a 'learning shift' would be one example of such a 'learning entity'. A group of students learning together on a project would be another.

While individuals and groups can both learn from experience within an organisation, this needs resourcing and managing, and the responsibility for this falls on the *Learning Manager*. The resources include all the techniques, tools and procedures of the Learning Conversation. They also include those that can usefully be invited to support some aspect of learning on the job. The Learning Manager monitors the processes of individual and group learning, by means of the evaluation measures described in Chapter 7 and referred to again at the end of this chapter. The SOL spreadsheet and the Personal Learning Biography are recruited to monitor the cumulative experiences of learning. It is also part of the Learning Manager's responsibility to ensure that the efforts of the SOL coach and the Domain Expert are being implemented in appropriate ways and that results are accruing that are valuable to the individuals, the teams and the organisation as a whole.

The Learning Manager reports to the *learning policy committee*. This committee is responsible for creating a 'learning policy' which contributes to the operational purposes of the organisation. It also oversees that the organisational objectives expand in response to the capabilities developing within the organisation.

We have now presented an overview of a system, illustrated in Figure 8.1, for maintaining and developing SOL in an organisation.

Let us now summarise the seven systems for operating SOL within an organisation.

- **System 1** The learner (node 2) and the learning domain (node 1).
- **System 2** The SOL coach (node 3) and the learner (node 2).
- **System 3** The SOL coach (node 3) and the tasks supervisor or Domain Expert (node 4).
- **System 4** The Learning Manager (node 5) and the SOL coach (node 3).
- **System 5** The Learning Manager (node 5) and the tasks supervisor or Domain Expert (node 4).
- **System 6** The tasks supervisor or Domain Expert (node 4) and the learning domain (node 2).
- **System 7** The Learning Manager (node 5) and the learning policy committee.

Together, these seven systems and five conversational nodes create an SOL environment which can facilitate change in an organisation. A quantum shift in skills, competences and attitudes takes place, resulting in improved business competitiveness and new visions.

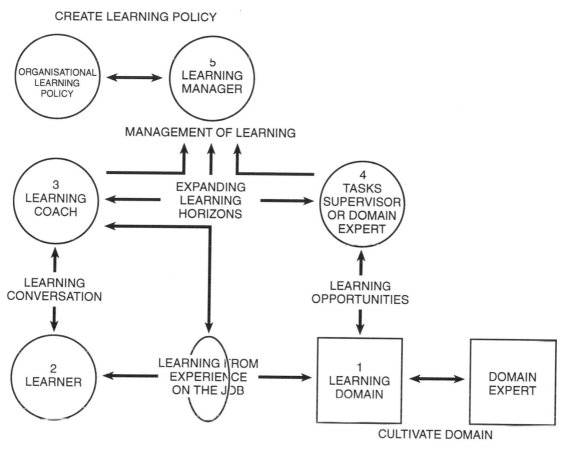

CREATE LEARNING POLICY

THE FIVE NODES OF SYSTEMS 7

Figure 8.1   *Developing SOL within an organisation: Systems 7*

System 1 represents the core Learning Conversation between each learner and his or her domain (work, study, leisure or social activities), always seeking improvement in performance and in learning competence.

System 2 represents the support Learning Conversations between each learner, or the learning group/team and their SOL coach, with the PLC as the primary tool.

System 3 represents conversations between the SOL coach and Domain Expert, seeking to explore ways of enriching the domain, expanding the horizons of learning.

System 4 represents conversations between the Learning Manager and the SOL coach for the effective management of learning with the SOL spreadsheet and Personal Learning Biography as the primary tools. As the system develops this conversation can be driven by the feedback-for-learning package referred to later in the chapter.

System 5 represents conversations between the Learning Manager and the Domain Expert, resourcing and creating more and more opportunities for learning.

System 6 represents conversations between the Domain Expert and the domain (people, artefacts, machines, paperwork, etc.) for an effective manipulation of that domain, ensuring better and richer learning opportunities.

System 7 represents conversations at executive level, generating an organisational learning policy.

There is also a 'hidden eighth' conversation which opens out the whole system into an ever-spiralling process of growth. This is generated by an insightful exploration of the creative tension which exists between work-focused organisational policies and learning-focused organisational policies. This can lead to fundamental changes in the trajectory of the enterprise. This, however, is rarely achieved, and we can count on one hand those world-class organisations that may have attained this collective 'peak experience'. Increasingly of late, enterprising small companies function on a policy of freedom-to-decide and freedom-to-learn for all their staff. This empowering process has already introduced a new dimension of quality but in itself this does not address learning.

Feedback-for-Learning: the engine for SOL

The power of the SOL Systems 7 for promoting an on-going capacity for change in an organisation can be augmented by a computer-based Feedback-for-Learning package devised and written by Thomas and Harri-Augstein. The package offers individual learners and learning teams systematic commentaries about their progress. The comments are generated by a range of people within the hierarchy of an organisation. By operating the package within an SOL Systems 7 environment the local values of work and professional effectiveness are identified. This is achieved by eliciting an interlocking system of criteria, which allows relative judgements to be made on a given scale. There is a variety of methods of analysis which can offer the following feedback:

1 To the learners so that they can diagnose their current capabilities in the context of those responsible for them.
2 To the learners and the SOL coach so that they can together initiate PLCs in relation to the judgements of the boss.
3 To the team of managers who are the local judges of performance, so that they can calibrate each others' subjective judgements and learn to improve them, as well as to use items 1 and 2 above to manage their teams more effectively.

It is important that the Learning Manager in Systems 7 should manage the operation of this Feedback-for-Learning package. This involves periodic collection of the evaluative data, and regularly monitoring and maintaining the process. Minimally, it involves a quarterly 'appraisal exercise' by those managers responsible for their teams and who are also responsible for developing each member of their team to improve total quality. The task requires computer analysis of the data, and communicating the results to all those involved. It requires that these results are acted upon and followed up by the learners themselves, the SOL coach and the Domain Expert. Finally, it also requires periodic updating of the locally elicited criteria to meet the changing local situations, values and needs.

The Learning Manager may require support for the above tasks. This suggests an interesting new role for the training practitioner.

- Who is responsible for the installation of the feedback-for-learning package within an organisation?
- Who is responsible for monitoring the quality of the results?
- Who is responsible for integrating the feedback-for-learning package into the SOL system as a whole?
- Who is responsible for resourcing this developing system?

These are some of the questions which the training practitioner needs to address. In addressing them, the practitioner can seek out new involvements, new responsibilities and new functions.

Part of the Institute of Personnel Management's 'Changing Frontiers' project has been to consider the role of personnel at top management level. We suggest that training practitioners familiar with the ideas, tools and practices of SOL should take up this challenge. They could become the enablers of learning organisations for today's competitive and fast-changing world. *To achieve this, training practitioners need to build new partnerships, and construct closer working relationships with the operational and support managers in an organisation.* They need to seek ways of maximising the integration of operations and learning on the job. They need to work within these partnerships to facilitate total ownership of organisational goals, particularly learning goals.

The training practitioner and learning organisations

Many attempts to create a learning organisation have failed, because intentions to change are organised around a theory or idea, and this is not enough. 'Total quality', 'empowerment' and 'leadership' are notions that can support those who have the insights and skills to translate them into action. But many managers do not possess these skills. Again, top management may produce a mission statement which is sold to their workforce in a communications exercise. But, often this exercise is one way, resulting in total failure or some minimal success. Without the shared understanding of the full operational implications of a new idea, they will flourish only to become 'fashions of the month'.

The capacity to take responsibility for one's own thoughts, feelings and actions, is the ability to organise one's own learning. An organisation made up of people who work together in this way is able to participate proactively in change. This is a learning organisation (Figure 8.2). The feedback-for-learning package briefly described is a mechanism by which the SOL Systems 7, made up of learners, the domain, the SOL coach, the Domain Expert and the Learning Manager working with leaders creating the learning policy can integrate these processes of learning which become the engine of change.

The training practitioner can resource this engine in many ways. The practitioner can work closely alongside the Learning Manager (or indeed, in some instances, becoming the Learning Manager at least temporarily), accepting responsibility for installing, maintaining and developing the SOL system as a whole. Such a fundamental change in the role of the training practitioner involves two paradigm shifts. The first involves a *fundamental shift in attitudes from a traditional view of training*, both centralised and local, *towards the more radical view of enabling learning*. This shift involves truly recognising the implications of a transformation in outlook from an instructional, expert-based mode to a learner-centred mode. The second paradigm shift is concerned with the *transformation in attitude towards learning itself.* 'Adaptive learning' sets a learning policy which is reactive, merely coping with changing events within a problem-solving, dealing-with-crises scenario. But 'generative learning', i.e. Self-Organised Learning, is proactive and opens up a more creative learning policy. This focuses on:

- anticipating future needs
- exploring new challenges
- inventing strategies for dealing with unexpected events
- new and creative ways of looking at the world
- new ways of competing successfully in the marketplace
- delivering total quality
- destructing inappropriate or old rules and regimes
- creating alternative futures with care and due regard for the environment.

The conversational evaluation of SOL

Many might philosophise that freedom to learn and to self-organise one's learning, for the individual, the team and the organisation, represents a *means and an end in itself*. However, let us stand back and *reconsider the various pay-offs*.

In the General Introduction we referred to some of the benefits to the individual, the learning team and the learning organisation. We end this chapter by reminding you of these within the wider context of action research and the need for evaluation. For over 20 years we have conducted action research in education, government, industrial, commercial and social contexts, based on developing a theoretical framework for SOL and the methodology of the Learning Conversation. The results

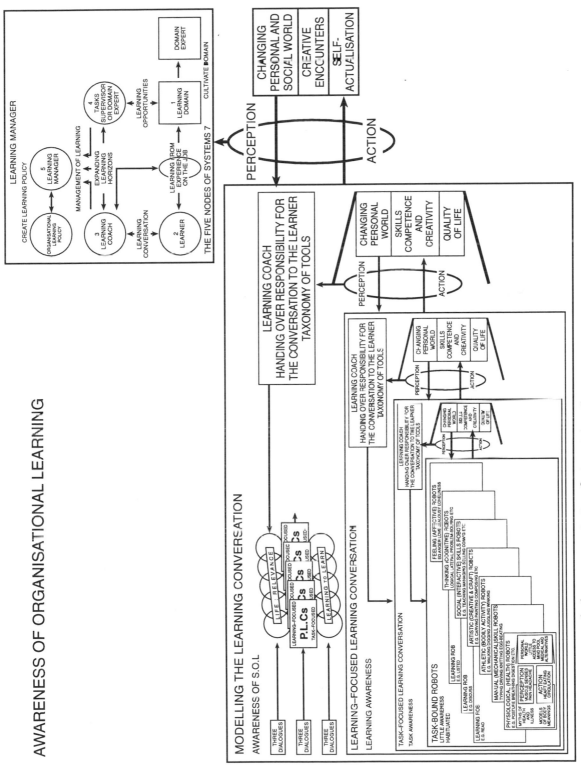

Figure 8.2 *Empowering the learning organisation: Systems 7 in action*

have been evaluated from many perspectives, in the short, medium and longer term. All we can do here is convey the flavour of these results, and refer you to the bibliography for fuller accounts.

In one project, higher education students used SOL techniques to improve their reading/writing and listening skills. Highly significant improvements were achieved, which were demonstrated to have transferred to other learning skills, such as learning by discussion, project work and preparing for examinations. A battery of measures based on a variety of pre- and post-tests and questionnaires all provided evidences which, together, corroborated to indicate highly significant advances in individual skills and competences. Examination results provided an additional measure of the success of SOL. The students involved in the project were in the highest quartile of exam grades, i.e. A and B for all the students examined in three academic subjects at the end of the year.

In one Ministry of Defence SOL project the eleven naval officers training to become air intercept controllers, all learnt to perform this very complex task to a much higher level of competence with greater skill and flexibility, and within a shorter time span than those trainees on the conventional training courses. They used both paper and pencil as well as computer-based PLC procedures as a resource for SOL. Each potential trainee goes through a stringent selection procedure prior to an intensive and expensive training, and normally less than one-third finally qualify. During the SOL project two-thirds of the trainees successfully completed the course and some of these became 'trainers' themselves.

One very experienced air intercept controller, who had been 'in action' in the Falklands war, used the Learning Conversation approach as a 'refresher' opportunity. He initiated a series of PLCs for himself, creating increasingly demanding and complex 'sorties'. He was able to experiment with hitherto unanticipated scenarios, flexibly initiate a variety of strategies and develop highly stringent criteria for evaluating his success. He valued the experience highly and became convinced that the SOL approach would have allowed him to have been more prepared for the demanding and unexpected situations he came across in the Falklands. In his words, no formal training could prepare him for the 'in anger' conditions, but SOL challenged him to compete with himself.

One major project involved installing and developing an SOL system in two large trial offices of the Royal Mail Letters business. This project also involved running a series of SOL workshops for operational managers to become SOL coaches supporting learning on the job. It also involved running seminars for senior managers enabling them to become Learning Managers. Over 350 SOL coaches attended these workshops, and over 150 senior managers attended the seminars. SOL was thus introduced to 82 offices throughout the country. Part of our brief was to develop an evaluation system, and to liaise with the Post Office steering committee to evaluate the results. *We developed a new model for evaluation: a matrix method for the 'conversational evaluation' of the results of SOL.* This was based on a development of the Personal Learning Biography procedure described in Chapter 7. Figure 7.1 (page 119) outlines the framework of the conversational model for recording and evaluating the results.

The conversational evaluation matrix for the Post Office project included three independent human observers, the learner's direct boss or the team leader, the SOL coach and the senior operational manager or chief inspector. Together, the learner's own view and others' observations corroborate the hypothesis that SOL activities and involvements initiated changes that are valued within the Post Office. Finally, in the Post Office additional 'objective measures' were also used as indicators of the success of SOL. In one of the trial offices during an 18-month evaluation period, productivity improved by 24 per cent. Quality of service improved by 2 per cent to 99 per cent for first-class mail, and by 5 per cent to 98 per cent for second-class mail, and over a 12-month period cost-effectiveness improved with costs per standard hour dropping by 19 per cent.

The original workshops for SOL coaches were evaluated by the Post Office as highly successful. All the coaches had attempted to implement some aspect of SOL in their office. Those that were supported by their Learning Manager went on to develop their own local brand of SOL. All these results of the project were evaluated in the short, medium and long term up to five years. A full report is available and is referred to in the Bibliography and Appendix C is an overview of an SOL Coach's job in the Post Office.

Summary

In this last chapter, we have only briefly been able to introduce you to the mechanisms, systems and technology through which an organisation can self-organise its learning. We have outlined the SOL Systems 7, and the feedback-for-learning technology which together power the engine for self organised change within an organisation. We have explored a new role for the training practitioner as a professional enabler of a learning organisation.

We have tried to convey some flavour of the range of benefits of SOL and to show how a conversational evaluation system has been developed for measuring its effects. Evidences from many of our projects have shown that SOL is not only valued for the qualitative results it achieves, but is also valued on measures based on objective assessments. *SOL is highly productive, cost-effective and contributes to improvements in total quality.*

This book is intended to be used as a tool for change by the training practitioner, training manager, operations manager, team leader, research and development manager, personnel manager, chief executive, teacher, lecturer, consultant and counsellor. Now that we are close to the end, we can only hope that the book has achieved this purpose, at least for some readers. We now invite you to engage in one last Learning Conversation involving two earlier activities you were asked to initiate in the General Introduction, Chapters 1 and 2.

Suggested activity

Constructing, deconstructing and reconstructing your job description: trainer or enabler of learning?

At the end of the General Introduction we invited you to produce specifications for a design brief for a 3-day event focusing on processes of learning for about 30 participants. The suggested activity in Chapter 1 indicated how you might take this further. We also invited you to return to this activity as you felt this to be appropriate. At the end of Chapter 2 we introduced you to an activity which enabled you to represent in a structured form your 'personal myths', i.e. your own beliefs, values, prejudices and attitudes towards the job of being a 'trainer'. We suggested that you continued to reflect on these personal myths as you worked through this book. In Chapter 3 we offered some mini-exercises to help you to model personal experiences of learning, and the activity at the end of that chapter showed you how you could use the repertory grid to elicit a model of managing people. You may by now have carried out a series of Personal Learning Contracts, as described in Chapters 4, 5 and 6, based on further developing your 'professional self' as a training practitioner.

You may feel that you have expanded your horizons and developed some new skills. In the General Introduction we stressed the importance of first experimenting on yourself, gaining personal insights of the SOL approach and method of the Learning Conversation before working with others. In this chapter our aim has been to challenge you further. We have outlined our vision of the changing role of the training practitioner—as a 'learning practitioner', i.e. a professional enabler of learning organisations. We have briefly described a systems approach to SOL to encourage you to consider the ways in which the training practitioner might support and resource this process in an organisation. Towards the end of this chapter we suggested that, depending on the current myths/values you may hold, two paradigm shifts were necessary for training practitioners to transform their views of their jobs.

Now, we suggest you begin this final activity by taking the following actions:

1 Review your personal myths
- Explore once more the pattern of relationships made explicit by your own 'structure of meaning', as revealed in the 'suggested activity' in Chapter 2.
- What does this pattern of representing your 'images of learning'

reveal about your values and myths as a training practitioner?

2 **Reflect on your approach to your job**

- Use this representation, which identifies 'where you were' when you began work on this book, to reflect on 'where you now are' and 'where you might ideally like to be' in terms of your job.
- Re-examine the original cards on which you recorded your tasks/ topics on one side and your thoughts/ feelings/'images of learning', on the other side.
- Keep a record of this original structure of meaning or personal map, showing how the cards clustered into a pattern of values representing your personal myths.
- Shuffle your original cards into a random order.
- Add new cards, i.e. those recording tasks/topics which are new to you and related thoughts/feelings—in other words, images of learning.
- Reflect on your reactions to each chapter of this book and use this experience to add further tasks/topics and images of learning.
- Reflect on all the activities you may have carried out.
- Continue to add as many cards as you can, until you 'exhaust your repertoire of items relating to personal experience'.
- Remember these can include imagined items as 'possible experiences in the future which seem right to me'.
- Now, when you feel ready, begin to sort out the cards into a NEW STRUCTURE—A NEW PATTERN OF MEANING. If you are unsure how to continue, please refer to the guide notes in activity on page 22. [*A word of advice. Do not look at your original representation, although you need to look at your original cards.*]
- As you reflect and the emerging clusters of cards begin to form, be prepared to discard any card or cards that you no longer consider to be appropriate.
- Continue until you have created a new STRUCTURE OF MEANING, recording the best possible representation of your current personal myths and values as a training practitioner.

3 **Compare the old structure of meaning with the new structure of meaning**

- Examine the cards you may have discarded.
- What do these tell you about your changing values?
- Compare each new cluster of cards against your original clusters.
- How different are the two clusters?
- Have your descriptions of the clusters changed?
- Have the items or cards been redistributed among the clusters?
- Where do the new cards locate in relation to the old?
- Explore the new pattern of relationships made explicit in your STRUCTURE OF MEANING.
- What does this pattern as a whole tell you about the 'images of learning you value'?
- Have your values/myths changed? If so how?

4 Review

- Use the results of this comparison to review the nature of how you approach your job, your tasks and your activities as you currently see them.
- Stay with the possibility that you may still need to make a paradigm shift in your ways of thinking about your job. In the first and last analysis, the decisions you make are truly your own. It is definitely not part of the philosophy of SOL to attempt to instruct, train or expertly insist that this approach is the 'new panacea' for trainers, managers and teachers. But it is in the spirit of SOL to challenge, to provoke, to encourage you to construct alternative viewpoints and to persuade, if not insist, that you develop stringent criteria to justify your own position, whatever this may be.

Creatively converse and spiral

This activity has been intended to invite you to engage in a Learning Conversation with yourself. It is designed to support your own quest for synergy, your personal exploration, generating a creative tension between 'where you have been', 'where you are now' and 'where you might choose to be' as a professional enabler of others' learning.

Epilogue

Through the medium of this book as a whole we have attempted to invite you to have a Learning Conversation with us. We hope that we have at least, to some extent, been successful. You might consider that one measure of success would be your own personal definition of SOL! Why not have a go at this right now!

So! What about your definition of Self-Organised Learning?

Towards the end of each chapter we have reviewed the CSHL definition of Self-Organised Learning. We choose to end as we began by reminding you of the original definitions, from earlier in the book:

Self-Organised Learning (SOL) is a process which has to be personally experienced in order to be properly understood. Here we shall start with a basic definition which will become more personally meaningful as readers work through the book. By using the book as a resource for their practice, readers can develop an appreciation of how SOL can empower the person, on the job and in life.

SOL is defined as:

*The personal construction of **meaning**—a system of 'personal knowing'*

and

*Meaning is the basis for all our **actions.***

Let us now expand on this definition, introducing a *new dimension*. Self-Organised Learning is:

The conversational construction, reconstruction and exchange of personally *significant, relevant* and *viable* meanings, with *purposiveness* and *controlled awareness*. The patterns of meaning we construct are the basis for all our actions.

Spiralling onwards and outwards we now present our own **personal** and idiosyncratic definitions!

Sheila's definition of SOL

LEARNING IS THE CONSTRUCTION OF PERSONAL COMPLEXITY. THIS PROCESS PROACTIVELY COUNTERACTS THE FORCES OF DISORDER. THE SELF-ORGANISED LEARNER RAGES AGAINST THE DYING OF THE LIGHT! LEARNING IS A CHALLENGING, PAINFUL, JOYOUS AND SELF-FULFILLING ACTIVITY. IT IS A PERSONAL STORY IN THE ADVENTURE OF LIFE. WE SHOULD ALL RESPECT THIS UNIQUE PROCESS IN OURSELVES AND IN OTHERS. IF WE STOP LEARNING WE MAY AS WELL BE DEAD!

Ian's definition of SOL

LEARNING IS ABOUT OUR PERSONAL VOYAGE OF DEEP INNER SELF - DISCOVERY. IT CANNOT BE REDUCED TO BLINDLY FOLLOWING RULES SET UP BY OTHERS. IT INVOLVES CHALLENGING AUTOMATIC, ROBOTIC BEHAVIOUR AND BEING DEMANDING AS A LEARNER BOTH OF OTHERS AND OURSELVES. SELF-ORGANISED LEARNING IS A LIFETIME'S WORK WITH TREMENDOUS PERSONAL PAY-OFFS. WITHOUT LEARNING WE REMAIN STATIC AND UNCHANGED.

Pob Lwc
Viel Glück
Good luck
Sheila

Good Luck!

Ian Webb

Appendix A: The CSHL Feedback-for-Learning package: an example

APPRAISER'S NAME:

Self-appraisal by top management team

PART A. MY RATING OF HOW WELL KNOWN THE colleague IS TO ME

Very well known to me											Unknown to me
RATED 1	1	2	3	4	5	6	7	8	9	10	RATED 5
	S t B	M i J	D a S	K e P S	I a K	J o J	C h D	A L	J o M	T o C	
RATED 1	1	2	3	4	5	6	7	8	9	10	RATED 5

PART B. MY RATINGS OF EACH colleague ON THE FOLLOWING CRITERIA

	1	2	3	4	5	6	7	8	9	10	
Achieves goals through cooperation											Dominates staff to achieve goals
Keeps everyone informed about what is going on											Keeps information to themselves
Helps others to discover their potential by involvement											Restricts the development of others by exclusion
Gives real consideration to other people's ideas											Dismisses other people's ideas
Believes employees should take initiative											Believes management should make all decisions
Readily responds to requests for help											Responds with reluctance to requests for help
Provides what is needed to get the job done											Provides inappropriate resources to help people
Seeks staff involvement in developing procedures											Requires staff to follow management devised procedures
Gets out of the way of those doing the job											Maintains a controlling presence
Really listens and communicates in a friendly way											Disregards other people's feelings when communicating
Allows capable people to do the job their way											Places limits on people's ability to do jobs
Actively promotes staff development											Appears to have no interest in staff development
Provides the right response when asked for help											Responds inappropriately when asked for help
Shows trust in ability of staff											Appears to distrust ability of staff
Is sensitive to the feelings of staff											Appears to disregard the feelings of staff
Listens to what staff have to say											Hears staff but does not listen

Self-appraisal by top management team

CSHL APPRAISER GRID BY Ch_____ D_____ (One appraiser's judgements of all colleagues)

SPACED (BY TOTAL OF RATINGS – EQUALLY WEIGHTED)

CONSTRUCT POLE RATED – 1 (left) / CONSTRUCT POLE RATED – 5 (right)

#	Construct (Rated 1)	Ke_ P (BEST)	Jo_ P (AVERAGE)	Jo_ M	Da_ M	Al_ S	St_ L	To_ B	Jo_ C	Ch_ J	Ila_ K_ D	Mi_ J (WORST)	Construct (Rated 5)
1	Achieves goals thro' cooperat'n ...	3	4	3	4	3	4	5	4	5	5	5	Dominates staff to ach' goals ...
2	Keeps everyone informed ...	2	2	3	4	4	4	4	4	4	4	4	Keeps info. to themselves ...
3	Helps others to discover pot'l ...	3	3	3	4	3	3	4	4	4	4	4	Restricts others' development ...
4	Real consideration to o' ideas ...	3	3	3	3	3	4	3	4	4	3	4	Dismisses others' ideas ...
5	Believes in employees' init've ...	2	3	4	3	3	4	4	5	4	4	4	Believes man't sh'd make decs ...
6	Readily responds to requests ...	4	4	5	5	5	5	4	4	5	5	5	Responds reluctantly to ...
7	Provides what is needed to ...	3	4	3	3	4	4	3	4	3	4	4	Provides inapprop' resources ...
8	Seeks staff involvement in ...	3	3	3	4	4	4	4	4	4	5	5	Requires staff to follow 'nan' ...
9	Gets out of the way of those ...	2	3	3	4	2	3	4	4	4	5	5	Maintains a controlling 'pres' ...
10	Really listens and com'ates in ...	3	2	4	4	4	5	4	4	3	5	5	Disregards others' feelings ...
11	Allows c' people to do own way ...	3	3	3	3	4	3	4	4	4	5	5	Places limits on people's ab' ...
12	Actively promotes staff devel' ...	4	4	5	4	3	5	4	4	4	5	5	No interest in staff develo ...
13	Right resp' when asked f help ...	3	3	4	5	5	5	4	4	5	5	5	Inapprop' response when asked ...
14	Shows trust in abil'y of staff ...	3	3	3	3	3	3	4	4	4	5	5	Appears to distrust ab'y o' st' ...
15	Is sensitive to staff feelings ...	2	3	4	3	3	3	3	4	4	5	5	Appears to disregard feelings ...
16	Listens to what staff ... say ...	2	4	2	3	3	3	4	4	5	5	5	Hears staff but doesn't listen ...

BEST colleague: Ke_ P_____ (1)
AVERAGE colleague: Jo_ P_____ (1)
Jo__ M_____ (1)
Da_ M_____ (1)
Al__ S_____ (1)
St_____ L_____ (1)
To_____ B_____ (1)
Jo__ C_____ (1)
Ch____ J_____ (1)
Ila_ K____ D_____ (1)
WORST colleague: Mi__ J _____ (1)

The numbers in the '( )' are the 'HOW WELL KNOWN' ratings

Colleagues not known to appraiser Ch_____ D_____ : NONE

© The Centre for the Study of Human Learning

Self-appraisal by top management team

CSHL APPRAISER GRID BY Ia_ K___ (One appraiser's judgement of all colleagues)

SPACED (BY TOTAL OF RATINGS – EQUALLY WEIGHTED)

CONSTRUCT POLE RATED – 1

Construct (pole rated 1)	E122	E106	E101	E103	E080	E085	E010	E094	E109	E010	E104	E017	E013
1 Achieves goals thro' cooperat'n ...	1	2	2	2	2	2	2	2	3	2	4	4	4
2 Keeps everyone informed ...	2	2	3	4	4	4	4	4	4	4	4	5	5
3 Helps others to discover pot'l ...	2	2	3	2	2	4	2	2	3	2	2	4	4
4 Real consideration to o' ideas ...	2	2	2	2	2	2	2	2	2	4	2	4	4
5 Believes in employees' init've ...	1	1	3	3	3	2	1	4	4	4	4	4	4
6 Readily responds to requests ...	2	2	2	2	2	2	4	4	4	4	2	2	4
7 Provides what is needed to ...	2	2	2	2	2	2	4	4	3	4	4	2	4
8 Seeks staff involvement in ...	2	2	2	2	2	4	2	2	4	2	4	4	4
9 Gets out of the way of those ...	2	4	3	2	4	2	4	4	4	4	4	4	4
10 Really listens and com'ates in ...	2	2	2	2	2	2	2	2	2	2	4	4	4
11 Allows c' people to do own way ...	1	1	2	1	1	2	3	2	2	2	2	2	4
12 Actively promotes staff devel' ...	2	2	4	4	4	4	4	4	4	4	4	4	4
13 Right resp' when asked f help ...	2	2	3	3	4	2	4	3	4	4	4	4	4
14 Shows trust in abil'y of staff ...	1	2	1	1	2	2	1	2	2	2	2	2	2
15 Is sensitive to staff feelings ...	2	2	3	2	3	4	2	2	4	2	2	2	4
16 Listens to what staff ... say ...	2	2	2	2	2	2	3	4	4	4	4	4	4

CONSTRUCT POLE RATED – 5

1 Dominates staff to ach' goals ...
2 Keeps info. to themselves ...
3 Restricts others' development ...
4 Dismisses others' ideas ...
5 Believes man't sh'd make decs ...
6 Responds reluctantly to ...
7 Provides inapprop' resources ...
8 Requires staff to follow man' ...
9 Maintains a controlling pres' ...
10 Disregards others' feelings ...
11 Places limits on people's ab' ...
12 No interest in staff develo' ...
13 Inapprop' response when asked ...
14 Appears to distrust abl'y of st' ...
15 Appears to disregard feelings ...
16 Hears staff but doesn't listen ...

Element labels:
- BEST colleague
- Mi__ J
- Jo__ J (1)
- Da__ J (1) — AVERAGE colleague
- Al__ S (1)
- Ia_ L (1)
- To_ K (1)
- Jo_ C (1)
- Ke_ M (1)
- St_ P (1)
- Ch_ B (1)
- ...D (1) — WORST colleague

The numbers in the '( )' are the 'HOW WELL KNOWN' ratings
Colleagues not known to appraiser Ia_ K___ : NONE

© The Centre for the Study of Human Learning

Self-appraisal by top management team

CSHL APPRAISER GRID BY Jo__ J____ (One appraiser's judgement of all colleagues)

SPACED (BY TOTAL OF RATINGS – EQUALLY WEIGHTED)

CONSTRUCT POLE RATED – 1   CONSTRUCT POLE RATED – 5

	E102	E121	E016	E009	E008	E003	E005	E010	E004	E007	E001	E011	E013	
1 Achieves goals thro' cooperat'n …	2	2	2	2	2	3	2	2	4	3	4	4	4	1 Dominates staff to ach' goals …
2 Keeps everyone informed …	2	3	4	3	4	3	4	3	3	4	5	4	4	2 Keeps info. to themselves …
3 Helps others to discover pot'l …	2	2	2	2	3	3	3	2	2	4	5	5	5	3 Restricts others' development …
4 Real consideration to o'ideas …	1	2	3	3	2	2	2	3	3	4	4	4	4	4 Dismisses others' ideas …
5 Believes in employees' init've …	2	2	2	2	2	2	2	2	2	2	2	2	2	5 Believes man't sh'd make decs …
6 Readily responds to requests …	1	1	2	2	2	3	2	2	2	2	3	3	3	6 Responds reluctantly to …
7 Provides what is needed to …	2	2	2	2	2	2	2	2	2	3	2	3	3	7 Provides inapprop' resources …
8 Seeks staff involvement in …	2	2	2	1	3	3	3	2	3	3	3	3	4	8 Requires staff to follow man' …
9 Gets out of the way of those …	1	1	3	3	2	3	3	3	4	4	4	4	4	9 Maintains a controlling pres' …
10 Really listens and com'ates in …	2	2	2	2	2	2	2	3	2	3	3	4	4	10 Disregards others' feelings …
11 Allows c' people to do own way …	2	2	3	2	2	2	3	3	2	3	3	3	3	11 Places limits on people's ab' …
12 Actively promotes staff devel' …	2	3	2	3	3	3	3	3	3	4	4	4	4	12 No interest in staff develo' …
13 Right resp' when asked f help …	2	2	2	2	2	2	2	2	1	2	2	2	2	13 Inapprop' response when asked …
14 Shows trust in abil'y of staff …	1	1	1	1	2	1	2	3	1	3	3	3	3	14 Appears to distrust aby of st' …
15 Is sensitive to staff feelings …	1	2	2	2	2	2	3	3	2	3	3	3	3	15 Appears to disregard feelings …
16 Listens to what staff … say …	2	2	2	2	2	3	3	2	2	3	2	4	4	16 Hears staff but doesn't listen …

BEST colleague — Mi__ J____
Jo__ J____
AVERAGE colleague — Jo__ J____
Al__ M____ (1)
Da__ L____ (1)
Ia_ S____ (1)
To__ K____ (1)
Ke_ C____ (1)
Ch__ P____ (1)
D____ (1)
St___ B____ (1) — WORST colleague

The numbers in the '( )' are the 'HOW WELL KNOWN' ratings
Colleagues not known to appraiser Jo__ J____ : NONE

© The Centre for the Study of Human Learning

Self-appraisal by top management team

CSHL APPRAISER GRID BY Ch_____ D_____   (One appraiser's judgement of all colleagues)

FULLY SPACE FOCUSED

CONSTRUCT POLE RATED – 1 (left poles):

C6 / C13	Readily responds to requests … / Right resp' when asked' help …
C1	Achieves goals thro' cooperat'n …
C11 / C14 / C8 / C12	Allows c' people to do own way … / Shows trust in abil'y of staff … / Seeks staff involvement in … / Actively promotes staff devel' …
C7 / C4	Provides what is needed to … / Real consideration to o'ideas …
C3 / C9	Helps others to discover pot'l … / Gets out of the way of those …
C16 / C15 / C5	Listens to what staff … say … / Is sensitive to staff feelings … / Believes in employees init've …
C2	Keeps everyone informed…
C10	Really listens and com'ates in…

CONSTRUCT POLE RATED – 5 (right poles):

Code	Right pole
C6 / C13	Responds reluctantly to… / Inapprop' response when asked…
C1	Dominates staff to ach' goals…
C11 / C14 / C8 / C12	Places limits on people's ab'… / Appears to distrust ab'y of st'… / Requires staff to follow man'… / No interest in staff develo'…
C7 / C4	Provides inapprop' resources… / Dismisses others' ideas…
C3 / C9	Restricts others' development… / Maintains a controlling pres'…
C16 / C15 / C5	Hears staff but doesn't listen… / Appears to disregard feelings… / Believes man't sh'd make decs…
C2	Keeps info. to themselves…
C10	Disregards others' feelings…

Elements (colleagues) — dendrogram order:

- Jo__ M_____ (1) — BEST colleague
- Ke_ P_____ (1)
- Al_ L_____ (1) — AVERAGE colleague
- Jo_ L_____ (1)
- Ch__ J_____ (1)
- Ia_ K___ D___ (1)
- To_ C_____ (1)
- St_____ B_____ (1)
- Da___ S_____ (1)
- Mi__ J_____ (1) — WORST colleague

The numbers in the '( )' are the 'HOW WELL KNOWN' ratings

Colleagues not known to appraiser Ch_____ D_____ : NONE

© The Centre for the Study of Human Learning

Self-appraisal by top management team

CSHL APPRAISER GRID BY Jo__ J____ (One appraiser's judgement of all colleagues)

FULLY SPACE FOCUSED

CONSTRUCT POLE RATED – 1 / CONSTRUCT POLE RATED – 5

Construct	Pole rated 1	E102	E109	E004	E010	E003	E008	E011	E016	E005	E017	E010	E01_	Code	Pole rated 5
C14	Shows trust in abil'y of staff …	1	1	2	2	3	1	1	2	2	3	3	3	C14	Appears to distrust ab'y of st …
C6	Readily responds to requests …	1	1	2	3	3	2	2	3	3	3	3	3	C6	Responds reluctantly to …
C15	Is sensitive to staff feelings …	1	2	3	2	3	2	2	3	3	3	3	3	C15	Appears to disregard feelings …
C7	Provides what is needed to …	2	2	2	2	2	2	2	2	2	3	3	2	C7	Provides inapprop' resources …
C5	Believes in employees init've …	2	2	2	2	2	2	2	3	2	2	2	2	C5	Believes man't sh'd make decs …
C13	Right resp' when asked f help …	2	2	2	2	2	2	2	2	3	3	2	2	C13	Inapprop' response wh'n asked …
C11	Allows c' people to do own way …	2	2	2	2	2	2	2	2	3	3	3	2	C11	Places limits on people's ab' …
C16	Listens to what staff … say …	2	2	2	2	2	2	2	2	3	4	4	3	C16	Hears staff but doesn't listen …
C1	Achieves goals thro' cooperat'n …	2	2	4	2	3	2	2	3	3	3	4	4	C1	Dominates staff to ach' goals …
C10	Really listens and com'ates in …	2	2	3	2	2	3	2	2	3	3	3	4	C10	Disregards others' feelings …
C4	Real consideration to o' ideas …	1	1	3	2	2	2	3	3	2	2	4	4	C4	Dismisses other's ideas …
C9	Gets out of the way of those …	1	1	4	3	3	2	2	1	3	4	4	4	C9	Maintains a controlling pres' …
C8	Seeks staff involvement in …	2	2	3	3	3	2	3	1	3	4	4	3	C8	Requires staff to follow 'man' …
C3	Helps others to discover pot'l …	2	2	2	3	3	3	3	2	3	4	5	4	C3	Restricts others' development' …
C12	Actively promotes staff devel' …	2	2	3	3	3	3	3	3	3	4	4	4	C12	No interest in staff develo' …
C2	Keeps everyone informed …	2	2	3	3	3	3	4	4	4	4	4	4	C2	Keeps info. to themselves …

Element columns (left to right), with 'HOW WELL KNOWN' ratings in ( ):

- Mi__ J____ — BEST colleague
- Jo__ J____
- Ke__ M____ (1)
- To__ P____ (1)
- Da__ C____ (1)
- Al__ L____ (1)
- Jo__ J____ — AVERAGE colleague (1)
- Ia__ K____ (1)
- Ch__ K____ (1)
- St____ D____ (1)
- B____ — WORST colleague (1)

The numbers in the '( )' are the 'HOW WELL KNOWN' ratings

Colleagues not known to appraiser Jo__ J____ : NONE

© The Centre for the Study of Human Learning

161

Self-appraisal by top management team

CSHL APPRAISER GRID BY Ia_ K___   (One appraiser's judgement of all colleagues)

FULLY SPACE FOCUSED

Code	CONSTRUCT POLE RATED – 1	E02	E12	E06	E03	E11	E15	E18	E13	E14	E17	E04	E09	Code	CONSTRUCT POLE RATED – 5
RC15	Appears to disregard feelings ...	4	2	4	4	4	2	2	4	3	4	4	4	RC15	Is sensitive to staff feelings ...
RC4	Dismisses others' ideas	4	2	4	4	2	4	4	4	4	4	4	4	RC4	Real consideration to o' ideas ...
C12	Actively promotes staff devel' ...	2	2	4	2	5	4	4	4	3	4	4	4	C12	No interest in staff develo' ...
C2	Keeps everyone informed ...	2	2	4	4	5	4	4	4	3	4	4	4	C2	Keeps info. to themselves ...
C10	Really listens and com'ates in ...	2	2	4	2	2	4	2	2	2	4	2	2	C10	Disregards others' feelings ...
C9	Gets out of the way of those ...	2	2	2	2	4	4	4	4	4	4	4	3	C9	Maintains a controlling pres' ...
C3	Helps others to discover pot'l ...	2	2	2	2	4	4	4	4	4	3	2	4	C3	Restricts others' development ...
C8	Seeks staff involvement in ...	2	2	2	2	4	4	4	4	4	3	2	4	C8	Requires staff to follow man' ...
C16	Listens to what staff ... say ...	2	2	2	2	4	4	4	4	4	4	4	4	C16	Hears staff but doesn't listen ...
C1	Achieves goals thro' cooperat'n ...	2	1	2	1	4	2	2	2	4	3	4	4	C1	Dominates staff to ach' goals ...
C11	Allows c' people to do own way ...	1	1	2	2	4	2	2	2	4	3	2	2	C11	Places limits on people's ab' ...
C14	Shows trust in abil'y of staff	2	1	1	1	2	2	2	2	3	4	2	2	C14	Appears to distrust ab'y of st' ...
C7	Provides what is needed to ...	2	2	2	2	4	4	4	4	4	4	3	4	C7	Provides inapprop' resources ...
C6	Readily responds to requests ...	2	2	4	3	4	2	3	2	4	2	2	4	C6	Responds reluctantly to ....
C13	Right resp' when asked f help ...	2	2	4	3	2	2	2	4	4	4	3	4	C13	Inapprop' response when asked ...
C5	Believes in employees' init've ...	1	1	4	4	2	3	2	4	4	4	4	4	C5	Believes man't sh'd make decs ...

Element labels:

- Mi__ J__ (1)
- Jo__ J__ (1) — BEST colleague
- Da__ J__ (1)
- Da__ S___ (1) — AVERAGE colleague
- Ia__ S___ (1)
- Ia_ K___ (1)
- Al__ K___ (1)
- St____ L ___(1)
- Ch____ B ___(1) — WORST colleague
- To__ D___(1)
- Ke_ C____(1)
- Jo__ M____(1)

The numbers in the '( )' are the 'HOW WELL KNOWN' ratings

Colleagues not known to appraiser Ia_ K__: NONE

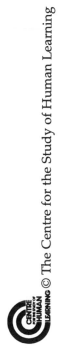

Self-appraisal by top management team

CSHL APPRAISER GRID FOR – AVERAGE APPRAISER VIEW –

SPACED (BY TOTAL OF RATINGS – EQUALLY WEIGHTED)

CONSTRUCT POLE RATED – 1

1	Achieves goals thro' cooperat'n ...
2	Keeps everyone informed ...
3	Helps others to discover pot'l ...
4	Real consideration to o' ideas ...
5	Believes in employees' init've ...
6	Readily responds to requests ...
7	Provides what is needed to ...
8	Seeks staff involvement in ...
9	Gets out of the way of those ...
10	Really listens and com'ates in ...
11	Allows c' people to do own way ...
12	Actively promotes staff devel' ...
13	Right resp' when asked f help ...
14	Shows trust in abil'y of staff ...
15	Is sensitive to staff feelings ...
16	Listen to what staff ... say ...

CONSTRUCT POLE RATED – 5

1	Dominates staff to ach' goals ...
2	Keeps info. to themselves ...
3	Restricts others' development ...
4	Dismisses others' ideas ...
5	Believes man't sh'd make decs ...
6	Responds reluctantly to ...
7	Provides inapprop' resources ...
8	Requires staff to follow man' ...
9	Maintains a controlling p'res' ...
10	Disregards others' feelings ...
11	Places limits on people's ab' ...
12	No interest in staff develo' ...
13	Inapprop' response when asked ...
14	Appears to distrust ab'y of st' ...
15	Appears to disregard feelings ...
16	Hears staff but doesn't listen ...

Dendrogram colleague labels (left to right):

- AVERAGE colleague
- BEST colleague
- To_ C___
- Al__ C___
- Da__ L___ (1)
- Mi__ S___ (1)
- Jo__ J___ (1)
- Jo__ J___ (1)
- Ia_ M___ (1)
- Ke_ K___ (1)
- St___ P___ (1)
- Ch___ B___ (1)
- D___ (1)
- WORST colleague

The numbers in the '( )' are the 'HOW WELL KNOWN' ratings

Colleagues not known to AVERAGE appraiser VIEW: NONE

© The Centre for the Study of Human Learning

163

Self-appraisal by top management team

CSHL COLLEAGUE GRID FOR Ch_____ D_____ (Each appraiser's judgements of one colleague)

SPACED (BY TOTAL OF RATINGS – EQUALLY WEIGHTED)

CONSTRUCT POLE RATED – 1 ... CONSTRUCT POLE RATED – 5

Construct (pole 1)	#	E12	E04	E08	E013	E10	E016	E09	E05	E07	E01	E13	#	Construct (pole 5)
Achieves goals thro' cooperat'n ...	1	2	2	3	2	3	4	3	4	4	4	4	1	Dominates staff to ach' goals ...
Keeps everyone informed ...	2	3	3	2	4	3	3	4	4	4	4	4	2	Keeps info. to themselves ...
Helps others to discover pot'l ...	3	3	2	3	2	3	4	4	2	4	4	4	3	Restricts others' development ...
Real consideration to o' ideas ...	4	2	3	2	4	3	2	3	2	2	4	4	4	Dismisses others' ideas ...
Believes in employees' init've ...	5	1	1	2	3	3	3	2	2	4	4	4	5	Believes man't sh'd make decs ...
Readily responds to requests ...	6	2	2	1	4	2	2	2	2	2	4	5	6	Responds reluctantly to ...
Provides what is needed to ...	7	1	2	2	3	2	3	3	2	2	5	4	7	Provides inapprop' resources ...
Seeks staff involvement in ...	8	3	4	3	3	3	4	3	3	4	4	5	8	Requires staff to follow man' ...
Gets out of the way of those ...	9	2	2	4	2	4	4	4	5	4	5	4	9	Maintains a controlling pres' ...
Really listens and com'ates in ...	10	1	1	3	3	3	3	3	3	4	4	4	10	Disregards others' feelings ...
Allows c' people to do own way ...	11	2	4	3	2	4	3	3	4	3	4	4	11	Places limits on people's ab' ...
Actively promotes staff devel' ...	12	1	1	2	1	1	2	2	2	2	4	4	12	No interest in staff develo' ...
Right resp' when asked f help ...	13	2	2	2	2	3	2	1	2	3	4	4	13	Inapprop' response when asked ...
Shows trust in abil'y of staff ...	14	2	2	4	4	3	3	2	3	3	4	4	14	Appears to distrust ab'y of st' ...
Is sensitive to staff feelings ...	15	2	2	3	3	4	4	4	3	4	4	4	15	Appears to disregard feelings ...
Listen to what staff ... say ...	16	2	2	3	3	4	4	4	3	4	4	4	16	Hears staff but doesn't listen ...

Appraiser views (BEST → WORST):

- Mi_ J___ (1) — BEST appraiser VIEW
- Ke_ P___ (1)
- Al__ L___ (1)
- Da__ S___ (1)
- St___ S___ (1)
- To___ B___ (1) — AVERAGE appraiser VIEW
- Jo__ C___ (1)
- Jo__ J___ (1)
- Ia_ M___ (1)
- Ia_ K___ (1)
- Ch__ D____ (1) — WORST appraiser VIEW

The numbers in the '( )' are the 'HOW WELL KNOWN' ratings
Appraisers not knowing the colleague Ch_____ D_____: NONE

Self-appraisal by top management team

CSHL APPRAISER CRITERIA CALIBRATION GRID FOR – Allows c' people to do own way –

(All appraisers' judgements of all colleagues on ore criteria)

FULLY SPACE FOCUSED

CONSTRUCT POLE RATED – 1		E1 2	E1 0 8	E0 8 6	E0 6 3	E0 1 1	E1 0 2	E0 0 7	E0 0 9	E0 0 4	E0 1 0	E1 0 0	E1 0 5	E1 – 13		CONSTRUCT POLE RATED – 5
BEST appraiser VIEW	C12	1	1	1	1	1	1	2	2	1	2	2	2	2	C12	BEST appraiser VIEW
Da__ S____	C3	2	2	2	2	2	3	2	2	3	4	3	5	5	C3	Da__ S____
Ke_ P_____	C4	1	1	1	2	2	3	2	4	1	4	4	4	4	C4	Ke_ P_____
Ia_ K___	C5	1	1	1	2	2	1	4	4	2	3	2	4	4	C5	Ia_ K___
St___ B____	C1	1	2	1	2	2	2	3	4	4	3	2	4	4	C1	St___ B____
Mi_ J ____	C2	1	2	1	2	2	1	2	4	4	3	2	4	4	C2	Mi_ J ____
Al_ L____	C8	2	2	2	2	2	3	3	3	4	3	3	4	4	C8	Al_ L____
Jo__ M____	C9	2	2	2	2	2	3	4	2	2	3	3	4	4	C9	Jo__ M____
Jo__ J____	C6	2	2	2	2	2	2	3	2	2	2	3	3	3	C6	Jo__ J____
AVERAGE appraiser VIEW	C11	2	3	2	2	2	2	3	3	3	2	3	3	3	C11	AVERAGE appraiser VIEW
To__ C____	C10	2	2	3	2	2	2	3	3	3	2	3	3		C10	To__ C____
Ch___ D____	RC7	3	2	2	2	2	1	2	3	3	3	2	2	5	RC7	Ch___ D____
WORST appraiser VIEW	RC13	3	2	2	2	1	1	2	2	3	3	1	1	5	RC13	WORST appraiser VIEW

BEST colleague
Al_ L____ (1)
Jo__ J____
Da__ S____
AVERAGE colleague VIEW
Mi_ J____
Ch____ J____
Jo____ D____
Ke_ P____ M____
To__ C____
St__ C____
Ia_ K____ B____
WORST colleague

© The Centre for the Study of Human Learning

Appendix B: Examples of PLC and grid forms

THE PERSONAL LEARNING CONTRACT FORM
PLAN – Negotiating the contract

BEFORE

NAME

TOPIC AND TASK FOR LEARNING

P U R P O S E — **PURPOSES FOR LEARNING:** What is my purpose?

S T R A T E G Y — **INTENDED STRATEGY:** What actions?

O U T C O M E — **DESIRED OUTCOME:** How shall I judge my success?

THE PERSONAL LEARNING CONTRACT FORM

AFTER – Reviewing the contract

NAME	Before and after differences		
	TOPIC AND TASK FOR LEARNING		
P U R P O S E	What actually was my purpose?	Compare purpose	What are my strengths?
S T R A T E G Y	What did I actually do?	Compare strategy	What are my weaknesses?
O U T C O M E	How well did I actually do?	Compare outcome	What shall I do next? Make plan for learning

© The Centre for the Study of Human Learning

169

Pair ✓	E1	E2	E3	E4	E5	E6	E7	E8	E9	E10	E11	E12	Singleton X	
C1													C1	
C2													C2	
C3													C3	
C4													C4	
C5													C5	
C6													C6	

Pair ✓	E1	E2	E3	E4	E5	E6	E7	E8	E9	E10	E11	E12	Singleton ✗
C7													C7
C8													C8
C9													C9
C10													C10
C11													C11
C12													C12

CSHL   Raw Repertory Grid Form

Construct pole rated – 5

	C1	C2	C3	C4	C5	C6	C7	C8	C9	C10	C11	C12
E1												
E2												
E3												
E4												
E5												
E6												
E7												
E8												
E9												
E10												
E11												
E12												

	E1	E2	E3	E4	E5	E6	E7	E8	E9	E10	E11	E12

Construct pole rated – 1

Appendix C: An overview of the SOL Coach's job in the Post Office

Conducting Learning Conversations in the Post Office

All SOL Coaches were full-time operational managers seconded into the SOL system. Most of those who applied were experienced first-line managers ready for promotion to the next grade who were genuinely interested in 'training' but had no formal experience as trainers. Part of the reason why the national SOL workshops were so successful was due to the open mind which the 350 participants each brought to the induction situation. *The SOL approach appealed because they could see their own learning mirrored in the process, albeit in an embryonic form.* They brought with them their operational experiences which turned out to be invaluable. Some offices interpreted the job as part-time but as experience of SOL spread many offices appointed two, three and up to five coaches.

The view of the SOL Coach's responsibilities presented on the workshops was that they were expected to conduct Learning Conversations on the job with staff at all levels, within their office. They were to work on a one-to-one basis, in small groups and with teams in specific sections, such as the mechanised areas and delivery areas. They were to set up a network of Learning Conversations throughout the office which would serve as a vehicle for departmental change. Acknowledging the variation in office management across the country most of the appointed SOL Coaches worked wholeheartedly at what they interpreted the job to be and at what they were allowed or enabled to do.

The national workshop offered three days of intensive exploration of SOL techniques followed by a two-day follow-up course. Individual SOL special projects on the job were backed up with support from CSHL staff as well as someone appointed by Post Office headquarters. This offered sufficient support for coaches to familiarise themselves with some basic skills and to develop these further on the job. To gain accreditation, SOL Coaches were expected to carry out one intense

it relates to their working environment. The interview is then used as a basis for an ongoing, critical, objective-setting exercise to improve their effectiveness and to move forward in setting Personal Learning Contracts in the context of a developing Learning Conversation.

7 Maintain a record of Learning Time, indicating daily the amount of time spent, where measurable, both at cost and no cost.

8 Maintain a constant understanding of any computer-based information which may have a bearing on the supervisors' working role and provide information for a learning aid.

9 Maintain a constant understanding of any work plans or control systems in operation.

10 Constant liaising with CSHL to set short, medium and long-term plans for installing Self-Organised Learning into the Post Office, and provide information and advice about the installation.

11 Constant liaising with the national coordinator for Self-Organised Learning providing information and advice regarding the whole of the trial project covering short, medium and long-term proposals.

12 Initiate the Cascade of Self-Organised Learning into other post offices by providing coaching experience and expertise and providing evidence of the success of SOL.

13 While carrying on Learning Conversations with individuals, identify special training needs required by them from the organisation.

14 Support and develop the Feedback for Learning package initiated in the trial by the CSHL.

15 Regular reporting to the Learning Manager to discuss past, present and future needs and directions of SOL in the trial.

16 Maintain and secure all records of SOL, remembering always that personal records are confidential.

17 Contribute evidence and facts towards the assessment of SOL when required.

18 Be aware of any developments in the strategic, tactical and operational policies within the organisation.

19 Provide evidence of the workings of SOL in the Post Office and use that evidence to persuade other sections of the Post Office e.g., Royal Mail Parcels, of the features and benefits of introducing SOL.

20 Teach yourself how to use computers to a stage where you can process the Feedback for Learning package or perform learning exercises with supervisors on the Post Office Simulator.

21 Planning a personal workload on a daily, weekly and monthly basis.

22 Constantly update your learning skills and techniques using all learning resources available.

23 Working closely with my Learning Manager on a day-to-day basis.

GB
SOL Coach

Bibliography

Amono, I. (1992) 'The bright and dark side of Japanese education', *RSA Journal*, CXL, No. 5425, January.

Bach, R. (1979) *Illusions: The Adventures of a Reluctant Messiah*, Pan Books, London.

Bannister, D. and Fransella, F. (1982) *Inquiring Man*, Penguin, Harmondsworth.

Bateson, G. (1980) *Mind and Nature, A Necessary Unit*, Bantam, New York.

Bentley, T. (1994) *Facilitation*, McGraw-Hill, Maidenhead.

Borger, R. and Seaborne, A.E.M. (1982) *The Psychology of Learning*, Penguin, Harmondsworth.

Boud, D. (ed.) (1985) *Reflection: Turning Experience into Learning*, Kogan Page, London.

Bruner, J. (1986) *Actual Minds: Possible Worlds*, Harvard Univ. Press, Cambridge, Mass.

Crick, F. (1992) *Astonishing Hypothesis: Scientific Search for the Soul*, Simon & Schuster, New York.

Diamond, P. (1991) *Teacher Education as Transformation*, The Open Univ. Press, Milton Keynes.

Edelman, G. (1992) *Bright Air, Brilliant Fire: On the Matter of the Mind*, Penguin, Harmondsworth.

Fontana, D. (1992) *Know Who You Are*, Harper/Collins, London.

Gell-Mann, M. (1994) *The Quarck and the Jaguar: Adventures in the Simple and the Complex*, Little, Brown, New York.

Gibson, B. and Gareth, M. (1979) *Sociological Paradigms and Organisational Analysis. Elements of the Sociology of Corporate Life*, Heinemann, London.

Handy, C. (1994) *The Empty Raincoat: Making Sense of the Future*, Century Business, London.

Harri-Augstein, E.S. and Thomas, L.F. (1978) *The Red Book of Learning: The Art and Science of Getting a Degree*, CSHL Pub., Brunel Univ., London.

Harri-Augstein, E.S., Smith, M. and Thomas, L.F. (1982) *Reading-to-Learn*, Methuen, London, New York.

Harri-Augstein, E.S. and Thomas, L.F. (1985) *Self-Organised Learning. Foundations of a Conversational Science for Psychology*, Routledge & Kegan Paul, London.

Harri-Augstein, E.S. and Thomas, L.F. (1991) *Learning Conversations*, Routledge, London.

Harri-Augstein, E.S. and Thomas, L.F. (1995) *Self-Organised-Learning and Management Effectiveness: A 7-Year Study with The Royal Mail*, CSHL Monograph, Brunel Univ., London.

Illich, I. (1971) *Celebration of Awareness*, Penguin, Harmondsworth.

Jung, C.G. (1974) *The Undiscovered Self*, Karnak Books,

Kelly, G.A. (1955) *The Psychology of Personal Constructs*, Vols 1 and 2, Norton, New York.

Kosko, B. (1991) *Fuzzy Thinking: The New Science of Fuzzy Logic*, Harper/Collins, London.

Langs, R.J. (1993) *Empowered Psychotherapy: Teaching Self-Processing*, Karnak Books, London.

Megginson, D. and Pedler, M. (1992) *Self-Development*, McGraw-Hill, Maidenhead.

Pask, G (1975) *The Cybernetics of Human Learning and Performance*, Hutchinson, London.

Penrose, R. (1991) *The Emperor's New Mind: Concerning Computers, Minds and The Laws of Physics*, Vintage, London.

Penrose, R. (1994) *Shadows of the Mind*, Oxford University Press, Oxford.

Prigogine, I. and Stenges, I. (1985) *Order Out of Chaos*, Flamingo, London.

Peters, T.J. (1985) *Liberation Management: Necessary Disorganisation for the Nanosecond Nineties*, Macmillan, London.

Peters, T.J. (1987) *Thriving on Chaos: Handbook for a Management Revolution*, Pan Books, London.

Phillips, D.C. (ed.) (1987) *Philosophy, Science and Social Inquiry*, Pergamon Press, Oxford.

Pirsig, R. M. (1976) *Zen and The Art of Motor Cycle Maintenance*, Corgi Books, London.

Polyani, M. (1966) *The Tacit Dimension*, Routledge & Kegan Paul, London.

Rogers, C.R. (1969) *Freedom to Learn*, Merrill, Columbus, Ohio.

Rogers, C.R. (1971) *On Becoming a Person*, Constable, London.

Rogers, C.R. (1978) *Carl Rogers on Personal Power*, Constable, London.

Salmon, P. (1980) (ed.) *Coming to Know*, Routledge & Kegan Paul, London.

Senge, P. (1990) *The Fifth Discipline – The Art and Practice of the Learning Organization*, Century Business, London.

Sowa. J.F. (1984) *Conceptual Structures. Information Processing in Mind and Machine*, Addison-Wesley, Wokingham.

Thomas, L.F. and Fransella. F. (ed.) (1987) *Experimenting with PCP*, Routledge & Kegan Paul, London.

Waldrop, M.M. (1990) *Complexity: The Emerging Science at The Edge of Order and Chaos*, Penguin, Harmondsworth.

Webb, I. (1990) 'The development of a conversational model for reflective talkback and planning of learning events', PhD Thesis, CSHL, Brunel Univ., London.

Weber, R. (1990) *Dialogues with Scientists and Sages*, Penguin, Harmondsworth.

Wertsch, J.V. (1985) *Vygotsky and the Social Formation of Mind*, Harvard Univ. Press, Camb. Mass. USA.

Zuber-Skerritt, O. (ed.) (1991) *Action Learning and Improved Performance: Proc. First World Congress on Action Research*, ABEIS Pub., Brisbane.

About the CSHL

CSHL acts as a networking global learning community. It supports SOL initiatives worldwide. It offers workshops, tutorials, seminars, courses, and consultancies to individuals, small groups, and organisations based on the principles and practice of Self-Organised Learning. It acts as an advisory body to agencies concerned with empowering people so that skills, competences and creativity are significantly advanced. Its members serve on advanced learning technology, educational, and organisational change think tanks. It offers certificates of learning competence for enablers of learning. CSHL offers various resources for Self-Organised Learners, including a system of reflective learning software.

1 An integrated repertory grid-based suite for eliciting personal and shared social models of the world.
2 The Personal Learning Contract suite for modelling change.
3 The reading-to-learn suite for advancing learning skills.
4 The feedback-for-learning suite for appraisal and self-development.
5 The SOL Systems 7 Personal Learning Biography suite for monitoring individual and group change over time.

Further details can be obtained by contacting the authors at CSHL, Brunel University, Uxbridge, Middlesex, UB8 3PH.

Index

Further titles in the McGraw-Hill Training Series

MEETING MANAGEMENT
A Manual of Effective Training Material
Leslie Rae
ISBN 0-07-707782-2

LEARNING THROUGH SIMULATIONS
A Guide to the Design and Use of Simulations in Business and
Education
John Fripp
ISBN 0-07-707588-9 paperback
ISBN 0-07-707789-X Disk

IMAGINATIVE EVENTS Volumes I & II
A Sourcebook of Innovative Simulations, Exercises, Puzzles
and Games
Ken Jones
ISBN 0-07-707679-6 Volume I
ISBN 0-07-707680-X Volume II
ISBN 0-07-707681-8 Set Ringbinder

TRAINING TO MEET THE TECHNOLOGY CHALLENGE
Trevor Bentley
ISBN 0-07-707589-7

CLIENT-CENTRED CONSULTING
A Practical Guide for Internal Advisers and Trainers
Peter Cockman, Bill Evans and Peter Reynolds
ISBN 0-07-707685-0

TOTAL QUALITY TRAINING
The Quality Culture and Quality Trainer
Brian Thomas
ISBN 0-07-707472-6

SALES TRAINING
A Guide to Developing Effective Salespeople
Frank S. Salisbury
ISBN 0-07-707458-0

CAREER DEVELOPMENT AND PLANNING
A Guide for Managers, Trainers and Personnel Staff
Malcolm Peel
ISBN 0-07-707554-4

DESIGNING AND ACHIEVING COMPETENCY
A Competency-Based Approach to Developing People and
Organizations
Edited by Rosemary Boam and Paul Sparrow
ISBN 0-07-707572-2

SELF-DEVELOPMENT
A Facilitator's Guide
Mike Pedler and David Megginson
ISBN 0-07-707460-2

TRANSACTIONAL ANALYSIS
A Handbook for Trainers
Julie Hay
ISBN 0-07-707470-X

USING VIDEO IN TRAINING AND EDUCATION
Ashly Pinnington
ISBN 0-07-707384-3

DEVELOPING WOMEN THROUGH TRAINING
A Practical Handbook
Liz Willis and Jenny Daisley
ISBN 0-07-707566-8

HOW TO SUCCEED IN EMPLOYEE DEVELOPMENT
Moving from Vision to Results
Ed Moorby
ISBN 0-07-707459-9

MAKING MANAGEMENT DEVELOPMENT WORK
Achieving Success in the Nineties
Charles Margerison
ISBN 0-07-707382-7

HOW TO DESIGN EFFECTIVE TEXT-BASED
OPEN LEARNING
A Modular Course
Nigel Harrison
ISBN 0-07-707355-X

HOW TO DESIGN EFFECTIVE COMPUTER-BASED
TRAINING:
A Modular Course
Nigel Harrison
ISBN 0-07-707354-1

EVALUATING TRAINING EFFECTIVENESS
Translating Theory into Practice
Peter Bramley
ISBN 0-07-707331-2

MANAGING PERSONAL LEARNING AND CHANGE
A Trainer's Guide
Neil Clark
ISBN 0-07-707344-4

DEVELOPING EFFECTIVE TRAINING SKILLS
Tony Pont
ISBN 0-07-707383-5

THE BUSINESS OF TRAINING
Achieving Success in Changing World Markets
Trevor Bentley
ISBN 0-07-707328-2

PRACTICAL INSTRUCTIONAL DESIGN FOR OPEN
LEARNING MATERIALS
A Modular Course Covering Open Learning, Computer Based
Training, Multimedia
Nigel Harrison
ISBN 0-07-709055-1

All books are published by:

McGraw-Hill Book Company Europe
Shoppenhangers Road, Maidenhead, Berkshire SL6 2QL, England
Tel: (01628) 23432   Fax: (01628) 770224

Learning Resources
Centre